C000065681

THE FRENCH IN LONDON

THE FRENCH IN LONDON

From William the Conqueror to Charles de Gaulle

ISABELLE JANVRIN
CATHERINE RAWLINSON

WILMINGTON SQUARE BOOKS
An imprint of Bitter Lemon Press

WILMINGTON SQUARE BOOKS
An imprint of Bitter Lemon Press

First published in 2016 by
Wilmington Square Books
47 Wilmington Square
London WC1X 0ET

www.bitterlemonpress.com

Copyright © 2013 Editions Bibliomane

First published in 2013 by Editions Bibliomane, Paris
www.editionsbibliomane.com

Translated by Emily Read

All rights reserved. No part of this publication may be reproduced in
any form or by any means without written permission of the publisher

The moral rights of the authors have been asserted in accordance
with the Copyright, Designs and Patents Act 1988

A CIP record for this book is available from the British Library

ISBN 978-1-908524-652

2 4 6 8 9 7 5 3 1

Designed and typeset by Jane Havell Associates
Printed in the UK by by T. J. International, Padstow

CONTENTS

PREFACE

'A city . . . in which Chateaubriand and Voltaire's genius was awakened, where Louis-Napoleon dreamt of a new Europe, where Verlaine wept – can such a city lack a soul?'

PAUL MORAND

Concealed within the great cosmopolitan metropolis that is London there lies a French city. Any visitor, whether French or English, wandering at random through its streets, could not fail to notice the many clues left behind: why do streets such as Beauchamp Place or Beaufort Street have French names? Why do the royal family have a French motto, 'Dieu et mon droit'? How did so many French works of art end up in London collections? Why are there commemorative plaques to Voltaire, Rimbaud and Verlaine, and a statue of Marshal Foch in London? To find the answers one must go back to the eleventh century, when William of Normandy, a vassal of the king of France, invaded England in 1066 in order to claim his inheritance. This invasion, which brought with it the language and culture of France, was the only one ever to succeed, and it would transform the course of British history. It marked the beginning of a long-lasting and uneasy relationship between the two countries, constantly veering between admiration and mistrust.

Since that time, French men and women of all social classes and professions have flocked to Britain, greatly contributing to the wealth of the country and of London in particular. Although many are now forgotten, others are still remembered, and their stories reveal an aspect of the British character that is rarely described, namely the warmth of the welcome extended to its so-called traditional enemies, when they came in search of asylum: persecuted Huguenots, royalists escaping from the French Revolution, political exiles in the nineteenth century, right up to the Free French during the Second World War. As well as these refugees, hundreds of French artists, writers and intellectuals came to seek inspiration in London. It is impossible to mention any but a few of these French visitors, but short portraits of some of the most captivating or strange characters can bring to life some of those who left their mark on the city. Even Napoleon, although he never came to London, left his traces. An English reader might perhaps be surprised to learn about the French origins of such famous Britons as David Garrick, Isambard Kingdom Brunel and Augustus Pugin as well as of the grandest hotels in London; also of how much the French influenced the renewal of English Catholicism in the nineteenth century.

After each chapter is a list of places (following the order of the text) in London and its outskirts where the French lived and worked – an opportunity for some interesting and unusual expeditions.

1

NORMAN ENGLAND
A LASTING FRENCH INFLUENCE

'England is an old French colony which turned out badly'
GEORGES CLEMENCEAU

Apart from the dig at 'perfidious Albion', Clemenceau's description of England as an ancient colony of France has a certain historical accuracy. It takes us back to the beginning of the last millennium when, in 1002, the English king Ethelred married Emma of Normandy. She had several children, one of whom was known, because of his great piety, as Edward the Confessor. After his father was deposed by King Canute of Denmark in 1016, Edward spent thirty years in exile in Normandy, before being recalled to England in 1042, where he married Edith Godwinson. When he died without heirs on 4 January 1066, his wife's brother Harold, an important figure at the court, claimed, with the support of the English barons, that he had been promised the throne. He pretended to have forgotten that he had been sent to Normandy by Edward to offer the crown to his nephew William, and that he had sworn allegiance to him.

The result of this betrayal was the Norman conquest of England. William, outraged by the usurper's coronation at Westminster Abbey on 6 January 1066 and assured of support from the pope, crossed the Channel in September, and won a great victory at the Battle of Hastings where Harold was killed. William, henceforth known as the Conqueror, was crowned on Christmas Day

1066 in Westminster Abbey. It took him five years to establish his authority. The agitated atmosphere of these times can be illustrated by one tragic misunderstanding: just after the coronation the Norman soldiers posted around the Abbey took the shouts of acclamation for cries of revolt, and began setting fire to the surrounding houses. In the ensuing panic the congregation fled and the ceremony was brought to a hasty and undignified end.

The Normans had to deal with several uprisings between 1067 and 1071: they were just seven thousand men, facing a hostile population of between one and two million people. In this precarious situation and to protect the Thames valley, they built a series of fortresses in and around London, including Baynard Castle, Montfichet, the Tower of London and Windsor Castle. At the beginning of his reign, however, the Conqueror made no attempt to change existing institutions, and addressed his new subjects with these words: 'William, the King, salutes all the burghers in London, French or English, in a friendly fashion. And I would have you know that I wish to leave with you the enjoyment of all the laws that were yours at the time of King Edward'.[1] However, in the course of suppressing one revolt after another, the King gradually wiped out the Anglo-Saxon aristocracy, and transferred their lands and the governance of the state and the church to Normans. By 1070 all Anglo-Saxon prelates had been replaced by Norman bishops. The king's friend and advisor, Abbot Lanfranc, from the Abbaye aux Hommes in Caen, became Archbishop of Canterbury.

In 1086, William ordered a census of all property throughout the kingdom, in order to fix rates of taxation. In this extraordinary document everything in the country is listed, from buildings and lands to animals, windmills and even duck ponds. The Domesday Book reveals a huge transformation in the ownership of property: more than four thousand small Anglo-Saxon landowners had already been replaced by fewer than two hundred barons, mostly Norman. They all retained their possessions across the Channel, too – England and Normandy would henceforth be a single state, dominated by the new Anglo-Norman aristocracy. That arrangment lasted until 1204, when John Lackland lost Normandy.

Introduction of a French feudal system

The Normans, having unified the country with their reforms, proceeded with the successful introduction of a French feudal system. The lord in his castle would ensure the protection of his people. In judicial matters, the local magistrates were replaced by a judge from the royal court assisted by a jury. The Confederation of the Cinque Ports organised coastal defences and transport between England and Normandy. French merchants and artisans developed commerce between England and the continent and their guilds were encouraged to organise the administration of the City of London, under the authority of the Lord Mayor. Romanesque and then Gothic art flourished and fortresses, churches, abbeys and public buildings were built throughout England. The addition of the territories of Anjou and then Aquitaine to the crown's possessions only served to increase the new masters' cultural domination; henceforth, until the thirteenth century, the English aristocracy spoke French. The Normans encouraged universities in Oxford and Cambridge. Jean de Ballieul, descendant of an Anglo-Norman baron who arrived at the time of William Rufus and was the father of the king of Scotland, founded Balliol College in 1263. The French Queen Marguerite d'Anjou, wife of Henry VI, founded Queen's College in 1448. These early Norman monarchs strengthened their personal authority and that of the Crown, but in 1215 the unpopularity of John Lackland led the barons to impose the Magna Carta on him, putting an end to absolute monarchy.

The Norman Conquest marked the beginning of a long period of instability in relations between England and France. The latter was now dealing with what was simultaneously an administrative dependency of the Duchy of Normandy and a kingdom with extensive possessions on the continent. For almost four centuries, until the end of the Hundred Years' War, the Anglo-Norman monarchs would continue to pursue their dream of uniting the two kingdoms. They did this by many different means, ranging from negotiation to force, and from marriage to outright conquest, and they very nearly succeeded in their enterprise.

Many of them spent the greater part of their lives outside England. Henry II (1154-89), husband of Eleanor of Aquitaine, spent only thirteen of his thirty-five years' reign in his English kingdom. Their son Richard the Lionheart (1189-99) was only there for six months of his ten-year reign. John Lackland (1199-1216) only resigned himself to life in England after losing almost all his French possessions in 1204. Edward I (1272-1307) held his court in Bordeaux until 1289. Finally, Henry V (1413-22), still trying in vain to gain the double crown, spent half his reign waging war in France.

The extent of English possessions on the continent fluctuated according to battles and royal marriages. The king of England, who was also the duke of Normandy, often owned more territory in France than the king of France himself, despite the fact that he remained his vassal and owed him allegiance. After the marriage of Henry Plantagenet to Eleanor of Aquitaine, English lands in France were larger than the French dominions, and remained so until John Lackland lost Normandy and Anjou.

The Anglo-Norman aristocracy, with its lands and relations in France, found its loyalties inevitably torn between the two opposing claims – the English one to the throne of France and the French to the throne of England. Each country attempted to profit from the mistakes and weaknesses of the other. So, in 1216, the English barons invited the French King Louis VIII to London to offer him the crown of England. The following year, after the death of John Lackland, Louis was forced to withdraw under pressure from Pope Innocent III and to make way for King John's nine-year-old son, Henry III.

England, for its part, laid claim to the French crown several times, and came close to obtaining it. When, in 1322, Charles IV le Bel died without an heir, Edward III claimed the throne as the son of Isabelle of France and therefore the legitimate heir. In order to justify their rejection of him, the French invoked the Salic law, which did not recognise a female line of inheritance, and installed a new dynasty by giving the throne to Charles IV's cousin, Philippe VI of Valois. The Hundred Years' War, which in fact lasted from 1337 until 1453, was the result of this crisis in the succession.

After the English victory at Agincourt in 1415, the English King Henry V married Catherine of Valois, daughter of the French King Charles VI, and had himself recognised as the heir to the French crown; he then awaited the death of the 'mad King' Charles VI in order, finally, to establish the double monarchy. Unfortunately, Henry V died at Vincennes in 1422, six weeks before the King of France. Since his son Henry VI was a nine-month-old baby, an English regent was installed in Paris. The wind then turned in favour of the French when Joan of Arc appeared, to take her place in history by helping the Dauphin Charles to 'kick the English out of France'; he was crowned in Reims in 1429, under the name of Charles VII. Since Henry V had died before Charles VI, the French felt that his son could not inherit a crown that his father had never worn. The English, however, crowned the young Henry VI King of France in Paris in 1431. But the French provinces eventually rallied round Charles VII, and the gradual loss of English possessions in France marked the end of both the English dream of a joint monarchy and the Hundred Years' War. And so the long period of confusion begun by the Norman Conquest came to an end.

The English possessions on French soil produced benefits on many levels. In the commercial field, Aquitaine and Anjou were able to trade their wines and salt for English wool, still the best in Europe, or for tin or wood. To this day, Bordeaux wine is known in England as claret, from the old French *clairet*, meaning a light red wine. Around 1300, 22 million litres were imported from Gascony, bringing great riches to the Anglo-Norman barons, who controlled production, trade and consumption. Most of the import–export businesses were run by Gascons living in London, although English merchants eventually took control of them and began to transform London into an international commercial centre.

The English even made profits out of the long years of fighting: simple soldiers as well as barons made fortunes from the pillage of the rich towns and lands of the continent, as well as the exorbitant ransoms demanded for the higher-ranking French prisoners (they were generally kept in the Tower while they waited for their families to decide to buy them back). The Savoy Palace was luxuriously rebuilt in the middle of the fourteenth century by Henry, Duke of Lancaster, with the proceeds of his French campaigns.

Honi soit qui mal y pense!

After its arrival with the Norman Conquest, the French language was spoken at the English court for more than three hundred years. It was the language of the aristocracy, the church and the administration, while English remained that of the common people. English only began to be spoken again by the ruling classes after the loss of Normandy at the beginning of the thirteenth century; it became re-established during the next century, reinforcing a new sense of national identity. The first English transcription of parliamentary debates appeared in 1362, and in the same year English became the official language of the law courts. After 1385, French was no longer used for teaching in schools. This movement was accelerated under Henry IV (1399-1413), the first king of England since the conquest whose mother tongue was English.

Under Henry V, the interminable quarrel with France brought about a popular rejection of all things French. However, the Norman imprint was by now deeply rooted in the language, and numerous traces remain in the English vocabulary, reflecting its past predominance, both cultural and political. These are found in judicial terms (mortgage, testament, litigation, judge, prison), commerce (commerce, account), the arts (music, poem, art, beauty, romance, colour), fashion (veil, collar, costume), religion (abbey, priest, saint, virgin), the court (baron, prince, marquess, duke) and even in sport. Tennis comes from the French *tenez*, from the *jeu de paume*, a precursor of the modern game popular at the French court. The common people, however, had never stopped speaking English. Saxon words were used to describe live animals such as the cow, pig and sheep, while the ruling and administrative classes referred to the same animals, once they arrived on their plates, by their French names of beef, pork and mutton. Many family and place names have inescapably Norman origins: Grosvenor (Grand Veneur), Beaumont, Beaufort, Beauchamp, Villiers and so on.

It is easy to spot other vestiges of the Norman administration in English institutions: juries still exist, and the British minister of finance is known as the Chancellor of the Exchequer, a title originating from the Échiquier de Normandie, an assembly of dignitaries surrounding the duke. Aldermen represent the guilds of the City of London, electing from among themselves a Lord Mayor who, in a procession that still appears medieval, rides through the City in November to inaugurate his function. The Confederation of the Cinque Ports, presided over by the Lord Warden (from the French *gardien*), has kept its original name, as has its president who, appointed by the sovereign, bears the honorary title of Admiral of the Cinque Ports and has his official residence at Walmer Castle.

One of the most striking examples of this impregnation is the motto on the English royal coat of arms: *Dieu et mon Droit*. This comes from a password or war-cry chosen by Richard the Lionheart at the Battle of Gisors in 1198. The message is clear: the king of England is not a vassal of the king of France and he recognises only God as his ruler. In the fifteenth century, Henry VI made it the royal motto. Just as famous, *Honi soit qui mal y pense* is the motto of the Order of the Garter created in 1348 by Edward III. The garter was a kind of thong attached to military equipment, but people generally prefer to connect the Order with a possibly apocryphal anecdote: Edward III was supposed to have gallantly said, 'Honi soit qui mal y pense,' when, in 1347, the Countess of Salisbury, before the mocking eyes of the courtiers, lost one of her blue ribbon garters while dancing. Her royal lover picked it up and tied it around his own knee. Such was the origin of the most ancient order of chivalry in Europe. Its members, which include a very few foreigners, are able to contemplate their coats of arms in St George's Chapel at Windsor. Like the gallant king, they tie a ribbon around their left knees when they are required to wear their full regalia at official ceremonies.

To this day, a great many of the heraldic devices of English aristocratic families are as French as their coats of arms. The first Anglo-Norman kings used the lion of Normandy flanked by a second lion representing England. Richard the Lionheart added a third to represent Aquitaine. The trio still adorns the royal coat of arms and the arms of England. The fleurs de lys of the French monarchy were added by Edward III when he claimed the French throne. They remained a part of the English coat of arms until the treaty of Amiens in 1802, when the English royal family finally gave up including among their titles that of king and queen of France.

Westminster and the Anglo-Norman palaces

The Normans were great builders, and they brought over from the continent artisans, masons and stone carvers to build churches, abbeys, fortresses and castles all in a specifically Anglo-Norman style. They imported stone from Caen for their earliest buildings, some of which have remained well preserved, while others have suffered or been rebuilt over the course of the centuries.

Westminster Abbey had its origins in a vow made by Edward the Confessor, the last but one of the Anglo-Saxon sovereigns, that he would make a pilgrimage to Rome if he recovered the throne of England. After his coronation, the pope relieved him of his vow on condition that he built a church dedicated to St Peter. There was already a chapel dedicated to St Peter in the west of London so Edward chose that place to build a monastery (or minster), hence the name Westminster. Inspired by the abbey of Jumièges in Normandy, he enlarged the existing structure in the Romanesque style which was already flourishing in France, and brought stone from Caen. Westminster Abbey was consecrated on 28 December 1065.

In the twelfth century, after the canonisation of Edward the Confessor, Henry III, who was devoted to his memory, decided to rebuild the abbey, enlarging and embellishing it. He admired the

Gothic style of the new cathedrals being built in France and charged the architect Henri de Reims with the project. Westminster Abbey became, over the centuries, the spiritual centre of the nation, and almost every monarch has been crowned and buried there.

Edward the Confessor had also rebuilt a Saxon palace that stood on the Thames beside Westminster Abbey, and made it his principal residence. The great Hall at Westminster Palace was the most imposing part of Edward's original construction, and William the Conqueror held a sumptuous banquet there after his coronation. In 1097 it was rebuilt by his son William II the Redhead (Rufus). It remained the centre for the monarchy until 1532, when Henry VIII moved to Whitehall. It burned down in 1834, leaving only two of the original buildings remaining: the great Hall and the Chapel of St Stephen. The Hall was incorporated into the new, nineteenth-century Palace of Westminster, the seat of Parliament. All of English history has been enacted within its walls.

William ordered the construction of the Tower of London to be begun shortly after his coronation. With its strategic position, within the walls of the newly conquered city and guarding the Thames, its purpose was to intimidate the newly conquered subjects. A temporary wooden fortress was erected at first in a restricted space, and then, in 1078, William asked the Norman monk Gandalf from the Abbey of Bec-Hellouin to build a fortress out of Caen stone which would also be a palace. Completed twenty years later, the Tower has been enlarged over the centuries, but the original building within its walls, the White Tower or Dungeon, remains intact since the days of the Conqueror. The Tower of London is the best preserved of all the medieval fortresses in England.

Numerous Frenchmen have spent time within its walls. In 1216, Louis, the French Dauphin and future Louis VIII (1187-1226), the son of and successor to Philippe Auguste, was called to help the English barons who wanted to depose King John. He held court in the Tower for a year. When it became a prison after the Battle of Crécy (1346), many French prisoners, including the six courageous Burghers of Calais, were locked up there. In the same year Charles de Blois, pretender to the duchy of Brittany, was taken prisoner by Sir Thomas Dagworth and placed in the Tower. He was handed over to the King of England in return for a ransom of 25,000 gold ecus. Without the slightest scruple, the King then demanded an even higher sum for returning him to France. In 1356, the French King Jean le Bon, his son the Dauphin Philippe and a large number of lords and knights were taken prisoner at the Battle of Poitiers. The knights were imprisoned in the Tower and Jean le Bon was held for three years in the Savoy Palace. In 1415 the 'poet prince' Charles, Duke of Orleans and nephew of the King of France, was captured at Agincourt; he remained a prisoner in England for twenty-five years, some of them spent in the Tower.

Another defensive fortress on the Thames, Windsor Castle, has been very well preserved: it soon became a royal residence and as such has been maintained and restored by successive kings and queens.

To the south-east of London the manor of Eltham, surrounded by moats, appears in the Domesday Book of 1086 as being the property of Odon, Bishop of Bayeux and half-brother of William the Conqueror. Edward I and Edward II often stayed there, and the latter gave it to his wife, Isabelle of France. The palace was then fortified and greatly improved. In 1316 their second son John was baptised there, and was subsequently known as John of Eltham; his handsome alabaster tomb can be seen in Westminster Abbey. Eltham became one of the most heavily used royal residences throughout the fourteenth century. King Edward III spent most of his childhood there, and returned often throughout his reign. The celebrations after the fall of Calais probably took place there, during which Edward III is thought to have created the Order of the Garter: the palace account books show that twelve blue garters, embroidered with gold and silver thread and the inscription *Honi soit qui mal y pense*, were the prizes for one of the jousting matches that took place beyond the moat. The royal apartments were enlarged between 1350 and 1360 and a huge park was laid out for the hunt. Richard II created a ballroom in the royal apartments and laid out a new garden. The kings' fondness for Eltham was such that Henry IV spent ten Christmases there in the thirteen years of his reign, while Henry VI, king from infancy, spent his entire childhood there. In 1445, he enlarged the queen's apartments in order to receive Margaret of Anjou, his new wife.

A religious revival arrives from France

In order to ensure the support of the pope, William the Conqueror and his successors set about reforming the Church in England, encouraging numerous monastic orders to come over and settle. Monks came from great Norman abbeys such as Le Bec-Hellouin, Jumièges and Saint Evroult, among them great mystics such as St Anselm of Bec, St Hugh of Lincoln and the great St Thomas Becket, son of a Norman merchant. Their abbeys and monasteries, established all over England, gained great reputations, bringing a religious revival as well as leaving behind magnificent examples of Anglo-Norman art.

In the eleventh century the Benedictine order of Cluny, which already enjoyed great intellectual prestige and renown in France, established an abbey to the south of London at Tooting Bec, which is mentioned in the Domesday Book. It was directed by the abbot of the ancient Benedictine abbey of Le Bec-Hellouin in Normandy, the future St Anselm, before he succeeded Lanfranc as Archbishop of Canterbury. The links between the monastery at Le Bec-Hellouin and the Archbishopric of Canterbury have continued to this day. Benedictines from La Charité-sur-Loire took over St Saviour's Abbey in Bermondsey in 1089, and William Rufus, son of William the Conqueror, gave them the adjoining manor. The French Queen Catherine of Valois, widow of Henry V, died there in 1437.

The Domesday Book also mentions a monastery in Southwark under the jurisdiction of Odon of Bayeux. In 1106 two Norman knights rebuilt the church and monks of the order of St Augustine were installed in the priory. The Bishop of Winchester, Henry of

Blois, William's grandson, built Winchester Palace beside the priory as his London residence, conferring added importance to the church and the priory.

After the execution of Thomas Becket, Henry II, smitten by remorse, founded several Carthusian monasteries in England. One of them, the Charterhouse, was established in London in 1371 in Smithfield. Other monastic orders were established early in the thirteenth century: the Dominicans, Franciscans and Carmelites installed themselves respectively in the priories of Blackfriars, Greyfriars and Whitefriars. The names, from the colours of their robes, became those of the areas of the city in which they were established. Despite their vow of poverty, these orders became extremely rich and wielded great authority over civil society and even over the crown itself. After the dissolution of the Order of the Templars, several of these monasteries took over their financial activities, which contributed to their prosperity. In the sixteenth century the richest orders were dissolved by Henry VIII, who appropriated their lands and wealth. All these religious orders had been generously endowed by the first Norman kings or their French wives, and had built their abbeys and churches in the same Romanesque or Gothic style as their monasteries back in France. Today a few remnants of this time can still be seen in London, both in the architecture and in the names of places.

The crusades gave rise to a new type of priest, the soldier monk. The Order of the Templars, founded in 1118 by the French Hugues de Payen to protect pilgrims in the Holy Land, settled in London in 1162. Its military spirituality inspired confidence among kings and the richer crusaders, who entrusted them with the management of their properties. The order became immensely rich and, forgetting their vow of poverty, its members transformed themselves into businessmen and bankers. When enthusiasm for the Crusades began to wane, the Order, deprived of its primary purpose, embarked on such blatantly temporal pursuits that it aroused a campaign of defamation which culminated in its dissolution. In France, where Philippe le Bel made unfounded accusations of criminal behaviour against it, its members were tortured and condemned to death. In England they were treated more humanely by Edward II, and the Temple was absorbed into the Order of the Hospitallers of St John of Jerusalem. This order, created in 1113 to care for the sick during crusades and pilgrimages to the Holy Land, exists to this day, running the St John Ambulances which supply first aid at large public gatherings.

Places to visit

THE TOWER OF LONDON

William the Conqueror ordered the building of the Tower as soon as he had been crowned king of England in December 1066. It is strategically placed overlooking the Thames and the newly conquered city. An earlier wooden fort was replaced in 1078 by a fortress of Caen stone that was also a palace with an adjoining chapel. It was protected on two sides by an old Roman wall and the river, with a ditch and a rampart on the other two sides. Completed twenty years later, the Tower of London was enlarged several times over the centuries but the original building, the White Tower with its four small towers, has remained intact since the days of William the Conqueror. It is the best preserved medieval fortress in England.

CASTLE BAYNARD

Castle Baynard Street EC4

In the south-west of the City, this fortress, named after its owner the Norman lord Ralph Baynard, was part of a series built to protect the city after the Conquest. The name of the street is the only surviving clue to its existence, as the castle was completely destroyed by the great fire of 1666. A large part of the action in Shakespeare's *Richard III* takes place in this castle.

MONTFICHET CASTLE

Blackfriars Thameslink Station EC4

To the north-west of Castle Baynard, Montfichet Castle was built by Gilbert de Montfichet of Rouen, a companion of the Conqueror, on the site of the present Blackfriars Thameslink station. It was destroyed during the reign of John Lackland.

WINDSOR CASTLE, BERKSHIRE

William the Conqueror chose the only raised ground in the area to build the artificial moat and dungeon here in 1080, in order to protect it from the Thames which flowed thirty metres below. The layout of the land allowed him to build two courtyards, the upper and lower wards. In 1170, Henry II replaced the wooden dungeon with a stone tower, the Round Tower, which still dominates the castle. Although it was originally planned as a defensive building, it became a royal residence thanks to its proximity to London and its hunting lodge, and thirty-nine sovereigns have lived there. The castle underwent many transformations over the centuries, with the addition of towers, royal apartments and chapels. King Edward III was the first to make changes in 1352, erecting new buildings in the lower ward for the College of St George's. This became the home of the Order of the Garter, whose patron saint is St George. The castle was damaged during the Civil War, when Cromwell made it his headquarters, and restored under Charles II. It was renovated once again under George IV in the nineteenth century and filled with numerous works of art sold after the French Revolution. Queen Victoria often stayed there. Restored once again after the fire of 1992, the castle is nowadays both a royal residence and one of the most popular museums in England. The reigning monarch spends a month there at Easter every year.

St George's Chapel, the chapel of the Order of the Garter. The coats of arms of the members of the Order can be seen on the choir stalls, with their names and French mottos. Every year in June the members of the Order hold a splendid service here, followed by lunch in the castle.

WESTMINSTER ABBEY

20 Deans Yard SW1

Rebuilt by Edward the Confessor, the abbey is the repository of English history. From William the Conqueror until the end of the Middle Ages, many signs of the French presence in London can be found in its various chapels.

St Edward's Chapel

- **Tomb of Edward the Confessor**, behind the sanctuary. His wife Edith Godwin is buried beside him.

- **Inscriptions in Old French** on the tombs of other kings and queens, among them that of Henry III Plantagenet, husband of Eleanor of Provence. Others are engraved on the tomb of Eleanor of Castile, wife of Edward I, who died in 1290.

- **Tomb of Edward III,** son of Isabelle of France.

- **Tomb of Philippa of Hainault**, wife of Edward III, marble statue by French sculptor Jean (or Hennequin) of Liège. The Burghers of Calais were spared thanks to her intervention.

- **Tomb of Henry V**, King of England and heir to the French throne after the Battle of Agincourt. The coffin of his French wife Catherine de Valois was only placed beside him in 1878.

Henry VII's Chapel. After Henry V's death, Catherine of Valois had three more sons from her marriage to a Welsh courtier, Owen Tudor. One of their grandsons became the first Tudor King, Henry VII. The chapel of Henry VII is famous for its fan-shaped roof. It is dedicated to the Order of the Bath, and several of the mottos of the knights are in French. This Order is sometimes bestowed on foreigners, such as President Jacques Chirac in 1996.

St Edmund's Chapel

- **Tomb of William of Valence**, Lord of Pembroke and Wexford (died at Bayonne in 1296), son of the French ex-Queen of England Isabelle d'Angoulême and of Hugues de Lusignan by her second marriage. His effigy, made of oak coated with bronze, is encrusted with Limoges enamels which can still be seen on the cushion, the shield and the belt.

- **Tomb of John of Eltham**, Earl of Cornwall, second son of Edward II and Isabelle of France. Alabaster recumbent statue; around the tomb, very damaged small crowned statuettes represent members of his family, Queen Marguerite of France, second wife of Edward I, and Queen Isabelle of France, his mother.

Chapter House. This octagonal room with a central pillar dates from the thirteenth century. It is remarkable for its proportions, its fourteenth-century frescoes and its original thirteenth-century paving on which one can see Edward the Confessor giving his ring to a beggar, King Henry III playing with a dog and his wife Eleanor of Provence with a falcon on her hand.

Crypt and Museum. The museum is in the crypt, the most ancient part of the abbey. The semicircular arches and the massive pillars supporting the crypt date from Edward the Confessor's Norman construction. At that time it was a communal hall used by the monks. Among the collection of funerary effigies is a moving one of Catherine de Valois, wife of Henry V.

PALACE OF WESTMINSTER

Parliament Square SW1. Of the original Palace of Westminster built by Edward the Confessor on the site of an ancient Saxon palace, only Westminster Hall and the crypt of St Stephen's chapel survived the fire of 1834.

Westminster Hall, behind the statue of Cromwell, embedded in the Parliament building. The most important building in Edward the Confessor's old palace, this was where feasts were held during the great religious festivals. Rebuilt in 1097 by William II Rufus, Westminster Hall was at the time the largest assembly room of all the courts of Europe. It was a centre for government, where the King's council and a court of justice were held until 1883, as well as all coronation banquets from William the Conqueror to George IV in 1820. The 'king's champion' would ride into the hall on a horse and defy anyone to challenge the legitimacy of a new king. In 1393, Richard II removed the Norman pillars and built a new wooden hammer-beam, one of the finest in England. Angels on each flying buttress bear his arms. Kings and queens lie in state in Westminster Hall before burial – an honour that was, exceptionally, accorded to Winston Churchill in 1965. The Queen Mother's coffin lay in state for a week in April 2002, to allow the British people to pay their last respects. Two French presidents have had the rare privilege of addressing Parliament in Westminster Hall: Albert Lebrun in 1939 and Charles de Gaulle in 1960.

St Stephen's Hall. St Stephen's Gate, the public entrance, and the Hall have the same layout as the splendid original chapel, inspired by the Sainte-Chapelle in Paris. It served as the chamber of the Commons from 1548 until the fire of 1834.

St Mary's Crypt. Many original sculptures and frescoes were discovered here, spared from the fire, during restoration works.

ELTHAM PALACE
Court Yard, Eltham SE9

To the south-east of London, the manor of Eltham, whose foundations can still be seen in the gardens, was built by Odon, William the Conqueror's half-brother. It was a royal dwelling under Edward II, and became the favourite home of the medieval kings. It seems that the Order of the Garter was created here after the celebration of the fall of Calais in 1348: the palace accounts tell us that twelve blue garters embroidered with silver and gold and inscribed 'Honi soit qui mal y pense' were awarded as prizes at a joust. Only the moats remain from the original medieval building. The Great Hall, built around 1475 by Edward IV, is very well preserved with its magnificent huge oak frame. Partly rebuilt by the Courtauld family in 1933, Eltham Palace has a remarkable Art Deco interior.

THE BURGHERS OF CALAIS
Victoria Tower Gardens SW1

The burghers of Calais were saved thanks to Philippa of Hainault, but were sent to the Tower of London. Rodin chose the position for this copy of his famous sculpture in 1915 (the original has been in Calais since 1895). After reading Froissart, Rodin chose to depict the moment when the six burghers are 'in shirts, bare-headed and barefoot, with ropes around their necks', before they are spared. Eustache de Saint-Pierre is their leader, surrendering the keys of the town. Rodin said of the work: 'I have rarely produced a sketch with so much vigour and solemnity. Eustache de Saint-Pierre alone, with his dignified movement, carries along his family and friends . . .'

WALMER CASTLE
Kingsdown Road, Walmer, Deal, Kent

The official residence of the Warden of the Cinque Ports. Because of their strategic positions on the south coast, these five ports – Hastings, Hythe, Dover, Romney and Sandwich – ensured maritime defences and transport between England and Normandy, supplying ships and equipment in exchange for privileges and tax exemptions.

SAVOY HOTEL
Strand WC2

A statue of Peter of Savoy, uncle of Queen Eleanor of Provence, overlooks the entrance. He is shown in medieval costume with a large shield and lance. The 1904 bronze sculpture is by Frank Lynn Jenkins.

COATS OF ARMS
100 Strand WC2

A series of coats of arms belonging to the king of England and the house of Savoy on the facade of Simpson's.

SAVOY CHAPEL
Savoy Hill WC2

After a fire, the chapel was partly rebuilt in 1864. Still with its original graveyard, it is now surrounded by large modern buildings behind the Strand. The chapel is endowed with the Royal Victorian Order and has special status as the queen's chapel. Inside are several mottos in French belonging to members of the Order.

NATIONAL ARCHIVES
Kew, Richmond, Surrey

The Doomsday Book is one of the most valuable objects from the Conquest era. Published around 1086, this inventory is the first land register made in England. It is extremely detailed and has served as a reference in litigations for centuries. It defines existing lands to this day.

THE WORSHIPFUL COMPANY OF BOWYERS

These companies still exist in the City as closed groups of businessmen sharing their experiences. They are extremely rich and own splendid ancient buildings. They still have power at the heart of London, under the aegis of the Lord Mayor, and run their own charitable enterprises. The Company of Bowyers have as their motto 'Crecy, Poitiers, Agincourt'.

AGINCOURT ROAD
Hampstead NW3

The Battle of Agincourt on 25 October 1415 saw Henry V's archers inflict a cruel defeat on the French who greatly outnumbered them.

BUCKINGHAM PALACE MENUS

To this day, menus at the royal table are in French, according to tradition.

RICHARD THE LIONHEART'S LIONS

Sculpted lions can be found everywhere in London, notably in the City and along the banks of the Thames. They are reminders of the Norman origin of this emblem chosen by the first Anglo-Norman kings for their armouries.

FLEURS DE LYS

These adorn the walls of many palaces and churches, in particular Westminster Abbey.

CHARTERHOUSE
Charterhouse Square EC1

After the dissolution of the monasteries, the Carthusians' headquarters became in turn a private house, an almshouse and a school. Today the Charterhouse shelters forty pensioners. The neighbouring hospital, St Bartholomew's, better known as Bart's, has taken back some of the monastery buildings for its medical students. Neighbouring streets are named Charter or Carthusian.

CHURCH OF ST BARTHOLOMEW THE GREAT
West Smithfield EC1

Unscathed by the great fire of 1666, the church is a rare and architecturally interesting example of the Anglo-Norman style in London. In front of the effigy of the founder, Rahere, to the left of the altar, is an angel bearing the coat of arms of the monastery: the two lions of Normandy with two crowns.

CHRIST CHURCH TOWER
Corner of Newgate Street and
King Edward Street EC1

The Franciscans, or Greyfriars, came to this area in the thirteenth century and their Gothic church was one of the biggest in London. Queen Isabelle of France and Queen Marguerite of France were buried there, as well as the heart of Eleanor of Provence, another French queen of England. When the order was dissolved by Henry VIII, the church was given to the City of London, and the monastery buildings used as a hospital. Destroyed in the great fire of 1666, the church was rebuilt by Wren in the baroque style. Once again destroyed during the Blitz, only four walls and the tower remained; the tower was converted into flats. The site, comprising just a few remains of the church and the graveyard, is now a memorial garden.

ST MARY LE BOW
Cheapside EC2

The church was built in 1080 by Lanfranc, who had come from the abbey of Le Bec-Hellouin in Normandy and was made Archbishop of

Canterbury by William the Conqueror. It was built in Caen stone. All that remains of that period is the well-preserved crypt, with its massive pillars and arches.

BLACKFRIARS BRIDGE
Blackfriars Lane EC4

On the site of Montfichet Castle, destroyed under John Lackland, the Dominican or Black-friars' monastery was built with stone from the castle in 1278. The area and the bridge were named after them. The Apothecaries' Hall now stands on the site of the monastery guest house.

- **Commemorative plaque**
  Carter Lane EC4
  This plaque commemorates the Blackfriars Priory founded at this spot in 1278

WHITEFRIARS STREET AND CARMELITE STREET EC4

The Carmelites, or Whitefriars, established their monastery between Westminster and the City, beside the Thames. Strategically placed between the two centres of power, the king and the City, it became an important building in which several kings held their councils. The two streets are now the only reminders of its presence.

SOUTHWARK CATHEDRAL
South Bank, London Bridge SE1

The original Norman structure was destroyed by fire in 1212 and rebuilt in the Gothic style with the help of the Bishop of Winchester who lived in the neighbouring palace. The first Gothic church in London, it was partially rebuilt in the nineteenth century but some Norman remains may still be seen.

WINCHESTER PALACE
Clink Street SE1

A short distance further along the Thames, a wall with a magnificent rose window is all that remains of Winchester Palace, built in 1140 by Henry of Blois, Bishop of Winchester and grandson of William the Conqueror. The palace had its own prison, the Clink, which came under the jurisdiction of the bishop. It was destroyed by fire in 1780, and the palace itself in another fire in 1814.

ABBEY STREET, ST SAVIOUR BRIDGE, ST SAVIOUR WHARF
SE1

These names commemorate the site of St Saviour's Abbey in Bermondsey, founded by the monks of Cluny in 1089.

TOOTING BEC
SW16

Tooting Bec, with its common and under-ground station, gets its name from the Norman abbey of le Bec-Hellouin. According to the Domesday Book, the land belonged to the abbey, which installed gallows there in 1258. It was seized by Edward II and returned to the French abbey by Edward III. Tooting Bec Abbey was built on the old road from London to Win-chester and Chichester, well situated and with an abundance of water. The buildings were at the junction of Bedford Hill, Hillbury Road and Tooting Bec Common.

- Becmead Road SW16
  This road gets its name from Bec Meadow.

ST ANSELM'S CHURCH
311 Balham High Road SW17

St Anselm was the prior of the abbey of le Bec-Hellouin before coming to Tooting Bec Abbey. The Roman Catholic church of St Anselm was rebuilt in 1933 on the site of a chapel at the corner of Tooting Bec Road and Balham High Road.

WANDSWORTH TOWN HALL
Wandsworth High Street SW18

St Anselm is depicted on a bas relief visiting the Totinges (Tooting) tribe.

TEMPLE CHURCH
Temple EC4

The Order of the Templars, supported by Henry I when it came to England, was well established by the second half of the twelfth century. Their first church was built in Holborn, and their second, the Temple Church, was built closer to the Thames and consecrated in 1185 by the Patriarch of Jerusalem in the presence of Henry II. The adjoining monastery has disappeared. This church is circular in shape, like most of the Templar churches, as a reminder of the Holy Sepulchre in Jerusalem. A rectangular choir and a chapel were added in the thirteenth century to enable Henry III to be buried there, but he changed his mind and is buried in Westminster Abbey. The church escaped the great fire of 1666 but has been restored several times over the centuries. In the oldest part, the rotunda, lie nine magnificent effigies of knights armed with chain mail, swords and shields. One of them is that of William Marshal, Earl of Pembroke and brother-in-law of John Lackland, who died in 1219. He is represented with his legs crossed, like most of the Crusaders. All around the circular church, grimacing masks are reminders of the strange and controversial Templar initiation ceremonies. At the junction of the rotunda and the choir, two narrow windows on the left opening on to the choir reveal a cell from which imprisoned Templars could hear Mass. One of them was locked in there until he died of hunger, for having disobeyed the orders of the Grand Master of the order. The windows, destroyed in the Blitz and replaced in 1954, depict the history of the Templars. In the Middle Ages justice was dispensed beneath the Romanesque entrance porch on the west side of the church.

EQUESTRIAN STATUE OF TWO TEMPLARS

In Temple Court, where the cloister used to be, a Gothic-style column bearing a statue of two knights on one horse was erected in the year 2000. This image was inspired by the Templars' seal and symbolised their vow of poverty. Later, when they stood accused of heresy, the symbol was interpreted as a sign of homosexuality. The statue is by Nicola Hicks.

THE TEMPLE DISTRICT

The surrounding area is now named after the Templars' church. When the Hospitallers took possession of the Templars' property, they let some of the buildings around the church to the clerks of justice, and the area has kept its legal connection to this day: many lawyers' chambers and law schools are based in this picturesque maze of courtyards, passageways and buildings. The two courts of justice, the Inner and Middle Temple, are responsible for the upkeep of the Templars' church according to a royal charter of 1608. The coats of arms in these courts illustrate their links with the history of the Templars.

CHURCH OF ST JOHN
St John's Lane, Clerkenwell EC1

The priory of the Hospitallers' Order was built at the beginning of the twelfth century, destroyed during the Peasants' Revolt in 1381, then rebuilt. The order was dissolved by Henry VIII in 1540. Stones from the building were used for the construction of Somerset House beside the Thames, and the church was put to various different uses through the centuries. The Order of the Hospitallers of St John of Jerusalem was rehabilitated in 1831, and reoccupied its church a century later.

- **Museum of the Order of St John**. The museum acts as a link between the order's past and present.

- **St John Ambulance Brigade**. Still active as a charitable enterprise, this offers emergency medical services dispensed by the Order of the Hospitallers of St John, successors to the Templars.

MUSEUM OF LONDON
150 London Wall EC2

Objects and explanations relating to the Norman Conquest can be found In the medieval section. There are also some displays in glass cases on the monastic orders of the time, and the closure of monasteries under Henry VIII.

VICTORIA & ALBERT MUSEUM
Cromwell Road SW7

The Becket Casket. Thomas Becket was a typical Anglo-Norman: the son of Norman parents who had arrived in London during the Conquest. He was a part of the entourage of the Norman court, and eventually became Archbishop of Canterbury, the highest clerical position in the English church. Although he was a friend and counsellor to King Henry II, he remained intractable when it came to the independence of the church. Henry, exasperated, had him assassinated in the cathedral. The murder caused a scandal throughout Europe and Thomas was canonised only three years after his death. His relics are divided among many caskets, mostly preserved in monasteries. The one in the VIctoria & Albert was manufactured in Limoges between 1180 and 1190, and represents several scenes from the murder of Thomas, as well as his burial and ascension into Heaven. It is one of the museum's most important treasures.

2

EXCEPTIONAL PEOPLE

'Princes, pass by without lingering: yours shall be the land of England, conquered in the past by a Norman. Valiant heart can at all times wage war'

EUSTACHE DESCHAMPS, *Oeuvres*, VI, 73

The Conqueror

The centuries following the Norman Conquest are populated with major figures and men of destiny on both sides of the Channel, the most important being of course the one introduced to us in that marvel of Western art and precursor of the comic strip, the Bayeux Tapestry. *Hic est Willelm Dux* ('Here is Duke William') proclaims the fifty-fifth panel. This complex and contrasted man, the founder of a legitimate dynasty, was himself the illegitimate son, born in Falaise around 1027, of Robert the Magnificent, Duke of Normandy, and Arlette, the daughter of a rich tanner of the town. However, the Duke had no qualms about naming him as his successor when he set off on a pilgrimage to Jerusalem. When he died during the homeward journey in 1035 William was only eight years old; the revolts of the petty barons made him fear for his life, and he was forced, when hardly old enough to bear arms, to battle against the turbulent Norman barons and the neighbouring princes.

Physically, the Conqueror was a tall man with a high forehead and a loud voice that would ring out during his terrible rages. He loved hunting and demolished villages without compunction in order to create the New Forest, which exists to this day in the south of England. We know something of his life from the writings of the chronicler William of Malmesbury: 'He loved the pleasures of the chase above all things […]. He would organise great entertainments during the main Christian festivals: when he was in England he would spend Christmas in Gloucester, Easter in Winchester and Pentecost in Westminster.'[2] He was energetic and could also be cruel: a revolt in the city of York was harshly suppressed in 1070, the town razed and the countryside around ravaged. When he was in England he lived in the Tower of London, and when he travelled to Normandy he would leave the governance of the country to his half-brother Odon, Bishop of Bayeux, to whom he gave the county of Kent.

William, however, could be merciful when he judged it necessary. We are told in one Anglo-Saxon chronicle that 'King William was a man of great wisdom and great power. He surpassed all his contemporaries in honours and in authority. He was exceedingly severe on those who resisted his will, but gentle with virtuous men who served God.'[3] He displayed admirable statesmanship in the way he organised the Conquest and rallied the church to his side by giving it an important part to play in the new order. In 1053, defying opposition from the Pope, he had married his fourth cousin Matilda, the daughter of Baudouin of Flanders and niece of the King of France, Henri I. He had her crowned Queen of England on Pentecost 1068, and he always remained faithfully attached to the mother of his nine children. Her death in 1083 was a severe blow: 'At her death, which occurred four years before his own, he had her buried with great pomp and shed so many tears, and for so many days, that he proved how harshly he suffered her loss; also, if we are to believe what they say, he never again enjoyed the pleasures of the flesh.'[4]

He was a pious monarch, attending Mass every morning; he built chapels in all his palaces and churches all over England: Winchester, St Albans, Norwich, Chichester, Gloucester, Durham and Battle, the scene of his victory over Harold. During his childhood he had strengthened his faith with Lanfranc, the impressive bishop of the abbey of Le Bec-Hellouin, whom he now made archbishop of Canterbury. He possessed a strong sense of justice: if one is to believe the chronicler Orderic Vital, nobody asked the King in vain for a fair judgement. He would only condemn when it would have been unjust not to. Many contemporaries, whilst recognising his exceptional qualities as war leader and statesman, criticised his greed, however, when it came to money: 'He seized every opportunity to procure it, it little mattered to him in what manner; he was capable of saying and doing certain things unworthy of such a great king when motivated by the prospect of financial gain.'[5]

William's life was overshadowed, even before the loss of his wife, by the death in 1074 of his son Richard in a hunting accident. He also had a difficult relationship with other members of his family, his son Robert Curthose in particular, whose thirst for power drove him to ally himself with the King of France. In 1079, in battle against his father, he went so far as to wound him with a sword-thrust to the arm which knocked him off his horse. Matilda was obliged to intervene in order to end the quarrel. William also had to punish his ambitious and very rich half-brother Odon for his abuse of power. In 1082 he personally arrested him and sent him for trial for corruption: Odon remained imprisoned in a tower in Rouen until the death of the King.

William the Conqueror, by now obese, died in 1087, aged sixty, from the consequences of a wound caused by the pommel of his saddle while once more suppressing a revolt in Normandy by nobles allied to the King of France. His funeral was comically grotesque: his body, in too narrow a coffin, exploded, giving out a pestilential odour which drove clergy and congregation from the church. His tomb is in the church of St Étienne in the Abbaye aux Hommes in Caen. His sons divided up his kingdom: Robert Curthose took Normandy, and William Rufus England. Henry I Beauclerc reunited the two when he took the English crown after the death of his brother William in 1100 after a hunting accident. He then recaptured Normandy in 1106 after capturing Robert

Curthose. The latter then remained in captivity for twenty-eight years, first in the castle at Devizes, and then in Cardiff until his death in 1134. He is buried in Gloucester Cathedral.

The story of the conquest and of William's life is told in the Bayeux Tapestry, and also in several chronicles – in English, that of William of Malmesbury, and in French, those of William of Jumièges, William of Poitiers, WIlliam's chaplain and Orderic Vital.

Miseries of the French Queens

From the middle of the twelfth century until the end of the Hundred Years' War in 1453, nine of the wives of the fifteen reigning sovereigns were French – twelve if one includes two princesses of Navarre and Philippa of Hainault. They often brought with them as dowries strategic and important territories: Matilda of Boulogne brought the county of Boulogne and Eleanor brought Aquitaine. Such provinces assured England of a considerable foothold in France. Isabelle of Angoulême added the county of Angoulême.

These queens were often betrothed at a very young age, with the only purpose of ensuring a link to the French royal family to seal an alliance after a war. Thus Henry V married Catherine of Valois, the daughter of the French King Charles VI, after the battle of Agincourt in 1415. Those kings who loved war and adventure – Henry II, Richard the Lionheart and Edward I – would take their wives with them on military campaigns and crusades: Eleanor of Aquitaine, Bérengère of Navarre and Margaret of France. The weaker ones – Stephen of Blois, Henry III, Edward II and Henry VI – would leave their wives to run the state more or less successfully: Matilda of Boulogne, Eleanor of Provence, Isabelle of France and Margaret of Anjou. The frivolous and unfaithful kings – Henry II, John Lackland and Edward II – drove their wives to take revenge, as Eleanor of Aquitaine did, or to lead a dissipated life, as was the case with Isabelle of Angoulême. As for Isabelle of France, she took a lover and deposed her husband, who came to a tragic end.

These 'French queens' were often severely tested in their new country. Henry V's early death left Catherine of Valois, mother of the heir to the throne, a widow after only eighteen months of marriage. Margaret of Anjou was exiled and several were imprisoned in various castles for treachery, infidelity or even murder. Eleanor was removed from power for fifteen years; Isabelle of Angoulême was placed under surveillance by her husband, as jealous as he was unfaithful; and Isabelle of France was exiled to Norfolk by her son for almost a quarter of a century. Such were the perils attendant on their important position, and they were only alleviated when it was a question of a second marriage for the king, once he had assured the succession and marriage could become simply a private affair. Edward I was sixty and had fifteen children when he married Margaret of France, with whom he had three more, but he never bothered to have her crowned queen. Richard II married Isabelle of Valois when he was twenty-nine and she had barely reached the age of reason. Henry IV had seven children when he married Jeanne of Navarre who was nine years old, and with whom he had no descendants.

Most of the wives helped their husbands through their energy and their personal assets, often against the will of their French families. They fully played their part in ensuring the continuity of the English monarchy. Catherine of Valois's second marriage to Owen Tudor even resulted in a change of dynasty. But it is the case that, over the course of four centuries, the aristocracy, originally French, had become integrated into its new environment and had adopted a fully English identity; the new queens arriving from France were held to be intruders in this new society and were often unpopular.

Fascinating Eleanor

Eleanor of Aquitaine holds a special place in the Western imagination. We are still fascinated today by her radiant femininity and her altogether modern way of combining intelligence with sensuality, as well as her taste for poetry and love. She was beautiful and almost recklessly brave; she was the heiress to the house of

Aquitaine, with a father and grandfather who were both warriors who loved literature. Brought up in a climate of freedom and poetic licence, she became Duchess of Aquitaine in 1137. Her marriage, in the same year, to the French King Louis VII considerably increased his territories, since Aquitaine covered a third of present-day France. Even though only fifteen, she held considerable sway over her husband and it was under her influence that he embarked on a war against the Count of Champagne. But disaster struck when his army burned down a church, killing over a thousand people taking shelter. The King decided that in order to expiate this crime he would take part in the second Crusade (1147–49). Eleanor, always adventurous, decided to take part in the journey. However, her marriage was failing: the King's great piety hardly suited her passionate temperament. She described her husband as 'a monk and not a king'.[6] Pope Eugene III succeeded in reconciling them at the abbey of Monte Cassino, so much that on her return to France Eleanor gave birth to a second daughter (the first was born in 1145). Louis VII, however, more and more anxious at not having a male heir, managed to have the marriage annulled by the pope in 1150, for reasons of consanguinity.

Eleanor, with her huge possessions, was besieged by suitors. Despite being ten years older than him, she chose Henry Plantagenet of Anjou, Duke of Normandy, the future Henry II of England. They married in 1152, and she was crowned alongside him two years later, at Westminster Abbey. She was both cultivated and refined: she embellished the royal palaces and surrounded herself with poets and scholars. The sumptuous court soon became renowned throughout Europe. For his part, Henry II restored order throughout the country, which had been devastated by years of anarchy. When he was away dealing with his French possessions, she would run the government of the country. She developed commerce with the continent, particularly the wine trade with Bordeaux. On her journey to the Holy Land, she had observed the existence of laws governing maritime movements; inspired by these, she set up, first at Oléron and then in England, the maritime code known as the Judgements or Rolls of Oleron,' which became the basis of maritime law in Europe.

Henry's and Eleanor's marriage was stormy but fruitful, producing eight children, two of whom, Richard the Lionheart and John Lackland, became kings of England. In 1170, having produced several successors to the throne, and tired of her husband's infidelities, notably his infatuation with Fair Rosamund, Eleanor decided to establish her court at Poitiers where, with the consent of Henry II, she was able to administer her own territories. Here she continued to surround herself with culture, arts and courtly love: she was a muse for the troubadours who sang her praises in some of the most beautiful love songs of the time.

The extent of English territories in France brought by the addition of Aquitaine had broken the geopolitical balance of power between the two countries, and resulted inevitably in tension and discord. For several years, Henry and Eleanor had hoped to unite the two countries under one crown with the marriage of their son Henry to Margaret, daughter of Louis VII's second marriage. This hope was dashed when, in 1165, King Louis finally conceived his long-awaited male heir from his third marriage – the future Philip Augustus. In 1173, with the support of several barons from Aquitaine and his father-in-law the King of France, the young Henry, heir to the English throne, rebelled against his father and, with the support of his brothers and his mother, demanded power. Henry II made some concessions to the rebel and sent Eleanor back to England. But, mistrusting her influence, he cut her off from her children and placed her under surveillance in several castles, notably at Winchester and Salisbury, for more than fifteen years.

In 1183, Henry took up arms against his father once again, but his troops were routed and he collapsed with acute dysentery. Before he died he begged his father to release his mother. The King then placed Eleanor in relative liberty and she resumed her position at the court; however, this was not the end of the dramas of her astonishing life. After the death of Henry II in 1189, his third son and heir Richard the Lionheart named Eleanor Regent of England while he was away on crusade. At the age of sixty-seven she ruled with a firm hand and gained the respect and affection of the English people. She worked hard to rally all possible support for her son's cause – Richard had spent most of his life in France, and was virtually unknown in England – and travelled throughout the country receiving oaths of allegiance, dispensing justice and managing public affairs.

Two years later, with unusual energy for her age, she set off on horseback to accompany her future daughter-in-law Bérengère of Navarre as far as Sicily, before the latter continued to Cyprus to marry Richard, who had set off a little earlier on crusade. Eleanor died at the age of eighty-two in 1204, and is buried next to her husband at the Abbey of Fontevraud in France. She is the origin of the Plantagenet line in England.

The Pious Eleanor and the 'She-Wolf of France'

The daughters of the Count of Provence were famous for their beauty and Henry III chose Eleanor whom he married in 1236. The couple had nine children, the eldest of whom became Edward I. The Queen was a good mother and a perfect wife, playing an active part in public life, supporting her husband, raising money and troops during the English rebellions. She did, however, manage to alienate barons and Londoners by imposing her French kinsmen on the court, whose demands eventually made her unpopular. She had come to London with her uncle Peter of Savoy, whose main aim was to enrich himself. The King ennobled him, endowing him with the title and lands of Richmond and a manor beside the Thames, the Savoy Palace, on a site now occupied by the hotel and the Savoy chapel. Later, Henry III intervened with the Pope in 1240 to name Peter's brother, Boniface of Savoy, Archbishop of Canterbury. The prelate spent only fourteen out of the twenty-nine years of his office in England; he came into conflict with the bishops and the King when he tried to impose taxes and reforms. He did, however, succeed in paying off the debts left by his predecessor, and in completing the construction of the chapel at Lambeth Palace, the seat of the archbishopric.

In 1255, the King of France Louis IX, the future St Louis, gave an elephant to Henry III and Eleanor, who was the sister of his wife Margaret of Provence; this caused a sensation in England. Exotic animals had often been represented in fantastic forms in bestiaries and on the doorways and capitals of churches. Only very important people were able to possess them, which became a symbol of their power. The elephant was kept at the Tower of London where, given wine to drink for two years, he finally died in a state of inebriation. He was first buried at the Tower and then his huge corpse was taken to the sacristy of Westminster Abbey. After Henry's death in 1272, Eleanor took on the Regency until her son Edward returned from the Crusades. In 1280, she took the veil at the convent of the Benedictines at Amesbury near Salisbury in Wiltshire, where she died and is buried.

Isabelle of France, daughter of the King of France Philip le Bel and Joan of Navarre, married Edward II at the age of thirteen. The King soon turned out to be a feeble man who was manipulated by his favourites. The Queen, tiring of her husband's weakness, fell in love with a prisoner in the Tower, Roger Mortimer, with whom she raised an army in Hainault, deposed her husband and imprisoned him in Berkeley Castle in Gloucestershire, while she occupied the Regency until her son came of age. The deposed King was tortured and killed in prison on her orders, and the populace was so horrified by her cruelty that the new King Edward III imprisoned his mother at Castle Rising in Norfolk, where she ended her days.

Isabelle, having been very popular on her arrival in England, went down in history as the 'She-Wolf of France'. She was buried in London at Greyfriars Church (now destroyed,) alongside Mortimer who was accused of usurping royal power and hanged at Tyburn on 29 November 1330. A statuette of Isabelle of France as a mourner adorns the tomb of her son John of Eltham in Westminster Abbey.

The misfortunes of Catherine and Margaret

Catherine of Valois suffered a no less dreadful fate. She was the daughter of the 'mad king' Charles VI and Isabel of Bavaria; she had an unhappy childhood, unloved by her mother. After his victory at Agincourt, Henry V married her in the renewed hope, forever disappointed, of uniting the two crowns; she gave birth to the future king Henry VI shortly before her husband's death in France. Widowed after only eighteen months, she oversaw her son's education and accompanied him to Paris where he was crowned King of France in 1431. Henry VI was, in effect, the only English sovereign ever to have worn, if only for a short time, the two crowns.

Ignoring the interdict on remarrying without the consent of parliament, Catherine secretly married a young Welsh nobleman, Owen Tudor, with whom she would have three sons. Parliament ordered her to withdraw to the Abbey of Bermondsey without her children, where it seems she died of grief. This marriage, however, was the origin of the new dynasty of the Tudors, with the accession to the throne of her grandson Henry VII in 1485. Catherine lies in Westminster Abbey, near the tomb of Henry V. When her coffin was opened in 1669 the diarist Samuel Pepys recorded: 'here we did see, by particular favour, the body of Queen Catherine of Valois; and I had the upper part of her body in my hands, and I did kiss her mouth, reflecting upon it that I did kiss a Queen, and that it was my birth-day, thirty-six years old, that I did first kiss a Queen.'[7]

The last of the French queens of that period, Margaret of Anjou brings the list to the most tragic of endings. Daughter of René, Duke of Anjou, and niece of King Charles VII of France, her reign was one of torment and trial: war, exile, restoration, the murders of her son and husband, prison . . . This Shakespearian fate places her at the centre of the *Henry VI* trilogy, and she reappears as an old woman in *Richard II*. She married Henry VI of England at the age of fourteen, but the King, who was revered for his great piety, was also subject to fits of madness and was incapable of governing his country. During the Wars of the Roses, Margaret, placed by fate in the Lancastrian camp against the house of York, showed enormous energy expending all her resources on ensuring the succession for her son Edward. Her husband's incapacity forced her to take matters of state into her own hands and, when all seemed lost, she succeeded several times in rebuilding the army, with the help of her allies and the support of France or Scotland. All the same, her French origins made her the target of a great many calumnies and plots and did not help the Lancastrian cause. In the end, Edward of York usurped the throne in 1471, and after being crowned Edward IV, he had Henry VI and his son Edward Prince of Wales executed, thereby permanently eliminating the Lancastrian threat.

Imprisoned at first in the Tower of London, Margaret was moved to Newmarket Castle in East Anglia. In 1477 her father paid her ransom and took her back to France. She ended her life retired at Saumur and is buried in the cathedral of Angers.

She shared her husband's intellectual interests and founded, during her reign, Queen's College Cambridge in 1448.

Prisoners in the Tower

Jean le Bon, the second king in the Valois dynasty, was the son of Philippe VI of Valois. He suffered all his life from the instability of such a recent dynasty, threatened as he was by the King of England Edward II's claim to the French throne, as well as by the many tensions within his kingdom. At thirteen he was married to Bonne of Bohemia, who would give him thirteen children. His health was fragile, and he preferred art and music to violent exercise. Easily angered, he lacked political flair and after his coronation at Reims in 1350, he was soon confronted by the English. In 1356 he set off in pursuit of the Black Prince, the son of Edward III, who had embarked on an expedition into France and met him at Poitiers. The French army, although superior in numbers, lacked discipline and was routed. When all seemed lost, Jean dismounted from his horse and continued to fight until he was exhausted. His young son Philippe at his side gave the celebrated cry: 'Father, look to your right! Father, look to your left!' He was finally captured with his son and many other Frenchmen, including an archbishop, thirteen counts, five viscounts, twenty-one barons and around two thousand knights.

The Black Prince treated the defeated King with great respect, going so far as to present him with a meal on his knees on the evening after the battle. Jean was held in Bordeaux, then an English possession, for several months, and then finally taken to England, where the victor was given a triumphal reception. In London they processed together through the streets and, in order not to humiliate his prisoner, the Black Prince rode a small black horse with Jean at his side on a splendid grey charger, normally the royal prerogative. Jean remained in England from 1357 until 1360 whilst lengthy negotiations on his conditions of release were pursued. He lived in the splendid Savoy Palace and could move around freely. His accounts reveal that he bought horses, animals and clothes, and that his domestic staff included an astrologer. Edward III and Queen Philippa sometimes visited him and took him hunting at Windsor. His mistress was the Countess of Salisbury, possibly shared with Edward III; however, this comfortable lifestyle came to an end when, in order to speed up the ransom negotiations, the King placed him in less comfortable surroundings, first at Somerton Castle in Lincolnshire and in 1360 in the Tower of London.

Finally, in May 1360, a huge ransom of three million gold écus (which was never fully paid) was agreed at the Treaty of Brétigny. Edward III renounced his claim to the French throne, but France lost many possessions, mainly Aquitaine and Gascony. Jean was finally allowed to return to France in October 1360 in order to raise his ransom, leaving three of his sons behind as hostages. He found his kingdom in chaos after the revolt of Étienne Marcel and the 'jacqueries'. In 1363 his son Louis escaped from England to join his young wife and Jean decided to return to London in mid-winter in order to save his honour. Apart from being a simple gesture of chivalry, little is known of the motives for his return. Was he unbalanced by the situation he had found in France? Or did he hope to persuade the English king to join a crusade that would never take place? He was welcomed back with great festivities and he died a few months later, in April 1364, in the Savoy Palace at the age of forty-four. After a splendid funeral at St Paul's Cathedral in the presence of the King of England, his body was taken to France, where it is buried in the Abbey of St Denis.

Another noble prisoner of the Tower was Charles of Orleans, the 'poet-prince', who was taken prisoner at Agincourt in 1415. He was the nephew of Charles VI, and third in line of succession to the French throne; for that reason the English kept him prisoner for twenty-five years. His first wife, Isabel of France, the daughter of Charles VI and widow of the English King Richard II, died at the birth of their daughter. The prince then married Bonne of Armagnac, with whom he was very much in love and to whom he remained faithful throughout his enforced stay in England, despite distance and solitude. She died in 1432, and after he was freed the widowed prince took as his third wife Mary of Cleves, the niece of the Duke of Burgundy.

At the beginning of his captivity Charles of Orleans was held in the Tower of London, which was still a royal palace, and later in the palaces of Westminster and Windsor. He was very well treated, out of respect for his rank, and was able to continue to manage the affairs of his duchy, with visits from his secretary and trusted friends. His books, personal effects and favourite wines were sent from France. In June 1417, Henry V removed him from London, where he would only return for brief visits, and banished him to remote castles. As his stay in England continued, he forced Charles to pay for his keep. The noble prisoner continued to receive visitors from France, but the melancholy and depression caused by the discomfort of his icy residences is reflected in his verses:

What do you intend,   *The most miserable of all men*
Boredom and Melancholy?   *must I be? I refuse you that.*
do you wish for my whole life *And what do you intend,*
to torment and anger me?   *Boredom and Melancholy?*[8]

All the same, Charles of Orleans bore his twenty-five years of captivity with remarkable strength of character. He had a fine and cultured intellect, a remarkable poetic gift, and all the charm of a witty philosopher. He also wrote in English; Henry VII so admired his poems that he had them illuminated and bound for his new wife Elisabeth of York, in an edition which can still be seen at the British Library. Many of the poet-prince's love poems were dedicated to his wife, who had remained in France, and to whom he sent the first Valentine while he was in captivity in the Tower. During his captivity he followed political developments in France and the story of Joan of Arc. He deplored the misfortunes of his country and the horrors of war, and constantly sought to promote peace between the two nations, just as he had become reconciled to his old French enemy the Duke of Bourgogne.

Henry V had, on his deathbed, forbidden Charles from ever being freed, but Henry VI, who was a friend of the poet-prince, showed himself more merciful and, after being paid a large ransom, sent him back to France to promote peace. Charles retired to Blois, where he entertained his fellow poets, the most famous of whom was Francois Villon. He died at Amboise in 1465. His son was the future Louis XII, who became king in 1498, and married, as his third wife, Mary of England, sister of Henry VIII.

Chronicles of France, England and neighbouring countries

Jean Froissart, the only commoner in this gallery of noble portraits, played just as important a part in the relations between the two kingdoms. He was born around 1337 in Valenciennes in Hainault. His family were comfortably off, but we know little about his life except that he was at one time destined for the priesthood. He devoted his life to writing the history of his times. Thanks to his accounts of the battles in the early part of the Hundred Years' War, notably Crécy in 1346 and Poitiers in 1356, he came to the attention of Queen Philippa of England, who was from Hainault like himself, and who engaged him as her secretary. Her court was at that time the most prestigious in Europe, and it was there that Froissart began to discover and admire the values of chivalry. He spent six years in London, from 1361 to 1367, writing poems and visiting England, Scotland and Wales as well as travelling to the continent on several occasions. On his return from one of these trips, in 1369, he learned that the Queen had died and he returned to France. Moving from one patron to another, he travelled widely, meeting and speaking to participants and witnesses of the wars and great events of the time, gathering material for his celebrated *Chronicles*. Froissart returned to London in 1395 to present them to Richard II. He spent the last years of his life at Chimay, in present-day Belgium, where he died around 1410.

Places to visit

WESTMINSTER ABBEY

Tomb of John of Eltham. Two statues beside the tomb, one of his mother Isabelle of France, in mourning; the other of his grandfather's second wife, Margaret of France.

Tomb of Catherine of Valois. After the reconstruction of the abbey in 1502, the badly closed coffin of Catherine of Valois was forgotten for several centuries. It was finally placed behind that of her husband Henry V in 1878. She is the only French-born English queen to be buried in Westminster Abbey.

Effigy of Catherine of Valois (crypt/museum). During royal funerals, a wooden effigy of the dead monarch replaced the body during the funeral procession.

QUEEN ISABELLA WAY
Off King Edward Street EC1
The name refers to Queen Isabelle of France, known as the 'She-Wolf of France', who was buried in Grey Friars Church. Now destroyed, the church has been replaced by a memorial garden beside this street.

VICTORIA & ALBERT MUSEUM
Cast Courts. These contain effigies of several French-born queens of England: Eleanor of Aquitaine, Bérangère of Navarre and Isabelle of Angoulême, as well as several of their husbands, kings of England. These plaster casts were created for the Great Exhibition of 1851, and were displayed in the medieval galleries. The one of Eleanor of Aquitaine is a copy of her effigy at Fontevraud in Maine-et-Loire. She is holding an open Bible, unusually for the Middle Ages, especially in the hands of a woman, as it is the symbol of education and literacy.

BRITISH MUSEUM
Great Russell Street WC1
Badge of Queen Marguerite of Anjou: she had adopted a white swan as her badge and her supporters wore one in homage to their queen.

GLOUCESTER CATHEDRAL
College Green, Gloucester
Tomb of Robert Curthose, Duke of Normandy, the eldest son of William the Conqueror. He is depicted as a Crusader as he had taken part in the First Crusade.

BAYEUX TAPESTRY
13 rue de Nesmond, 14400, Bayeux, France
This tapestry, or rather embroidery, measures 62 x 0.5 metres. A precursor of the comic strip, it tells the whole story of William's Conquest of England in 58 scenes. Probably commissioned by Bishop Odon of Bayeux to adorn his cathedral, it is also a work of propaganda to justify the Conquest.

FONTEVRAUD ABBEY
49590 Fontevraud-l'Abbaye,
Maine-et-Loire, France
Effigies of Eleanor of Aquitaine, her husband Henry II, their son Richard the Lionheart and their daughter-in-law, the wife of John Lackland, Isabelle of Angoulême.

ABBAYE AUX HOMMES
100 rue de l'Ancienne Mairie
ABBAYE AUX DAMES
Place Reine Mathilde
14100, Caen, France
When William married Matilda of Flanders, the Pope condemned the marriage for reasons of consanguinity. He finally absolved them and imposed as a penance that they should found two monasteries, the Abbaye aux Hommes and the Abbaye aux Dames. William the Conqueror is buried in St Etienne church in the Abbaye aux Hommes. His tomb was destroyed many times over the centuries and only the tombstone remains. Queen Matilda's tomb is in the choir of the abbey church of the Holy Trinity in the Abbaye aux Dames.

3

BOURBONS AND STUARTS
A FAMILY AFFAIR

'That enemies should come
from a thousand corners of the earth,
that I concede; but that England
should wish that our two kings should cease to be friends,
that is something I cannot believe'

LA FONTAINE, *Le Pouvoir des Fables*

After the bloody Wars of the Roses, the five kings of the Tudor dynasty greatly increased the power of their kingdom. The first of them, Henry VII, the grandson of Catherine of Valois, laid the foundations for the great reigns of his successors, Henry VIII and Elizabeth I. Now freed from French influence, England gradually became a great European power, and consequently France's greatest rival, with the two countries sometimes in open conflict as when Henry VIII tried, in 1544, to take back Boulogne and Calais. However, the two countries were also brought together by peace treaties and marriages: in 1514, Henry VII's fifth child and sister of Henry VIII, Mary, married the King of France, Louis XII, the son of Charles of Orleans. In 1520, in a sumptuous encampment that came to be known as the Field of the Cloth of Gold, Henry VIII and Francis I signed a treaty uniting them against the Emperor Charles V of Hapsburg. Subsequently, a marriage was planned between his daughter Elizabeth I and François, Duke of Anjou, despite the fact that she was forty-six and the young man twenty-four. This plan for a union with a French Catholic prince was abandoned, not because of the age difference, but because it was rejected by the English people and by Elizabeth's council. The Queen, in her poem *On Monsieur's Departure,* expressed the pain of an impossible love – 'I love and yet am forced to seem to hate'[9] – for the man she nicknamed her 'frog' after a frog-shaped jewel he had given her. Providing another complication in Anglo-French relations, France and Scotland became more closely linked by the marriages of Marie of Guise to James V of Scotland and that of their daughter Mary Stuart to the future King Francis II of France.

Across the Channel, the arts were stimulated by competition with France, a rivalry illustrated by the extravagant displays at the Field of the Cloth of Gold. Henry built the castle of Nonsuch near Epsom in Surrey as a response to the splendour of Chambord, making use of a great many foreign artists, especially French Protestants who had begun to arrive in England in order to flee increasing persecution.

When Elizabeth I died without an heir, the crown passed to James VI of Scotland, who then became James I of England. Thus the son of Mary Stuart, by uniting the two thrones, founded the Stuart dynasty, which became linked by blood to that of the Bourbons. When his son Charles I, who reigned from 1625 to 1649, married Henrietta Maria, daughter of the French King Henri IV, he became the brother-in-law of Louis XIII. Thus in the next generation Charles II and James II were first cousins of Louis XIV. La Fontaine, in the poem quoted at the head of this chapter (which he dedicated to Paul de Barillon, the Sun King's ambassador to London), refused to contemplate for a moment any conflict between the cousins' kingdoms, now that Anglo-French relations had become a family matter. The parents on either side of the Channel helped each other in difficult situations: Charles I welcomed Henrietta Maria's mother Marie de Médicis in great style for nearly three years, while Ann of Austria, Louis XIII's widow, welcomed Henrietta Maria during the Civil War with Cromwell; and when James II lost the English crown he benefited from lavish

French hospitality with all the respect due to his rank. If necessary, the related monarchies added secret clauses to the treaties that linked them. Thus, when Charles I and Charles II were in desperate need of money in order to maintain their supremacy in the face of Parliament, Louis XIII and then Louis XIV discreetly promised them an income in exchange for a commitment to support Catholicism, thus keeping England on their side and allowing them to extend their domination of the rest of Europe.

The Very Catholic Henrietta Maria, 'Her Majesty Generalissima'

James I's decision, tired as he was of religious strife, to marry his son, the future Charles I, to a Catholic had grave and disastrous consequences. Henrietta Maria of Bourbon (1609–69) was the youngest daughter of the French King Henri IV and Marie de Médicis. She was not highly educated, but had been solidly brought up in the Catholic faith. She was lively and headstrong and soon demonstrated her determined character. The marriage took place at Notre Dame in Paris on 11 May 1625. She was never crowned as queen and did not even attend her husband's coronation the following year. She arrived in England aged fifteen and not speaking a word of English. She was soon faced with Protestant intolerance of 'Papists', and throughout her life she never ceased to support persecuted Catholics. Her husband kept her at a distance, and only had eyes for his favourite, the Duke of Buckingham. After the latter was assassinated in 1628 he returned to his wife and from then on remained loving, tender and faithful towards her. She gave him nine children, including the future kings Charles II and James II. The couple lived a peaceful life, punctuated by visits to their various residences.

Since her marriage contract allowed her to practise her religion, she had two Catholic chapels built by Inigo Jones, the greatest architect of the time, at the heart of St James's Palace and in Somerset House. Henrietta Maria took a lively interest in the decoration of the palaces and chapels assigned to her and employed many French artisans. During the early years of her English life she resided with her entourage at St James's Palace. She would entertain the court at Somerset House, acting herself in 'masquerades', masked spectacles, and putting on plays that had done well in France. Thanks to her, Corneille's work was performed at the same time in London and Paris, and his play *Le Cid* was a huge success. In 1629 King Charles I gave her an unfinished house in Greenwich, which was completed by Inigo Jones in 1635. Le Nôtre, after designing the gardens at St James's Palace, made the park surrounding the Queen's House at Greenwich. However, Henrietta Maria had little time to enjoy this 'palace of Delights', as her peace of mind was gradually destroyed by the threat of an uprising of Parliament and people. She decided to leave in 1642, and departed from London on the pretext of accompanying her daughter Mary to Holland to marry William of Orange. She returned a few months later to England at the head of troops intended to reinforce the royalist army. She joined the Catholic nobles loyal to the king and rode at their head to meet the Parliamentarians, who nicknamed her 'the Generalissima of all traitours'. She finally rejoined her husband at Oxford, where she spent several surprisingly untroubled months, before setting off for exile in France when faced with Cromwell's increasing success. She gave birth to her youngest child, Henrietta Anne, during the journey on 16 June 1644 in Exeter. Eventually she reached Paris, ill and exhausted, where she was kindly welcomed by her sister-in-law Ann of Austria, who had become regent after the death of Louis XIII the previous year. In 1649 Henrietta Maria learnt with horror the news of the beheading of Charles I. She returned to London for two years after the restoration of her son Charles II, living in Somerset House. She died in Paris in 1669 at the age of sixty. Louis XIV granted her a state funeral and she was buried in the basilica of Saint Denis.

After the death of Oliver Cromwell, Charles II (1630–85) returned to England in 1660 and the monarchy was restored. He had lived in exile since his childhood, and he returned accompanied by his French or French-speaking entourage. He had become accustomed to French taste and was inspired by the luxury of the court of Louis XIV to replicate its grandeur at his new court. He founded the Royal Academy of Music and engaged French musicians such as Nicolas Lanier, who was of Huguenot origin, Robert Cambert and Louis Grabu. French music was very much in fashion, especially that of Lully. Handel, inspired by one of his motets, composed a very similar one which is believed by some to be the origin of the national anthem, *God Save the Queen*. Theatre, forbidden under Cromwell, was revived and the court and English public were delighted by performances of plays by Molière.

Charles II had inherited his French grandfather Henri IV's jovial nature, and was soon known as the 'Merry Monarch'. His court, reacting against the puritanism of the Cromwell years, became careless and dissolute, as is well illustrated in the pages of Anthony Hamilton's *Memoirs of the Comte de Gramont*.

Women played an important part in the life of Charles II. His mother, his sister and both his mistresses, Louise de Keroualle and Hortense Mancini, were all French. Like his father he married a Catholic woman, Catherine of Braganza, a member of the Portuguese royal family. He was more tolerant than his father and tried to settle religious conflicts in a more flexible manner. He was much attached to his sister Henrietta Anne, whom he nicknamed Minette and with whom he conducted a lengthy correspondence. She was both cousin and sister-in-law of Louis XIV and represented a link between the two monarchs. Louis XIV sent her to England so that she could further his interests in his war against the Dutch by signing the Treaty of Dover with Charles II. Her sudden death, fifteen days after her return, inspired Bossuet's funeral oration with the words: 'Madame is dying, Madame is dead . . .' Charles was plunged into despair by her death. Louis, who knew his cousin to be untrustworthy when it came to treaties, sent Louise de Keroualle over under the pretext of distracting him from his grief, but in reality so that she too could further the interests of France.

Louise de Keroualle 'almost queen'

This Frenchwoman would demonstrate conclusively that a royal
mistress could play as important a role as a wife as regards Franco-
British relations. Louise de Keroualle, twenty-one years old and
from an aristocratic Breton family, had accompanied Henrietta
Anne to Dover. For several months she allowed herself to be
courted by the King without succumbing to his advances, until
finally in the course of a grand reception she became his mistress,
giving birth nine months later to a son, Charles Lennox. In 1673
she was given the title of Duchess of Portsmouth, and the King
conferred on their son the titles and honours of the Richmond
family, which had become defunct. He also intervened with Louis
XIV to ensure that the titles and lands of the Duchy of Aubigny
in the Berry region, which had been attached to the Richmond
name, should be transferred to Louise. The latter wisely treated
Catherine of Braganza with the greatest respect, and tolerated the
King's infidelities with his two other official mistresses, the
unavoidable Barbara Villiers and Nell Gwynn, a lively actress with
a sharp tongue. Nell Gwynn nicknamed Louise 'squintabella'
because of her slight lazy eye, and 'the weeping willow' because of
her easy tears, particularly when asking for a favour.

Was Louise de Keroualle, Duchess of Portsmouth, secretly
hoping to wear a crown? Queen Catherine had not given Charles
an heir, and he was tempted to repudiate her. And Louise's position as mediator between the two sides of the Channel put her in
an important political position. However, she was disliked by a
great many courtiers and, more generally, by the English public,
who saw her as surrounded by a Catholic, pro-French clique. Her
enemies wanted to remove her from the court in order to loosen
the bonds between Louis XIV and Charles II and strengthen the
Protestant cause. But by the end of the reign she had come to
enjoy all the powers and prerogatives of a queen of England: she
was privy to all state secrets, she received distinguished guests at
the side of the king, held audiences and receptions in her apartments, and even arranged dynastic marriages, such as that of Anne,
James's daughter and future queen of England, to Prince George

of Denmark. She lived in apartments in the palace of Whitehall, luxuriously decorated and enlarged several times over the years. Visitors never failed to admire the magnificence of the Gobelin tapestries, Charles le Brun's decorations and furnishings, and paintings by her protegés such as the Frenchman Henri Gascar. These works of art were the foundations of the great present-day collection at Goodwood House, near Chichester, which belongs to a descendant of the Duke of Richmond. Charles II, under Louise's influence, created two institutions in London inspired by those in Paris: the Royal Observatory at Greenwich and, in 1682, the Royal Hospital at Chelsea, in imitation of the Hotel des Invalides created by Louis XIV for impoverished ex-soldiers.

Louise was almost ruined by her extravagant way of life, despite the very generous allowance she received from the King; this behaviour increased the resentment of her enemies, who saw in her the embodiment of the debauchery of the court, and of the King himself. However, he continued to love her until the end. In 1682, impatient for her return from a visit to France, he wrote: 'It is impossible to express all the true passion and tenderness I feel for my beloved Fubs.'[10] The nickname, from the old word 'fubsy' meaning plump, referred to her figure. The death of the King in November 1685 put an end to Louise's career at the court and she retired to Aubigny, crippled by debt. Louis XIV gave her a pension and she died in Paris in 1734 at the age of eighty-five.

Hortense Mancini, a free spirit

Charles II, unable to resist the charms of Frenchwomen, also succumbed to those of Hortense Mancini when she arrived in London in 1675; Louise was forced to put on a brave face and to accept her into the royal circle. The most beautiful of Cardinal Mazarin's five nieces, she was born in Rome in 1646 and went to Paris at the age of eight. Henrietta Maria, living there in exile at the time, developed a plan to marry the little girl to her son, the future Charles II. Hortense, however, was the heiress to the Cardinal's enormous fortune, and the latter was not disposed to give his niece to a deposed prince. He married her, when she was

fifteen, to the Duke de la Meilleraye who then became the Duke
de Mazarin, and with whom she had four children; however, this
unbalanced and fanatically jealous husband made her life impossible. After several years in exile in Rome and at Chambéry, Hortense travelled to London, ostensibly to visit her cousin Marie of
Modena, the wife of James, Duke of York, the king's brother. Her
real intention was to renew her ties with the man his mother had
wanted her to marry. She was bold and unconventional, and
determined to get the most out of life; she could be seen taking
fencing lessons in St James's Park, dressed in men's clothes. Charles
was soon attracted by her flamboyant personality and cultured
entourage when he met her at the home of Marie of Modena, and
she very quickly became his mistress. Unlike Louise de Keroualle,
the beautiful Hortense was not interested in politics, and she was
perfectly happy to share her lover with others. She had installed
herself in Covent Garden on her arrival in London, and was soon
surrounded by brilliant people such as Charles de Saint-Évremond, a libertarian philosopher exiled to London under the protection of Charles II who granted him a pension for the role of
'comptroller of the ducks of St James's'. On his advice, she started
a salon which became one of the most famous in Europe, and
their deep friendship endured until Hortense's death in 1699. In a
letter to Saint-Évremond of 18 December 1687, La Fontaine
wrote: 'You describe her, telling me it is impossible to do so,' and
took up the challenge with four lines:

> *Hortense received from Heaven her share*
> *of grace, beauty and wit; but that was not all:*
> *qualities of the heart; that was still not all*
> *for a thousand other charms the whole world adored her.*

As her husband had appropriated all her money, Hortense
found herself in financial trouble when she lost her royal pension
at the accession of William and Mary in 1688. She was forced to
move, first to a smaller house in Kensington Square, and then to
modest lodgings in Chelsea. Her circle of admirers was dispersed,

but she continued to receive a few friends such as the Dutch scholar Isaac Vossius and the French philosopher Pierre Bayle. After twenty-four years in London, she died there in July 1699 at the age of fifty-three.

She was mourned by the most faithful habitué of her salon, twenty years older than her, Charles de Saint-Évremond. After being compromised by a satirical letter about Mazarin, he had taken refuge in London where his libertarian philosophy could be freely expressed within the licentious court of Charles II. His shabby physical appearance concealed a sharp and witty mind and all his life he maintained links with the best writers of the time, both in France and in England. He lived in London for forty years and died there at the age of ninety; England paid him the honour of a tomb among the great historical figures that lay in Westminster Abbey.

The Tyburn martyrs

Queens, royal mistresses and other important persons were not the only French characters to enrich the London scene. On a very different level we must mention two memorable Frenchmen hanged at Tyburn.

The first was Claude Duval, also spelt Duvall or du Val, who was born at Domfront in Normandy in 1643 and worked as a groom for some English people in Rouen. He crossed the Channel after the Restoration as footman to an aristocrat. As his taste for drink, gambling and women demanded far more than a servant's wage he soon took to thieving and then highway robbery on the roads north of London in Holloway, between Islington and Highgate. He became famous for his eccentric methods: he would strip his victims with the greatest of courtesy. He often picked on members of high society heading for the races at Newmarket, and would ask them to advance him enough to bet on a favourite, promising them with a smile that he would pay them back out of his winnings. He was so charming to the women that, once they knew their lives were safe, they willingly opened their purses for him. It was said that one of them had her ransom considerably reduced after agreeing to dance with him in the middle of the road. This story has often been retold, notably after the pamphlet-eer William Pope published *The Memoirs of Monsieur du Val* shortly after Duval's death. One day, after the brigand had captured the King's huntsman and tied him hand and foot to a tree, a search warrant was issued for him and he decided to disappear to Paris, where he once again began to exercise his talents and his charm. But with the French police now on his tracks, he was forced to return to London where he was finally arrested in a tavern in Chandos Street in Covent Garden – being completely drunk he was unable to escape in time. He was condemned to death despite intercessions to the King, and hanged high and short on the Tyburn gibbet on 21 January 1670. He was twenty-seven and became a legend. Although he cannot be found in the register, several sources assert that he was buried at Saint Paul's Covent Garden with the following epitaph:

> *Here lies Du Vall: Reader, if male thou art*
> *look to thy purse; if female to thy heart.*
> *Much havoc has he made of both; for all*
> *men he made stand, and women he made fall.*
> *The Second Conqueror of the Norman race,*
> *knights to his arms did yield, and ladies to his face.*
> *Old Tyburn's glory; England's illustrious thief,*
> *Du Vall, the Ladies Joy; Du Vall, the Ladies Grief.*

His legend has been amplified by all sorts of exaggerated tales of his exploits; a film about him was produced by Gaumont in 1924, called *Claude Duval*.

Another Frenchman who finished up at the end of an English rope was Robert Hubert (1640–66), a silversmith originally from Rouen. He was in London in 1666, the year of the Great Fire. It had begun in a bakery but the cause was unknown, and suspicion soon fell on foreigners, particularly the French of whom there were many in that quarter. In this atmosphere, hostile to French and Catholics, Robert Hubert was arrested at Romford in Essex, accused of trying to leave the country. He confessed, possibly under torture, to being part of a group of twenty-three conspirators who had planned the fire in Paris and travelled to Sweden before arriving in London in August. He told of how he had thrown a 'ball of fire' made out of gunpowder and flammable materials through the window of Thomas Farriner's bakery in Pudding Lane. His confused and contradictory confessions convinced the judge that he was not entirely sane. The baker gave evidence in his favour, saying that there was no window in the place where the accused had claimed to throw the 'ball of fire', but despite an absence of witnesses and the weakness of the case the judge and jury condemned Robert Hubert to death by hanging on 27 October 1666. After the execution, new information brought conclusive proof of his innocence: the captain of a Swedish boat asserted that the condemned man had been on board his ship coming from Sweden, and that he had disembarked in London two days after the fire. A parliamentary enquiry finally concluded that the fire had been caused by 'an unfortunate spark from the baker's chimney' or 'great wind and a very dry summer'. And so of the two Frenchmen hanged at Tyburn, one had brought honour to his nation by his courtesy, and the other was the victim of a miscarriage of justice.

Places to visit

WESTMINSTER ABBEY

Jerusalem Chamber. Negotiations about the marriage of Charles I and Henrietta Maria of France took place in this chamber. An English Protestant present at the occasion was heard to remark prophetically: 'One must observe that a French queen has never brought any good fortune to England.'

Poets' Corner, in the south transept. Tomb of the philosopher Charles de Saint-Denis, Lord of Saint-Évremond.

QUEEN'S CHAPEL, ST JAMES'S PALACE
Marlborough Road SW1

The Royal Chapel, now Anglican, was once attached to St James's Palace by a gallery, now removed. A magnificent portrait by Van Dyck of Henrietta Maria hangs in the great gallery in which the Queen could attend Mass. Originally built by Inigo Jones for a Spanish marriage for Charles I, it was completed for Henrietta Maria in 1627. A congregation of French Oratorians was first installed there, followed by Benedictines, hence Friary Court which adjoins the existing chapel. It was the first Catholic chapel in England after the Reformation, and also the first built in the Palladian style. Excavations have revealed the presence of a graveyard connected to the chapel beneath Marlborough Road, a rare burial place for Catholics, who were considered outlaws.

SOMERSET HOUSE CHAPEL
Strand WC2

The only remains of the beautiful and luxurious chapel built for Henrietta Maria are four tombstones built into the walls of an underground passage beneath the central courtyard. Names of members of Henrietta Maria's entourage are engraved on them in French and Latin.

THE QUEEN'S HOUSE
Romney Road, Greenwich SE10

Set among later buildings by Christopher Wren, the beautiful Queen's House is a perfect example of the Palladian architecture introduced to England by Inigo Jones. Henrietta Maria insisted that her view of the Thames should never be blocked by other buildings. On the first floor, in the Queen's bedroom, one can still see Henrietta Maria's coat of arms on the painted ceiling. The building now houses a collection of paintings, including a portrait of the future King James II, dressed as a Roman hero, by the French painter Henri Gascar.

GREENWICH PARK

The gardens between the Queen's House and the Observatory were designed by Le Nôtre.

ROYAL OBSERVATORY
Blackheath Avenue, Greenwich SE10

Louise de Kérouaille persuaded Charles II to found the Observatory in 1675, with the purpose of solving the problem of longitude, crucial for navigation.

ALBERT MEMORIAL
Hyde Park SW7

Monument put up in memory of Prince Albert by Queen Victoria, designed by George Gilbert Scott. The Parnassus frieze around the base, made up of 169 larger-than-life statues, represents musicians, poets, painters, architects and sculptors, including many French artists (especially from the nineteenth century). On the southern panel of musicians and writers there are several seventeenth-century Frenchmen, including composers Lully and Rameau and playwrights Corneille and Molière.

ROYAL HOSPITAL CHELSEA
Royal Hospital Road SW3
A hospital for veterans founded by Charles II in 1682, the building was copied from the Invalides in Paris, created in 1670 by Louis XIV.

HENRIETTA STREET
Covent Garden WC2
This street is named after Henrietta Maria, and the neighbouring King Street after her husband Charles I.

INSCRIPTION
11 Kensington Square W8
The name of the Duchess of Mazarin is inscribed on the cornice above the porch of this house. Hortense Mancini is thought to have lived here from 1692 to 1698, although the sources are unclear. It seems more likely that she lived at number 15 where, according to the parish register, one of her ladies-in-waiting, Mme Claudine de Bragelone, died.

THE MARQUIS PUB
51–52 Chandos Place, Covent Garden WC2
Site of the seventeenth-century 'Hole in the Wall' tavern in which Claude Duval was arrested in 1669. A plaque on the left of the entrance tells his story.

NATIONAL PORTRAIT GALLERY
St Martin's Place WC2

Stuart Room. Portraits of the principal characters of the reigns of Charles I and Charles II: Henrietta Maria, Louise de Kéroualle, Henrietta Anne of England (Charles II's sister, Minette).

MUSEUM OF LONDON
In the Great Fire of London section, a panel tells of the arrest and hanging of the falsely accused Robert Hubert.

GOODWOOD HOUSE
Chichester, West Sussex
Bought by the first Duke of Richmond, son of Louise de Kéroualle. Louise created the foundation for the great collection with the furnishings of her apartment and her many commissions from artists of the time, such as her portrait and that of Minette, Henrietta Anne

4

A COUNTRY FOR
THE HUGUENOTS

VALUABLE IMMIGRANTS FOR ENGLAND

*'And so France lost around 500,000 inhabitants, a huge
variety of people, especially from the arts, thus enriching her
enemies'*

VOLTAIRE, *Le Siècle de Louis XIV,*
chapter XXXVI, 1751

The great reform of the church instigated by Luther and
Calvin, in rebellion against the excesses of the Roman
church, cut a huge swathe through political and religious life in
Europe long before its crucial effect on the economies of both
France and England. In France it influenced all levels of society,
with the exception of the peasantry. From 1560 onwards, the term
'Huguenot' was regularly used to describe French Calvinists. The
origins of the word are controversial, but in the generally accepted
version the word derives from the German *Eidgenossen*, 'confed-
erates, linked by an oath'. A term of abuse in France, in England
it described believers who were proud of their identity.

A generous welcome
Persecution soon led many Huguenots to leave France in search
of asylum with their co-religionists, notably the English Protes-

tants. As early as 1536, forty-seven Frenchmen obtained English citizenship under Henry VIII. Periods of tolerance and persecution alternated in France, culminating in the St Bartholomew's Day Massacre in Paris on the night of 24 August 1572. A year later there were already 9,000 Huguenots living in London, the majority from aristocratic or bourgeois families. The first to arrive established welcoming committees to help those who followed and who lacked social standing and financial means. They settled at first in Westminster, close to the court and to the centre of power, developing high-level contacts and thus ensuring vital support.

When the Protestant Henri of Navarre became King of France in 1589, he was forced to convert to Catholicism for the coronation – for him 'Paris was worth a Mass.' He was a naturally tolerant man and in 1598 he passed the Edict of Nantes, which recognised freedom of conscience and worship, and enshrined the notion of equality among all citizens. The Protestant emigration ceased for a time, but the persecutions began again under Louis XIII and more refugees arrived in England in successive waves. The repression became draconian under Louis XIV, with the 'dragonnades' which, from 1681 onwards, were an attempt to impose a return to Catholicism. After the Revocation of the Edict of Nantes in 1685, all Protestant churches were closed or destroyed and their pastors sent into exile. Despite the difficulty of leaving France, between 40,000 and 50,000 Huguenots took refuge in England. By 1700 almost 25,000 refugees were living in London and its surroundings, representing about 5 per cent of the population. Towards the end of the seventeenth century the Huguenot nobles and rich bourgeoisie began to build themselves houses on land hitherto reserved for the royal hunt, north of St James's Palace. The new district was called Soho.

Successive English monarchs set themselves up as protectors of the Huguenots, out of a combination of sympathy and political interest. As early as 1550, Edward VI had signed a royal charter permitting the opening of places of worship for 'the strangers banished and exiled from their own country for love of the Gospel of Christ'.[11] Elizabeth I had provided military and financial help to the Huguenots in France. Henri IV, as a token of gratitude, gave her an elephant in 1591 – like the one given three centuries earlier by St Louis to Henry III, it was installed in the Tower of London.

The links between the Huguenot community and the court earned the goodwill of Charles II, who gave them the 'little chapel' of Savoy in 1661, with the one condition that they should accept Anglican communion. They were also given the 'Greek church' in Crown Street (now Charing Cross Road) in Soho, so named because it had originally been intended for the Greek Orthodox community. The painter William Hogarth chose it for a satirical engraving of the French coming out of church.

In 1687 the Catholic James II reluctantly recognised the right to religious freedom with a Declaration of Indulgence, which attracted a new wave of French refugees to London. William and Mary set up the Royal Bounty for them, alms which were distributed until 1804. Finally, Queen Anne intervened personally to negotiate the release of about 180 Huguenots condemned to row in the French king's galleys. The English government passed several laws protecting the refugees and their communities, setting aside its usual suspicion towards foreigners, and showing remarkable generosity towards them.

Successful integration

At first, when they believed that their exile was only temporary, the Huguenots retained their French language and customs. Religious instruction was the most important priority for the Calvinist church, and it opened several schools in London and its surroundings. Many educated Huguenots taught in them, such as Claude de Saintliens (later Claude Holyband), who wrote the first French manual for the use of high-society English speakers. The last French Protestant School in Westminster survived until 1920, and the Westminster French Protestant School Foundation and The Educational Fund of the French Protestant Church of London give grants to this day to the descendants of Huguenots. With their high moral standards and strict discipline they were able to establish an extremely efficient mutual aid system. The Huguenot community was developed and preserved largely thanks to charitable enterprises and other benevolent associations. In 1718 it founded La Providence hospital, which moved to Rochester in 1960, retaining its name as a French hospital in the form of a retirement home for the descendants of Huguenots.

At the beginning there were very few mixed marriages but they multiplied as time went on, so much that it is thought that one in three English people may have Huguenot blood today. The Huguenot Society, an offshoot of the mutual aid societies, can help trace the origins of many families – a difficult task given the almost systematic anglicisation of surnames, either by translation or transformation: Blanc became White, Carpentier Carpenter, Delacroix Cross, Dubois Wood and so on. Other family names became, in their original form, household names – Courtauld (the Courtauld Institute, Courtauld textiles) or Dollond (Dollond and Aitchison).

The newcomers practised a version of Protestantism that was different from that of the English, who asked them to adopt the Anglican liturgy and use the Book of Common Prayer in a French translation. This brought about a division at the heart of the French community between the 'conformists' who accepted this, and the 'non-conformists' who refused to change their practice; the hierarchical Calvinist structure of the French Reformed Church in London was deeply shaken by this. At the end of the seventeenth century, the two communities founded the General Assembly of French Churches in order to re-establish unity and form a link between the thirty churches in and around London.

By giving the Huguenots legal status and facilitating their naturalisation, the English enabled them to integrate completely into society. The more prosperous among the newcomers, installed as they were at the centre of political and cultural life, became integrated more rapidly than their less prosperous compatriots who lived on the edges of the City, in Spitalfields. The area they lived in, the language they spoke and whether or not they were 'conformist' became the determining factors for success and influence in their new country.

By the end of the eighteenth century integration was complete. The success of the Huguenots in their respective individual or family businesses can be seen on the walls of London, where one can still read the names Cazenove (stockbroking), Minet (insurance) and Courage (brewing). These tradesmen, artisans and artists brought abilities and talents which allowed them to seek out and obtain important positions, and to make their mark in many different trades. John Houblon, a third-generation Huguenot, became the first governor of the Bank of England and then Lord Mayor of London. The numerous ex-army and navy officers distinguished themselves in the ranks of the British forces, improving their discipline and strategy in the wars against Louis XIV. In 1757, Jean-Louis de Ligonier became commander-in-chief of the British army. Nowadays, during the Trooping of the Colour celebrating the Queen's birthday every year, the band plays a tune from Meyerbeer's opera *The Huguenots*.

Intellectuals in the community took an interest in the movements that followed the Reformation and played an active part in the philosophical and religious debates of the time. Thomas Vautrollier was publishing books at Blackfriars by the 1570s. His widow married Shakespeare's publisher, and it is thought that she might well have been consulted by Shakespeare about the use of French expressions in his plays, notably *Henry V*. Abel Boyer published a Franco-English Royal Dictionary which remained an authority for more than a hundred years. Isaac Casaubon, a librarian and great scholar, worked at St James's and Lambeth palaces and is buried at Westminster Abbey. Peter Mark Roget compiled the celebrated Thesaurus, dictionary of synonyms; trained as a doctor, he also helped to create a medical school in Manchester and to found London University.

Many of the descendants of the original refugees regrouped according to political or religious affinity. In the 1720s two French masonic lodges were founded in London. The members were mostly Huguenot, the most famous being the experimental philosopher J. T. Desaguliers, Master of the French lodge in 1724.

From banks to silk, a rich contribution
to English life and economy

Huguenots participated in politics, becoming diplomats and members of Parliament (there were sixty-five between 1734 and 1832) as well as, sometimes, spies and even pirates. Some became distinguished lawyers, such as Samuel Romilly, who campaigned against slavery and the death penalty. Others became distinguished scientists. Theodore de Mayerne, one of the founders of the Society of Apothecaries, was Queen Henrietta Maria's private doctor. The Chamberlen family of obstetricians became famous for the invention of the forceps, kept secret for a long time. The opticians Dollond and Aitchison owe their reputation to the Dollond family who perfected optical instruments. The first director of the Royal Society was none other than Denis Papin, inventor of the pressure cooker. John Desaguliers, an Anglican vicar, philosopher and engineer, installed the first ventilation system in the House of Commons, and the engineer Charles Labelye designed Westminster Bridge in 1738.

When it comes to the arts, many works can be seen in London by Huguenot sculptors such as Maximilian Poultrain-Colt, Hubert Le Sueur and, above all, Louis-François Roubillac. Originally from Lyon, Roubillac worked all his life in England, arriving in 1732; here he became one of the greatest baroque sculptors of his adoptive country. He was a great portrait-sculptor, and he made busts of a great many of the important intellectual and political figures of his time in his studio in St Martin's Lane in Soho. These included the composer Handel, the poet Alexander Pope, the writer Jonathan Swift, the mathematician Isaac Newton and the actor David Garrick. He also carved numerous funerary monuments in Westminster Abbey.

The painter Philippe Mercier, who arrived in London around 1716, lived first in Leicester Square and then Covent Garden. He became a specialist in small group paintings, known as 'conversation pieces', an English version of Watteau's *fêtes galantes*. These intimate scenes and their informal style influenced a great many English painters in the eighteenth century, notably Gainsborough and Reynolds. In the nineteenth century, the painter John Everett Millais was one of the founders of the Pre-Raphaelite movement.

The illustrator and cartographer Jacques Le Moyne worked with Sir Walter Raleigh to draw up the first maps of the New World. Jean Chardin, son of a jeweller and himself a jeweller, spent fifteen years travelling in the Middle East, becoming one of the great oriental specialists of the seventeenth century. He became the official court jeweller and was ennobled by Charles II; he was also a member of the Royal Society and an agent of the East India Company. In 1686 he published *Voyages en Perse et autres lieu de l'Orient*, which remains one of the best sources of information on Persian culture at that time. Paul de Lamerie, who was in the service of George I in 1716, was one of the greatest goldsmiths of the eighteenth century. In around 1745 two Huguenot goldsmiths, Nicholas Sprimont and Charles Gouyon, set up a porcelain factory at Chelsea, the first in England to compare in quality with those in France and Germany. They were influenced by the porcelain produced at Chantilly and Saint-Cloud, and later that of Sèvres. The factory was transferred to Derby in 1784.

Finally, the Lanier family produced many generations of musicians: Nicolas Lanier was a flautist at the court of Elizabeth I in 1564. His grandson, also called Nicolas, was the first bearer of the title 'Master of the King's Music' in 1626. Pierre Prelleur was in charge of the music at Christ Church in Spitalfields. David Garrick, a third-generation Huguenot (the original name was Garrigue), the greatest of actors and directors, was a huge influence on the world of theatre in his time. He is one of the best examples of the deep integration of Huguenots into English society, confirming Saint-Simon's words: 'The Revocation of the Edict of Nantes ... this awful act which depopulated a quarter of the kingdom, and ruined its commerce ... sent our factories abroad, making their countries flourish and prosper at our expense, and helped them to build new cities.'[12]

The success of all their different activities led the Huguenots to play a particularly important part in the development of the City. As well as Sir John Houblon, first governor of the Bank of

England from 1694 to 1697, the Bosanquet and Minet families ran several insurance companies throughout the eighteenth and nineteenth centuries. And the Bosanquets and Romillys oversaw several important legal reforms.

In Greenwich, the Fortreys (originally Forterie) and the Lethieulliers became important merchants. Several glass manufacturers established themselves there and by the eighteenth century their descendants had built themselves handsome houses around the park. The Marquis de Ruvigny, an ex-courtier of Louis XIV, lived in the Queen's House. His presence there and that of his two high-ranking army officer sons drew other officers and aristocrats to the area. He organised French-language services in St Alphege's church, which took place after the end of the Anglican ones.

King William of Orange and Queen Mary employed two Huguenots to create the Privy Garden at Hampton Court. Daniel Marot, a disciple of Le Nôtre, designed the parterres, while the ironsmith Jean Tijou made the magnificent gate to the garden, comprising several panels symbolising England, Wales, Ireland and Scotland. With his *New Book of Drawings*, published in 1693, Jean Tijou completely transformed wrought-iron work in England.

No less important was the contribution made by those Huguenots living in poorer areas of London. French weavers established and developed the silk industry, and in 1684 Jean Larguier, a refugee from Nîmes, introduced a shiny black form of silk called 'Alamode', as well as another shimmering version. Spitalfields silk, with its fine and complex patterns, became highly sought after. Another fabric imported from Nîmes by the Huguenots is still today known as 'denim'. The Huguenots also made ribbons that were cheaper and of better quality than their English equivalents, a direct competition that caused some conflict with English weavers in 1675. By 1630, Huguenots had also established workshops for the manufacture and dying of felt and hats – ironically, they even supplied hats for the cardinals in Rome!

And so, as Saint-Simon said, French intolerance resulted in the gift to England of a great fortune in all areas of human endeavour.

Places to visit

SOHO AND WESTMINSTER

If the streets, churches and buildings could speak they could tell us about Paul Crespin, a goldsmith who lived at the corner of Greek Street and Old Compton Street, or Abraham Meure who opened a school in 1691 at 12 Greek Street which became well known in the eighteenth century. Some schools already existed such as the one founded by Metre in Long Acre and another in 1680 by d'Agard on the Strand. A bit further on towards Covent Garden were the taverns in St Martin's Lane patronised by such men as the sculptor Louis-François Roubillac and the mathematician Abraham de Moivre. Other illustrious Huguenots lie in the churches: Théodore de Mayerne, Charles I's doctor; the sculptor Roubillac, and the musician Nicolas Lanier. The scholar J. T. Desaguliers and a certain Louis Duras or Durford, Grand Chamberlain to Catherine of Braganza, wife of Charles II, are buried in the now-destroyed Savoy Chapel.

Huguenot Society
Ruislip, Middlesex HA4 4GU
The society was created in 1885 by the directors of the French Hospital to maintain links with the descendants of the Huguenots in England.

- **The Huguenot Library**
  National Archives, Kew, Surrey
  The library contains a large archive going back to the earliest times of the immigration.

Huguenot churches
Most of the Huguenot churches – such as the Savoy Chapel, the Patent, the Tabernacle and the Greeks – have now disappeared, but some have left the occasional trace, through a sign, a plaque or a building.

- **Congregational Chapel**
  Orange Street SW1
  Huguenots of the district opened a chapel in 1693 known as the Leicester Fields

Temple. Its first pastor was Daniel Chamier. In the eighteenth centry one of the pastors spoke seventeen languages, and another taught French to Queen Charlotte and her daughters. The chapel was eventually taken back and rebuilt by the Methodist Church.

- **Commemorative plaque**
  24 West Street WC2
  Recalls the existence of a chapel on this site in 1700.

- **French Protestant Church**
  8–9 Soho Square W1
  Offshoot of the first Huguenot church allowed by King Edward IV in 1550 in Threadneedle Street in the City. Built in Soho in 1893, it is today the only French Protestant Church in London. To celebrate its four hundredth anniversary, a sculpture was placed on the tympanum in 1950: it depicted the Huguenots flight across the Channel, and their arrival at Dover carrying the tools of their trades, followed by the granting of the Royal Charter by Edward VI. The sculpture is surmounted by a dove and the Huguenot cross.

Street names in Soho and Westminster
Reminders of the Huguenot presence in the district.

- **Romilly Street**. The Romillys were lawyers.

- **Foubert's Place**. Solomon Foubert founded and ran a famous military academy.

- **Garrick Street**. The Garrick Theatre and the Garrick Club are named in memory of the famous actor David Garrick, who was of Huguenot origin.

- **Petty France** or 'Petite France', near St James's underground station, so-called because of the French atmosphere of the neighbourhood. A plaque on the facade of the Adam and Eve pub recalls the presence of French wool merchants in the district.

Westminster Abbey

Several works by Huguenot sculptors Maximilien Poultrain (or Colt), Hubert Le Sueur and Louis-François Roubillac. Also tombs of important Huguenots: Maréchal de Lligonier, Isaac Casaubon (a great scholar and librarian to the French King Henri IV), as well as the actor David Garrick.

Westminster Bridge

The engineer Charles Labelye built the first Westminster Bridge using new techniques in 1739. It was only the third bridge in London at that time, after London Bridge and Putney Bridge.

Courtauld Institute

Somerset House

Augustin and Samuel Courtauld were famous eighteenth-century silversmiths, whose descendants founded a worldwide textile business. Samuel Courtauld, a great collector of French Impressionists, created this gallery and left his collection to it in 1931. It contains the largest collection of French Impressionist paintings in England.

Palace of Westminster

House of Commons

- **The Speaker's carriage** was built for King William III from designs by Huguenot Daniel Marot. It is still used for ceremonial occasions such as coronations and jubilees.

Statues of the painter John Everett Millais

- **John Islip Street SW1**. Of Huguenot origin, he was one of the founders of the Tate Gallery.

- **Victoria & Albert Museum**. On the facade of the entrance, a full-length statue.

David Garrick medallion

27 Southampton Street WC2

A bronze medallion representing the actor, who lived at this address.

Blue plaques

- **Sir John Everett Millais**, painter
  2 Palace Gate W8

- **Paul de Lamerie**, goldsmith
  40 Gerrard Street W1

- **David Garrick**, actor
  Adelphi Terrace WC2

- **Sir Samuel Romilly**, lawyer
  21 Russell Square WC1
  6 Gray's Inn Square WC1

SPITALFIELDS

The French Church

59 Brick Lane E1

On the corner of Fournier Street and Brick Lane, the church was built in 1743, as can be seen above the sundial on the facade. Large vaulted cellars beneath the church were used as depots by Huguenot merchants. After becoming a synagogue, the church is now a mosque for the Bangladeshi community, the new weavers of Spitalfields.

Christ Church

Commercial Street E1

Eighteenth-century tombstones with French names indicate the Huguenot presence in this church. The oldest is that of the Lefèvre family, on the ground at the entrance. Many other memorials bearing French names – Vaux, Fournier, Désormeaux, Chabot, Dubois – can be seen on the staircase leading to the gallery and in the arches beneath the church. The Huguenot Pierre Prelleur was the first organist of this church.

Fournier Street, Princelet Street, Wilkes Street E1

The houses in these streets show the particular characteristics of Huguenot weavers' dwellings: wooden shutters on the outside, typically French and unique in London. The large windows on the top floor let in the light for the looms, and pulleys outside these windows were used to bring merchandise in and out. There is a fine gutter on a house in Fournier Street, decorated with a fleur de lys and dated 1725.

Severs House
18 Folgate Street W1

This house recreates a typical Huguenot weaver's dwelling. The house is candle-lit and silent, with quiet voices in the background as if the original inhabitants were still there. A canary sings in a cage, as they did in Huguenot days to drown the sound of the looms which were usually on the top floor.

Streets in Spitalfields
Fournier Street
Huguenot Place
Calvin Street
Fleur-de-Lis Street
Navarre Street
Chambord Street
Rochelle Street

THE CITY

Bank of England Museum
Bartholomew Lane EC2

The Bank of England was built on property belonging to the Huguenot John Houblon, its first governor, who lived in Threadneedle Street. In a street behind the bank, the museum displays portraits, letters and documents relating to its history.

- **£50 note.** In 1994, to celebrate its 300th anniversary, the Bank of England issued a £50 note showing John Houblon and his house.

St Paul's Cathedral
St Paul's Churchyard, EC4

The wrought-iron railings and balustrades were made by ironsmith Jean Tijou. A monument in the crypt is dedicated to Royal Navy captain Édouard Riou, a second-generation Huguenot. His father, Étienne Riou, had introduced Vauban-style fortifications to England. John Everett Millais's ashes are interred in St Paul's.

Bouverie Street EC4

The street bears the name of a Huguenot family, the first of whom, Laurens de Bouverie,

arrived in London in 1567. Almost all his descendants, many ennobled or members of parliament, have been governors of the Providence French Hospital.

Blue plaques
53 Threadneedle Street EC2
St Martin's Le Grand EC1

These two plaques commemorate the history of the French Protestant church. After the Royal Charter allowing the opening of churches for foreigners in 1550, the chapel of the old St Anthony's Hospital in Threadneedle Street became the first French Protestant church in the sixteenth century. Destroyed in the great fire of 1666, it was rebuilt and reopened in 1669. When it closed in 1840, the congregation rebuilt the community in a nearby church in St Martin's Le Grand where they worshipped from 1841 to 1888. They finally moved to a new church in Soho Square in 1893.

WANDSWORTH AND PUTNEY

Huguenot communities established themselves in the countryside surrounding London, where life was cheaper. After 1630, the first arrivals in Wandsworth set up felt-manufacturing workshops beside the river Wandle in order to use the water. They founded their conformist church around 1682 and, at the beginning of the eighteenth century, represented 20 per cent of the population of Wandsworth. Rich Huguenots from the City also built splendid country houses there. A century later, this Huguenot community had been completely assimilated to the local population.

Huguenot cemetery (Mount Nod)
Huguenot Place SW18

A romantic little island of greenery surrounded by the South Circular Road, this was used by the Huguenots from 1687. On the north side, a commemorative plaque explains the history of the Huguenots in this cemetery: 'Here rest many Huguenots who on the revocation of the Edict of Nantes in 1685 left their native land for conscience's sake and found in Wandsworth freedom to worship God after their own manner. They established important industries and added to the credit and prosperity of the town of their adoption.' Unfortunately the inscriptions on the tombs are difficult to read. This cemetery remains an important historical site for the Huguenots in London.

Wandsworth Town Hall
The sculpted frieze on the facade shows the history of Wandsworth, including the Huguenot presence. On the Wandsworth coat of arms, drops of water on a golden background symbolise the tears of the Huguenot refugees escaping persecution.

Winchester House
10 Lower Richmond Road, Putney SW15
Now the Putney Constitutional Club, the elegantly decorated house was built beside the Thames in 1726 by the Huguenot Jacques Baudoin, born in Nîmes. One of its fireplaces is now in the Victoria & Albert Museum.

Street names

- **Wandsworth**
  Huguenot Place
  Barchard Street
  Ferrier Street
  Nantes Close
  Louvaine Road
  Rochelle Close
  Eglantine Road
  Osiers Road

- **Putney**
  Ruvigny Garden. Henri de Massue de Ruvigny was a Huguenot officer in William III's army.

CHELSEA

Royal Hospital Chelsea
Monument to Isaac Garnier who was Apothecary General to the Hospital, where he is buried. His son, with the same name, was also Apothecary General.

Commemorative plaque
Lawrence Street SW3
This plaque indicates the site of the Chelsea porcelain factory, which moved to Derby in 1784.

Street name
Sprimont Place bears the name of the founder of the Chelsea porcelain factory.

Victoria & Albert Museum
Examples of Chelsea porcelain, Spitalfields silks, gold and silver by Paul Crespin and Paul de Lamerie, and ironwork by Jean Tijou.

GREENWICH

Royal Observatory
In the museum, eighteenth-century telescopes by Dollond, a Huguenot refugee.

St Alphege's Church
Greenwich Church Street SE10
The ironwork of the altar railings and the gallery balustrade have been attributed to Jean Tijou. In the cemetery is a monument to Sir John Lethieullier, a rich Huguenot merchant.

Crooms Hill SE10
Alongside Greenwich Park, fine houses here belong to several families of Huguenot descent.

National Maritime Museum
Romney Road SE10
Several portraits of Huguenots such as the engineer J. T. Desaguliers and Navy captain Édouard Riou, as well as the diary of a ship's captain describing the La Rochelle expedition of 1628, embarked upon to support the Huguenot cause.

FRENCH HOSPITAL
41 La Providence High Street
Rochester, Kent
The French Hospital, or 'La Providence', was transferred to Rochester and is a retirement home for the descendants of Huguenots. It has

recently raised money to open an information centre and a small museum explaining the Huguenot heritage.

FAMOUS HUGUENOTS

Hubert Le Sueur, sculptor

- **Trafalgar Square**. Equestrian statue of Charles I. The 1633 equestrian statue was inspired by that of French King Henri IV on the Pont Neuf in Paris, on which Hubert Le Sueur had worked before coming to England. Imperturbable amidst the traffic, Charles I appears to be riding his horse towards the Banqueting Hall in Whitehall, his old palace and the scene of his execution. Sold by Parliament during the Civil War to be destroyed, the statue survived and was re-erected during the Restoration of Charles II.

- **Westminster Abbey**. In St Paul's Chapel, a bronze bust by Le Sueur of Lady Cottington on the tomb of Lord and Lady Cottington. Lord Cottington was a confidant of Charles I. In the first chapel around the choir of the Henry VII Chapel, a bronze monument of Charles Villiers, first Duke of Buckingham, and his wife. In the fifth chapel of the north ambulatory, a bronze tomb for the family of Ludovic Stuart, Duke of Richmond and Lennox. In Poets' Corner, a bronze bust of judge Sir Thomas Richardson, 1635.

- **Victoria & Albert Museum**. In the British Galleries, the bust of Charles I is the only marble bust known to have been made by Le Sueur. In the small sculptures gallery, a bronze statuette of Louis XIII on horseback.

Louis-François Roubillac, sculptor

- **Westminster Abbey** contains a great many works by Roubillac, who was a much sought-after baroque sculptor of his time. In the north transept, a white marble statue of Admiral and MP Warren. In St Michael's Chapel, a marble monument to Sir Joseph and Lady Elisabeth Nightingale, one of Roubillac's masterpieces. In Poets' Corner, a statue of the Duke of Argyll, soldier and orator, and another of George Handel, with the face modelled from his death mask. In the nave, marble busts of General George Wade and General James Fleming, with martial emblems and allegorical figures, and monument to General William Hargrave, Governor of Gibraltar. On the south side of the cloister, memorial plaque to Colonel Frances Ligonier, a Huguenot who fought under the English flag. It was commissioned by his brother, General Sir John Louis Ligonier, whose monument is also in the Abbey.

- A great many Roubillac sculptures can be found in London museums: the Victoria & Albert (statue of Handel), the British Museum (statue of Shakespeare), the Royal Academy, the National Portrait Gallery, the Guildhall Art Gallery and the Foundling Museum in Brunswick Square.

- Roubillac's works can also be seen in the churches of St Mary's Battersea, St Botolph Aldersgate, in Golden Square and in the Queen's House in Greenwich.

- Portraits of Roubillac are in the National Portrait Gallery, Dulwich Picture Gallery and the Garrick Club. Medallion bust of Roubillac on the north facade of the National Portrait Gallery. Portrait of Roubillac on the Albert Memorial (north panel, sculptors).

Jean Tijou, ironworker

- **Hampton Court**, East Molesey, Surrey. The gate into the Privy Garden is divided into twelve magnificent wrought-iron panels with the national emblems of the different parts of the United Kingdom (rose, thistle, harp, fleur de lys). The Privy Garden and the Great Fountain Garden, designed by Daniel Marot, were restored at the end of the twentieth century following the original designs.

- **Kensington Palace,** Kensington Gardens W8. Ironwork inside the palace, notably the balustrade of the king's staircase.

- **St Paul's Cathedral.** Wrought-iron railings in front of the altar, magnificent choir screens, readjusted in the nineteenth century, and balustrades for the galleries in the dome.

- **St Alphege's Church.** See page 71, col. 2.

- **Victoria & Albert Museum.** Examples of Hampton Court ironwork by Tijou.

Philippe Mercier, painter

Works by Philippe Mercier, with his innovative Conversation Pieces, can be seen in several London Museums: the Courtauld Institute, the National Gallery, the National Portrait Gallery, the Royal Academy and Tate Britain.

Jean Chardin, traveller and jeweller to the king

- **Westminster Abbey.** His funerary monument in marble near the grille separating the nave from the choir bears the inscription *nomen sibi fecit eundo,* 'He made his name by travelling.'

- **National Portrait Gallery.** Portrait of Chardin by Godfrey Kneller, showing a map of the Middle East held by a young black boy.

Maréchal Jean-Louis de Ligonier

- **Westminster Abbey.** In the north ambulatory, a white marble monument to this commander-in-chief of the British army. The four medallions surrounding him represent the English sovereigns under whom he served, and the commemorative plaque lists his principal battles.

- **National Army Museum**
  Royal Hospital Road, Chelsea SW3
  Oil portrait of the marshal in his uniform of Colonel of the Royal Regiment of Horse Guards.

Nicolas Lanier, musician

- **Lanier Road,** Lewisham SE13

- **British Museum.** In the museum archives, scores by Lanier (the second).

John Dollond, optician

- **Royal Observatory.** Around fifty objects from the Dollond factory for optical instruments, with numerous telescopes (the oldest dating from 1760) as well as many navigational instruments.

- **Science Museum**
  Exhibition Road SW7
  Several instruments signed by Dollond.

5

ENLIGHTENMENT VS 'SIÈCLE DES LUMIÈRES'
DIALOGUE AND ARGUMENT IN THE EIGHTEENTH CENTURY

'I believe that an Englishman who thoroughly knows France and a Frenchman who thoroughly knows England are both the better for that knowledge'

VOLTAIRE, *Lettre à l'Abbé Blanc*[13]

In the eighteenth century the established order was shaken by the new ideology of the 'Lumières', and its British equivalent the Enlightenment, while at the same time the two kingdoms went to war with one another. Two traces of these battles remain in French folklore: the song *Malbrouk s'en va-t-en guerre* (after the Battle of Malplaquet in 1709 General Marlborough's name was gallicised), and the famous call from the commander of the French guard in 1745 at the Battle of Fontenoy: 'Messieurs les Anglais, tirez les premiers!' Louis XV even went so far as to plan an invasion of England, and spies and emissaries from both sides would pass by one another on the streets of London.

The flood of foreign arrivals, particularly from France, sparked a new kind of chauvinism, satirically illustrated by William Hogarth in his painting *The Gates of Calais*, also known as *The Roast Beef of Old England*. This was inspired by the fact that, while staying in France and drawing at Calais, the artist had been arrested and accused of spying. He furiously responded with his paintbrush, contrasting the superiority and prosperity of the Englishman – symbolised by the roast beef – with the miserable indigence and poor fare of the Frenchman. Known to eat frog's legs, the French became known as the 'Frogs', a term used for the first time as an insult in Fanny Burney's novel *Evelina*.

The mutual animosity at this time is copiously illustrated in the memoirs of both English and French travellers. The writer Tobias Smollett is one example: 'If a Frenchman is capable of real friendship, it must certainly be the most disagreeable present he can possibly make to a man of a true English character.'[14] However, this antagonism had one positive result: it inspired a great deal of reciprocal curiosity.

Crossbreeding influences

In the century of the Enlightenment, the influence of the court of Versailles was all-powerful throughout Europe, dictating the fashion in all other courts. Dresses and suits *à la française* were all the rage, coquettes painted their faces with rouge and adorned their heads with extravagant coiffures. The English vocabulary describing clothing reflected these fashions. We find words such as brassière, camisole, corset, corsage, cravat, décolletée, déshabillée, négligée, etc. Beyond the world of fashion it was considered smart to speak French and to decorate one's home with French materials and furnishings. This happened in the opposite direction as well, as Madame de la Tour du Pin, a lady-in-waiting to Marie Antoinette, describes: 'Everything had to be copied from our neighbours, from the Constitution to horses and carriages. Some young people even affected an English accent when speaking French and studied, in order to imitate them, Englishmen's gauche habits, their way of walking, and their general physical appearance.'[15] Women wore hats *à l'anglaise* or *à la jockey*, while men wore *catogans* and hats *à l'anglomane*. The French word *redingote* is derived from 'riding coat'.

When it came to gardens, the great English landscape designers, inspired by the much-admired paintings of Claude Lorrain, advocated a return to nature, echoing the ideas of their contemporary Jean-Jacques Rousseau. Later, English gardens became the fashion in Paris, notably those of the Petit Trianon and of Bagatelle.

Intellectual exchanges were just as fruitful. While the French, introduced to English thought by translations made by Huguenots living in England, became inspired by dreams of the freedom and tolerance that reigned across the Channel, rich British aristocrats and artists completed their education with a Grand Tour, a journey across continental Europe. Laurence Sterne and Tobias Smollett describe these travels in *The Sentimental Journey* (1768) and *Voyages through France and Italy* (1766). These visits encouraged an exchange of ideas and knowledge, which took place at gatherings in Parisian salons and in London coffee houses.

The French encyclopaedists and the English pamphleteers attacked their respective societies with relish. Their high-powered conversations, helped by the distribution of newspapers, fuelled attacks on the regimes in power. In England, Parliament had well and truly won in the matter of sharing power with the monarch, but this was not the case in France where, under the regency which followed the death of Louis XIV, the development of ideas and the general relaxation of attitudes were beginning to undermine the foundations of a divinely elected monarchy.

There were numerous correspondences between French and English intellectuals. Madame du Deffand, whose Paris salon was famous, maintained an intellectual and amorous exchange of letters with Horace Walpole, a political writer and aesthete twenty years younger. This mingling of ideas gradually transformed the spirit of each nation; rationalism and scepticism gave way to romanticism, while across the Channel the French Revolution was brewing, causing much anxiety in England.

The most widely read English novelist in France in the eighteenth century was Samuel Richardson, who was a great influence on those writers who wanted to escape from the classical form.

His most fashionable novels, *Pamela* (1740) and *Clarissa* (1748) were the inspiration for Voltaire's *Nanine* (1749) and Rousseau's *La Nouvelle Héloise* (1761); Diderot, too, paid tribute to him with *Eloge de Richardson* (1762). In the opposite direction, the great English poet Alexander Pope (1688–1744) was fascinated by Boileau, while William Wordsworth (1770–1850) was inspired by Rousseau. The only book that the latter recommended the young to read in his *Émile* was Daniel Defoe's *Robinson Crusoe*. This game of mirrors manifests itself in the very similar sensibilities of works such as *Les Liaisons Dangereuses* by Choderlos de Laclos and Daniel Defoe's *Moll Flanders*. Similarly, Diderot's *Encyclopédie* (1751–72) is the counterpart to Samuel Johnson's *Dictionary* (1755); and Voltaire's *Candide*, with its lessons on life, echoes Jonathan Swift's *Gulliver's Travels*.

In the theatre, Aaron Hill's *Zara* is inspired by Voltaire's *Zaire*, which he translated, while *Zaire* has strange resemblances to Shakespeare's *Othello*! English theatre directors kept a watch on the Parisian stage and adapted successful plays to the tastes of their own audiences. Molière was regularly performed in the three main theatres in Drury Lane, Covent Garden and the Haymarket. Works by Destouches, Marivaux, Beaumarchais and Voltaire were all very successfully performed in London. Samuel Foote wrote *The Englishman in Paris* in 1753, adapted from Louis de Boissy's *Français à Londres* (1727).

As far as the arts were concerned, Joshua Reynolds, Thomas Gainsborough and Thomas Rowlandson were influenced by Watteau, Fragonard and Boucher. The rococo style spread through the world of decorative art, influencing Chippendale furniture and the porcelains of the Bow factory.

Eminent writers in London

Throughout the eighteenth century, French men of letters were drawn to London and the *modèle anglais*. Voltaire, after a quarrel with the Chevalier de Rohan in 1726, was ordered into exile at the age of thirty-two, and went to spend three years in London. He already had friends there, one of whom was Lord Bolingbroke, an English politician he had met in France. He settled in Wandsworth at the home of Everard Falkener, a rich merchant he had met in Paris, and when he came to the centre of town he would stay at the White Wig hotel at 10 Maiden Lane in Covent Garden. He also lived in Billiter Square in the City. He quickly mastered the English language with the help of a young Wandsworth Quaker, and for a time considered pursuing his writing career in England. He rapidly made friends at court, thanks to his letters of introduction, and was presented to George I and invited to great English houses. With the same devouring energy as he had shown in France, he discovered Shakespeare, by whom he was inspired to the point of plagiarism; he adapted *Julius Caesar* for the French stage and began to write a Shakespearean tragedy, *Brutus*, which he dedicated to his friend Lord Bolingbroke. He began *The History of Charles XII*, took notes for his *Lettres Philosophiques* and re-wrote his epic poem *La Ligue*, about the wars of religion. It was published in 1728 under the title *La Henriade,* with a dedication to Queen Caroline of England, and was a huge success.

In the dedication of his *Zaire* to Everard Falkener, Voltaire observed that the English realise how important merchants are to national prosperity: 'You are English, my dear friend, and I was born in France. [. . .] I therefore offer you this tragedy as to a compatriot in literature, and as to my close friend . . . At the same time I have the pleasure of being able to tell my own country of how merchants are regarded in your country; in what esteem a profession is held which makes the glory of England, and with what a superior manner some of you represent their country in Parliament, and as legislators.'[16]

Voltaire, struck by the spirit of tolerance in England, published his *Lettres Philosophiques* or *Lettres Anglaises* there in 1733. When they appeared in France the following year they caused a scandal, causing the writer to leave Paris to live prudently close to a frontier. He never lost his interest in England. At the end of his life a Major Broom came to visit him at Ferney near Geneva, and reported in his diary that the entire conversation had taken place in English.

Another eminent anglophile in the literary world was Montesquieu who, after the success of *Lettres persanes* in 1721, divided his time between Bordeaux, where he practised law, and Paris, where he frequented intellectual circles and literary salons. He was elected to the Académie Française in 1728, and decided to travel; after visiting most of Europe, he settled in London for almost two years, from 1729 to 1731. He had been introduced to British culture thanks to his friendship at school with the Duke of Berwick, Charles I's illegitimate son, and he had met several important English francophiles in Paris, notably Lord Bolingbroke and Horace Walpole. On his arrival in London, he lodged at 18 St James's Square, the home of Lord Chesterfield, who introduced him into society. He dined several times with George II and Queen Caroline. His *Lettres persanes*, already translated into English, were reprinted during his stay in London. He was admitted into the Royal Society, and read the British press and watched debates in the House of Commons and the House of Lords. In *L'esprit des lois*, Montesquieu paints an admiring picture of the British political system, with its balance between the executive, the legislative and the judiciary: 'They are the only people in the world who have been able to make use of these three great things at once: religion, commerce and liberty.'[17]

Abbé Prévost, who achieved literary fame in a quite different manner, also found asylum in England at the same period. Having joined the Benedictine order, he left his monastery without permission, and fled first to Holland and then to London in 1728. He quickly learned English and discovered Elizabethan theatre, which he introduced to France through his translations. He became the preceptor to Francis Eyles, the son of a rich and influential family, frequented coffee houses and began to write his *Mémoires et aventures d'un homme de qualité qui s'est retiré du monde*. An illicit love affair forced him to leave London in a hurry, and the book was published in Holland. *Manon Lescaut*, a brief story taken from the last volume, became a huge success, although (or perhaps because) it was seen as immoral. On his return to London, Prevost started a literary magazine, *Le Pour et le Contre*, with the purpose of spreading English culture and literature in France. He fell into debt and was imprisoned for a time before returning to Paris in 1734, where, forgiven by his order, he returned to the monastery. He was a prolific writer and a subtle translator who owed his fame to his most controversial work, while the rest of his copious oeuvre has been consigned to oblivion.

In 1765, following the scandal caused by the publication of *Émile* and *Du contrat social* in France, Jean-Jacques Rousseau in his turn came to seek refuge in England. He had met the Scottish philosopher David Hume in Paris, who had urged him to join him in London. Shortly after his arrival, Horace Walpole published, as a joke, a supposed anonymous letter claiming to inform Rousseau that the English government, acting on information from Hume, was planning to arrest him. Rousseau, who had a naturally suspicious nature, suspected his friend of conspiring against him. This Rousseau–Hume quarrel developed from frivolous beginnings into a public event, and he felt extremely wounded by it; although fêted in London, he turned against the capital and installed himself at Wootton in Staffordshire at the home of Richard Davenport. Convinced that he was being persecuted and that he would be assassinated, he left England after eighteen months, despite the fact that George III had just granted him a pension.

Baroque and rococo

Many artists as well as men of letters came to London. The painter Louis Laguerre (1663–1721) settled in England in 1683, where he acted as assistant to his Italian colleague Antonio Verrio, working at Windsor Castle. He was much admired as a great colourist and baroque painter, and was widely commissioned by the English aristocracy to paint frescoes on the ceilings and staircases of castles and stately homes. King William III commissioned paintings for Hampton Court and Buckingham House, now Buckingham Palace. Although he was the godson of Louis XIV, he was quite happy to paint scenes of English victories over his godfather's armies, particularly at Marlborough House in London. He also painted portraits and religious subjects, as at St Lawrence's church near Harrow; he became director of the Academy of Painting founded in 1711 at Lincoln's Inn Fields. He was commissioned by Sir Christopher Wren to decorate the cupola of St Paul's Cathedral, but the commission was cancelled because of tensions between the two countries. He married the daughter of the wrought-iron artist Jean Tijou, and died at a theatrical performance in which his son was performing. He was buried at St Martin-in-the-Fields.

Antoine Watteau (1684–1721), the greatest of the rococo painters, arrived in England in 1719. He suffered from tuberculosis, and came over to be treated by the celebrated Richard Mead, doctor to the English royal family as well as to Isaac Newton. The latter commissioned two paintings from him: *Les Joueurs Italiens* and *La Toilette*. Watteau's paintings were a great success in London, but the climate caused his illness to worsen, and he died in 1721, shortly after his return to France.

Born in Paris, Hubert François Bourguignon (1699–1773) is better known as Gravelot. A precocious draughtsman, he was a pupil of François Boucher before spending thirteen years in London, from 1732 to 1745. He became a well-known engraver and illustrator, and taught alongside William Hogarth at the St Martin's Lane Academy, the precursor of the Royal Academy of Art; one of his pupils was Thomas Gainsborough. Like Watteau, Gravelot was a leading promoter of the rococo style in England. He provided sketches for silversmiths, furniture makers such as Thomas Chippendale, the porcelain manufactures in Chelsea and the tapestry makers in Soho. He also put his pencil to the service of literature, illustrating Samuel Richardson's *Pamela*, Gray's *Fables* and Fielding's *Tom Jones*. His most remarkable achievement was his contribution of thirty-five engravings to the complete edition of Shakespeare in eight volumes, published by Theobald in 1740. He died in Paris in 1773.

The painter Philippe-Jacques de Loutherbourg (1740–1812), the son of a miniaturist, was admitted with an age dispensation to the Academy of Painting in 1767, and practised his art at the court of Louis XVI. Alongside his painting, he developed a method of three-dimensional representation of natural phenomena on miniature stages. He arrived in London in 1771 and was hired by David Garrick to make the sets for the Royal Theatre; he was the first to create special effects there. By 1781 he had become a master of illusion, and he perfected the Eidophusikon, a miniature mechanical theatre open to the public in Leicester Square. In a room holding 130 spectators he created changing landscapes, using more and more sophisticated techniques. Three-minute-long scenes would show dawn rising over the Thames at Greenwich, a view of Gibraltar in the midday heat, or a sunset over the Bay of Naples. The Eidophusikon, precursor to the diorama and the cinema, caused a sensation. He continued to paint as well as working in the world of show business. His theatrical style, which favoured dramatic landscapes and the violence of the elements, heralded the advent of romanticism, and proved to be a powerful influence on his Hammersmith neighbour J. M. W. Turner, who came to his studio regularly to seek inspiration, despite Madame de Loutherbourg's mistrust. He was admitted to the Royal Academy in 1781, and held successful exhibitions. One of the books he illustrated was David Hume's *History of England*. Towards the end of his life he became obsessed with occult sciences: he became a healer and was visited by hundreds of patients in his Chiswick house until his death in 1812.

The king's tailor: from rags to riches

Jean-Louis Bazalgette (1750–1830) was an economic migrant. A modest tailor from the Lozère region, he came to London in the mid-1770s where he established a business making clothes and selling silk. Well connected both in his commercial dealings and in the Huguenot community in London (he married a Huguenot, Catherine Métivier), he made his fortune from working for, among others, the Prince of Wales. His son joined the Royal Navy to fight in the Napoleonic wars and his grandson Joseph (1819–91) was the celebrated engineer who had the single greatest impact on the city of London in the nineteenth century: in order to purify the water from the Thames after several cholera epidemics, he built a network of sewers along the side of the river, creating the Embankment. This network, although ageing, has continued to function despite the massive expansion of the city.

Revolutionaries, spies and plotters

One of the French visitors to London at the time, a man who became tragically celebrated thanks to the French Revolution, was Jean-Paul Marat (1743–93). He was born to a family of Protestant converts who had taken refuge in Switzerland. Self-taught, he studied medicine, optics and electricity. He was drawn to England and settled in London in 1768, where he practised medicine. He was interested in philosophy, and published, anonymously, *Essai sur l'âme humaine* (1771), *Essai philosophique sur l'homme* (1772) and *Les chaînes de l'esclavage* (1774). His works were enthusiastically received in the English press, and he was admitted to the London Grand Lodge. He spent some time in Newcastle, then Edinburgh and the University of St Andrews, which awarded him a diploma as Doctor of Medicine in 1775. Back in Paris, he was made official doctor to the Comte d'Artois's guards. Fascinated by experiments in physics, he submitted his results to the Academy of Sciences, which rejected his candidature because he cast doubt on Newton's theories. Influenced by what he had observed in England and by his contacts with English republican groups, he denounced despotism and called for it to be brought down by violence. On the eve of the Revolution, Marat worked on the newspaper *L'Ami du Peuple*, in which he spelt out his revolutionary ideas. He was twice forced to flee to London, in 1790 and 1791, and once he had returned to Paris he played a leading role in the Terror, until his assassination at the hands of Charlotte Corday in 1793.

Charles d'Éon de Beaumont (1728–1810) was remarkable not for his talents but for his singular life. More commonly known as the Chevalier d'Éon, he was a mysterious and complex character. Drafted by Louis XV into his secret service, he carried out several missions, notably in Russia, dressed sometimes as a man, sometimes as a woman. The King, then still pursuing his invasion plans, sent him to England in 1762 as a plenipotentiary minister at the French embassy. The King's favour made him many enemies at Versailles, who would have liked to eliminate him, but his secret missions kept him in England, living in his house at 38 (now 71) Brewer Street, where he devoted himself to his writing. People were fascinated by his sexual ambiguity, and many bets were laid as to whether he was a man or a woman. Queen Sophie-Charlotte, whom he had met a few years earlier between Paris and Moscow, granted him late-night audiences, feeding rumours of a romance between them. Since he had become a liability, he was ordered by Paris to dress henceforth as a woman. After the death of Louis XV, the writer Beaumarchais was charged with negotiating conditions for the return of the Chevalier to France. After some difficult years, he returned to London shortly before the Revolution. He was financially ruined and was forced not just to sell his important library, but also to take part in duels, encumbered by his skirts. In the most spectacular of these, in 1787, at the age of fifty-nine, he faced the Chevalier de Saint-Georges – twenty years younger, a famous musician of mixed race at the court of Versailles, and known as a brilliant swordsman. D'Éon challenged him to a duel at Carlton House and invited the Prince of Wales to watch his triumph. He spent the last years of his life at 33 Westminster Bridge Road, and then at 26 New William Street, always dressed as a woman. He lived, in financial difficulties, in the company of Mary Cole, the French widow of an English sailor, until his death in May 1810, at eighty-two. He had spent forty-nine years as a man, and thirty-three as a woman. Such was the fascination this dual character exerted that the word eonism to denote transvestism is in the Concise Oxford Dictionary.

Charles Théveneau de Morande (1741–1805), son of a Burgundian lawyer, was an unsavoury character who earned his keep on the proceeds of a malevolent pen, helped by a fertile imagination and the use of blackmail. Pursued by the law in France, he went into exile in London around 1770, and in 1771 produced a book, *Le Gazetier cuirassé, ou Anecdotes scandaleuses sur la Cour de France*, which provoked panic in the royal family and among the mistresses of Louis XV. The French government even organised an attempted kidnap (it failed), in order to prevent the publication of *Mémoires secrets d'une femme publique*, which was about Madame du Barry. Théveneau de Morande cried scandal, invoking the sacred rights of the exile, and again the writer Beaumarchais was sent to London to buy his silence. Morande, without any scruples, agreed to stop writing about the royal family in exchange for a pension. He then sold his services as a spy, and wrote for several French newspapers in London. He was editor of the *Courrier de l'Europe* from 1784 to 1791, in which he carried on publishing defamatory libels.

Both the Chevalier d'Éon and Théveneau de Morande had dealings with the writer Pierre Augustin Caron de Beaumarchais, who, during the course of an incredible life, was sent several times to London as a secret agent in the service first of Louis XV and then Louis XVI. Always conscious of being watched and followed, he preferred to deliver his reports to the king in person rather than risk having his correspondence intercepted. Using the name M. de Ronac, an anagram of his middle name Caron, he carried out several missions between the two capitals between 1774 and 1776. He bought the silence of pamphleteer and blackmailer Théveneau de Morande, and later negotiated with the Chevalier d'Éon for the return of compromising papers concerning Louis XV's secret plan to invade England. In 1775, Beaumarchais accepted a mission with the purpose of supplying arms and equipment to the American revolutionaries. He came to London to find out about the situation of the British colonies in America, and defended the revolutionaries in the first issue of the French paper *Courrier de l'Europe*, which earned it the name 'the Beaumarchais paper'. From 1792 until 1795, the writer and adventurer was implicated in 'the affair of the 60,000 rifles', arms trafficked to America. After travelling extensively during this affair he was imprisoned for debts in London in 1792. During his imprisonment he addressed a petition to the Convention, defending himself against the accusations against him; freed after three months, he returned to Paris where he died on 18 May 1799.

Bringing up the rear of this parade of notorious French visitors to London, one should mention one aristocrat who went astray, Comtesse de Valois de la Motte (1756–91), a descendant of Henri II, who felt that her situation was unworthy of someone from such an illustrious family. In 1784 she plotted against Cardinal de Rohan and Queen Marie-Antoinette, with a notorious swindle known as the Affair of the Queen's Necklace, which inspired a novel by Alexandre Dumas. She heard that the Queen admired an exorbitantly expensive necklace, made by the jeweller Charles Boehmer, but had no intention of buying it. She also knew that Cardinal de Rohan wanted to get back into favour with the Queen, and persuaded him that he could do so by giving her the piece of jewellery. The cardinal handed over a large sum of money; she gave a small amount to the jeweller as a deposit, and took the necklace. When the jeweller demanded the full amount, the scandal broke. It went beyond the Queen, who was of course perfectly innocent in the affair, and gravely discredited an already damaged monarchy. After a resounding trial, the Countess was imprisoned in the Salpêtrière Hospital, which also served as a prison mainly for prostitutes and the mentally disabled. She escaped, disguised as a man, and fled to London, where her husband, who had gone ahead with the necklace, was living in Chester Square. After selling the necklace off in pieces, the Countess set out to take her vengeance on the Queen by publishing a venomous version of the affair under the title *Mémoires justificatifs de la comtesse de Valois de la Motte*. The book, published in French and English, was a great success. When she was about to be arrested for her debts, she shut herself in her house, climbed out of a third-floor window and jumped. After several weeks in agony, she died of her injuries in August 1791, and was buried in the churchyard of St Mary's Lambeth.

Two Corsican partisans

Two other visitors to London at this period would eventually be linked forever by their connection to an island that was briefly English – after Napoleon, they are the most important figures of

Corsican history. Theodore de Neuhoff (1694–1756) was the son of a German baron living in exile in France. When his father died, he was protected by the Duchess of Orleans who had him made a lieutenant at the age of seventeen. Instead of embarking on an honourable career in the army, he chose the life of an adventurer and undercover diplomat, first in the German army and then in the service of the kings of Sweden and Spain. In Italy he came into contact with Corsican revolutionaries who wanted to get rid of the Genoese. Theodore promised to help on condition he was made king of Corsica. He obtained money and ships and landed on the island in March 1736; elected monarch, he had some success against the Genoese. But he then re-embarked in November, promising to return with reinforcements. This he failed to do after three attempts and, after several years of wandering in Europe, he went to England where he was acknowledged as a monarch in exile. He had no money, fell into debt, and was imprisoned for a time at King's Bench prison in Southwark. Weakened by illness and privation, he died in December 1756 at the age of sixty, and was buried in the graveyard of St Anne's in Soho, where one can read Horace Walpole's epitaph:

> *The grave, great teacher, to a level brings*
> *Heroes and beggars, galley slaves and kings.*
> *But Theodore this moral learned ere dead*
> *Fate poured its lessons on his living head,*
> *Bestowed a kingdom, but denied him bread.*

Pasquale Paoli (1725–1807), another key figure from Corsican history, also took refuge in England. At the age of fourteen he accompanied his father into exile in Naples. He returned to Corsica in 1755 to organise resistance against the Genoese and, elected 'General of the Nation', he persuaded his compatriots to adopt a constitution inspired by Jean-Jacques Rousseau. In 1764 Genoa secretly sold Corsica to France. Paoli led the resistance against the troops of Louis XV and, after their decisive victory at Ponte Novo in 1769, he took refuge in England where he was welcomed as a hero and granted a pension by George III. In London the writer James Boswell,[18] whom he had met in Corsica, brought him into a club of assembled liberal spirits around Samuel Johnson. To occupy himself during his exile, Paoli enlarged his already vast cultural knowledge. Regarded as a symbol of liberty and democracy, he was recalled by the National Assembly when the French Revolution came but, by 1793, disappointed by its excesses, he once again asked for the protection of England. He also wanted England's help in detaching Corsica from France, which by now was at war with England. In 1794 an English fleet was sent to Corsica and for two years the island was an English protectorate. However, the viceroy Sir Gilbert Elliot kept Paoli out of power and in 1795 he returned into exile in England, where he received a pension until his death in 1807. He was buried in the cemetery of St Pancras, but his remains were repatriated in 1889 to his native village, Morosaglia. There is a stele in his memory in Westminster Abbey.

A chess champion

A final name in this list of the French who lived and worked in England in the eighteenth century is that of Francois Danican-Philidor (1726–95), now regarded as the founder of comic opera. Among other works for the stage he composed *Tom Jones*, after Henry Fielding's novel. However, his fame in England was not only due to his music. When he was very young he had learned to play chess and defeated all his adult opponents. Paris in those days was the capital of chess, and players would meet at the Club de la Régence. Philidor, who had astonishing powers of concentration, took on champions in Paris, Holland and London. In 1749 he wrote *Analyse du jeu des échecs* which was reprinted several times in his lifetime. From 1774 onwards, the members of the Parsloe Chess Club in London engaged him to come, all expenses paid, every year from February to June to give lessons and take part in tournaments. He carried out this engagement for twenty years, also giving demonstrations of playing 'blind' against two or three opponents at once. He often won against the robot known as 'the Turk', which was thought to be unbeatable. In England his reputation as a chess player was greater than his musical fame, but he did compose an *English Ode* and an *Ode for the Convalescence of the King*, dedicated to George III. Philidor died in 1795 and is buried in St James's Church, Hampstead.

Places to visit

'MALBROUK S'EN VA-T-EN GUERRE'

Windsor Castle. In the Guard Room, a white ensign bearing three French fleurs de lys recalls the exploits of the Duke of Marlborough ('Malbrouk' to the French) in his wars against France. Every year, on 13 August, the anniversary of the Battle of Blenheim in 1704, the Duke of Marlborough gives the Queen a new standard.

Blenheim Palace
Woodstock, Oxford
After his victories in the Wars of the Spanish Succession against France, Queen Anne gave the Duke of Marlborough the Woodstock estate and money to build a palace, which was named after the Battle of Blenheim. The paintings and tapestries in the palace reflect the history of the Duke's battles and there are many French works of art, Boulle furniture, Sèvres porcelain and frescoes by Louis Laguerre.

VOLTAIRE

Victoria & Albert Museum. European galleries: marble bust by Houdon of the ageing philosopher.

Wallace Collection
Manchester Square W1
The museum, rich in French eighteenth-century art, also possesses a touching gold and carnelian snuffbox which Voltaire had made after the death of his life's companion, the Marquise du Chatelet. Their two miniaturised portraits play hide and seek on the base of the box.

Commemorative plaque
10 Maiden Lane WC2
Voltaire stayed at this address at the White Wig inn between 1727 and 1728 when he needed to be in central London.

Street names
Voltaire Road, Clapham SW4
Voltaire Court, near Longhedge Street SW11
Voltaire Studio, Garatt Lane SW18
These addresses record his stays in London, in particular in Wandsworth with his friend Everard Falkener, whose house, now demolished, was in Garatt Lane.

Voltaire Foundation
Oxford University, 99 Banbury Road, Oxford
This academic foundation specialises in the study of Voltaire and the eighteenth century. A new edition of his complete works is planned. The foundation has also completed an edition of the complete works of Montesquieu in twenty-two volumes.

JEAN-JACQUES ROUSSEAU

Blue plaque
10 Buckingham Street WC2
He lived at this address in 1766, with the philosopher David Hume.

LOUIS LAGUERRE

Marlborough House
Pall Mall, SW1
In the square saloon and on the stairs, murals by Laguerre representing battles won by the Duke of Marlborough against Louis XIV of France.

St Lawrence Church
Whitchurch Lane, Little Stanmore,
near Harrow
Baroque church with trompe l'oeil ceiling and probably two panels on either side of the organ by Laguerre.

National Portrait Gallery
Victoria & Albert Museum
Works by Louis Laguerre.

Houses with murals by Laguerre
Frogmore House, Windsor
Petworth House, West Sussex
Chatsworth House, Derbyshire
Fetcham Park House, Surrey
Burghley House, Lincolnshire
Blenheim Palace, Oxfordshire, where Louis Laguerre painted himself on the west wall of the palace, above his signature on the mural in the dining room.

ANTOINE WATTEAU
Paintings and drawings by Watteau in the Wallace Collection, National Gallery, Dulwich Picture Gallery, Courtauld Institute, British Museum.

HUBERT GRAVELOT
Works by Gravelot in Tate Britain, Courtauld Institute and British Museum.

PHILIPPE-JACQUES DE LOUTHERBOURG
Paintings by Loutherbourg are in the Royal Academy, National Maritime Museum, Tate Britain, National Portrait Gallery, Courtauld Institute and the Victoria & Albert Museum.

Dulwich Picture Gallery. Portrait by Gainsborough of Loutherbourg.

Old Chiswick Cemetery
Corney Road, Chiswick W4
Surrounded by railings, the tomb of Philippe-Jacques de Loutherbourg and his wife is attributed to Sir John Soane. There is a long epitaph on one side.

JOSEPH BAZALGETTE

London sewers. Bazalgette brought salubrity to London with his hugely complex work: he installed pumping stations and built miles of new brick-lined sewers alongside the Thames which connected with the old pipes.

Albert, Victoria and Chelsea Embankments. The new embankments along the Thames were built by Bazalgette to cover the new sewers. They are now roads. By narrowing the Thames they increased its flow, thereby improving the quality of the water.

Commemorative monument
Victoria Embankment
near Northumberland Avenue WC2
Plaque and bust in memory of Joseph Bazalgette, erected in 1901.

Blue plaque
17 Hamilton Terrace NW8
Joseph Bazalgette's house.

St Mary's Cemetery
30 St Mary's Road, Wimbledon SW19
Bazalgette family tomb, where Joseph is buried.

THE CHEVALIER D'ÉON

Burdett-Coutts Sundial
St Pancras Old Church
St Pancras Road NW1
A listed commemorative monument, inaugurated in 1879, in the graveyard/garden beside the church. Names listed on it of French people who died in London and were buried here, including the Chevalier d'Éon.

National Portrait Gallery
Portrait of the Chevalier d'Éon by Thomas Stewart, after Jean-Laurent Mosnier, 1792.

Southside House
3–4 Woodhayes Road
Wimbledon Common SW19
Framed letter from the Chevalier in the music room.

The Beaumont Society
Organisation for support of transexuals and transvestites, named in memory of the Chevalier, Charles d'Éon de Beaumont.

JEAN-PAUL MARAT

Madame Tussaud's
Marylebone Road NW1
Death mask in the Chamber of Horrors.

KING THEODORE OF CORSICA

St Anne's Church
55 Dean Street W1
On an outside wall is a plaque inscribed: 'Near this spot is interred Theodore King of Corsica, who died in this parish, December 11, 1756, immediately after leaving the King's Bench prison, by the benefit of the Act of Insolvency, in consequence of which he registered his kingdom of Corsica for the benefit of his creditors.'

PASQUALE PAOLI

Westminster Abbey
Bust and plaque by sculptor John Flaxman.

Burdett-Coutts Sundial
St Pancras Old Church
Pasquale Paoli is among the French people listed on the monument in the churchyard.

Blue plaque
77 South Audley Street W1
Plaque unveiled in 2008 on the house he lived in during his long exile in London.

Association of Pasquale Paoli
Founded in 1994, the association, renamed ACRUPP (Association des Corses du Royaume-Uni Pasquale Paoli) welcomes Corsicans and friends of Corsica in Great Britain.

6

REFUGEES FROM
THE REVOLUTION
CROSSING THE CHANNEL TO
ESCAPE THE GUILLOTINE

*'Shelter so nobly granted, help offered as a duty towards the
unfortunate, all filled our hearts with admiration and gratitude
towards this England which was for us a haven after the
shipwreck'*

DUCHESSE DE GONTAUT[19]

Less than a century after the arrival of the Huguenots, England
once again became a land of asylum for the French. Among
the 130,000 to 150,000 who fled abroad at the Revolution, between 20,000 and 40,000 crossed the Channel. When the troubles
in France began England was delighted, but the violent turn of
events provoked a change of opinion. By 1792, relations had deteriorated and the death of Louis XVI on the scaffold horrified
everybody in England: the court went into mourning and theatres
closed. The French ambassador was expelled and on 1 February
1793, France declared war on England. The war continued until
1815.

Escape to England
The first refugees were aristocrats, followed by their servants and
suppliers such as Marie-Antoinette's dressmaker Rose Bertin,

Louis XVI's valet Jean-Baptiste Cléry and the court painter Henri-Pierre Danloux. After the arrest of the King and his family at Varennes in 1791 and the massacres of 1792, those threatened by the Terror left en masse. A large part of the clergy who had refused to sign the civil constitution[20] landed in England, as well as so-called 'constitutional' aristocrats, supporters of an English-style parliamentary monarchy. Among the richer refugees were about eighty Creole families, landowners from the French West Indies. Then followed, in the wake of the first arrivals, soldiers, sailors, intellectuals and journalists, artisans and modest tradesmen, all of whom shared with the grandees their loyalty to the King.

After a period of exile in continental Europe, the Comte d'Artois – younger brother of Louis XVI and the future Charles X – was the first member of the royal family to reach England in 1794. The English royal family received him with great respect and allowed him to live in Holyrood Castle in Edinburgh in 1796, before he settled in London. The Comte de Provence, who had been named Louis XVIII by the royalists after the death of the Dauphin in the Temple prison, had first emigrated with his loyal followers to Coblenz, but then, seeing the warm welcome received by his younger brother, left Germany for England in 1807. He installed himself at Hartwell House in Buckinghamshire with his wife the Comtesse de Lille and his niece the Duchesse d'Angoulême. The Comtesse de Lille died three years later and her funeral was celebrated with great pomp in the French chapel in London. Louis XVIII remained at Hartwell until the restoration in 1814. He was without doubt the most anglophile of all the French sovereigns and despite the initial reservations of the British royal family he developed a warm relationship with the Prince Regent, the future George IV.

The three sons of the Duc d'Orléans, Louis XVI's cousin (the Duc de Chartres, future Louis-Philippe; the Duc de Montpensier and the Comte de Beaujolais) arrived in London only in 1800. They lived at High Shot House in Twickenham and spent their time gardening, reading, painting and attending theatrical evenings with their neighbours. The two younger brothers died of tuberculosis in 1807 and 1808, leaving Louis-Philippe the only survivor of the House of Orleans,

About 8,000 of the 22,000–25,000 so-called 'non-juring' priests, who had refused to sign the civil constitution of the clergy, took refuge in England. Monsignor Douglass, the Catholic Vicar General in London, complained to Rome about the difficulties he had in lodging this horde, which included five archbishops, twenty-seven bishops and thirteen vicars general. The Anglican authorities and the government took an interest in their fate, and the anti-Catholic laws, until then extremely severe, began to be relaxed. In 1791, Parliament voted in the Catholic Relief Act which allowed greater freedom of practice to Catholics in England. As a result, about ten French chapels were established, five of which exist to this day.

One important member of the expatriate clergy was Monseigneur de la Marche, Bishop of Saint-Pol-de-Léon, who emigrated at the age of sixty and placed his organisational talents at the service of the exiled priests until his death in 1806. He lodged at the home of an English widow, Mrs Dorothy Silburn, at 10 Queen Street, in Bloomsbury. Her house became a centre of refuge for the penniless priests. The Abbé Baruel paid tribute to her in his *Histoire du Clergé*: 'at the mention of Mrs Silburn's name, all French priests would raise their hands to Heaven, calling for blessings on the woman who became the mother and the first port of call for their brothers when they arrived in England.'[21] Encouraged by George III's support, Monsignor Douglass showed particular goodwill towards the French clergy, and there was a surge of generosity from political and aristocratic circles. Famous writers denounced the horrors of the Revolution and roused public opinion. Edmund Burke and Monseigneur de la Marche launched a fund-raising appeal. The sums given by all classes of English society were such that the Wilmot committee, named after its president, was established to administer them. The committee, composed of about thirty members of the aristocracy and the government, extended its scope with a network of sub-committees. A wing of the Middlesex Hospital in Soho was placed at the disposal of sick priests; consultations and medicines were free. Later, faced with such an influx of refugee priests, the government decided that henceforth the French clergy would be looked after by the state.

The English people, faced with the distress of the émigrés, had behaved with great compassion, and the British government now decided to grant the most needy a shilling a day per person. This grant was distributed from 1794 until the Peace of Amiens in March 1802.

Resource and imagination: surviving as an émigré

In 1792, the Republic stripped the émigrés of their property and rights in France, and condemned to death any who attempted to return. Coutts, the English bank, opened a French department for the richer members of the community – the future king of France Louis-Philippe had an account with them. Other richer refugees were eventually forced to sell property and works of art in order to support themselves. At the beginning of their exile aristocrats, wanting to recreate life at court, continued to lead worldly and frivolous lives, but as time passed they found themselves obliged to restrict their expenditure, sometimes quite dramatically. 'Ladies from the highest rank were working ten hours a day in order to buy bread for their children,' observed the Comtesse de Boigne. 'In the evenings they would get themselves up, and gather to sing, dance and entertain themselves late into the night – that was the fine side. The ugly part was that they were unpleasant about one another, denigrating their work, complaining that one produced more than another, just like ordinary working women. This mixture of ancient pretension and modern pettiness was disgusting.'[22]

The émigrés who arrived in the later waves were for the most part totally destitute and had to face the bleak misery described by Chateaubriand, exiled in London from 1793 until 1800: 'I was devoured by hunger; I burned; I could not sleep; I sucked pieces of cloth dipped in water; I chewed grass and paper. When I passed in front of bakers' shops the torment was horrible. One cold night in winter I stood for two hours in front of a shop selling dried fruit and smoked meats, devouring everything I saw with my eyes: I would have eaten not just the edible food, but the boxes and baskets it lay in.'[23]

Many aristocrats took up crafts in order to survive. The manufacture of straw hats was a great success; some refugees made up bouquets, others became lace makers and embroiderers. The Marquise de la Tour du Pin became a specialist in fine linen. English ladies opened shops purveying the work of these noble ladies in order to spare them the humiliation of selling it themselves. The Comtesse de Guerey made sorbets and kept a café in Oxford Street, while M. de la Rivière made pastries and M. d'Albignac made money by seasoning salads at grand parties. Madame de Menerville painted fans and M. de Canisey horses, which were very popular, while the Duc and Duchesse de Gontaut decorated brooches. The Vicomte Leroy de Barde, who had arrived in London at the age of fifteen, painted still lifes and became one of the founder members of the Society of Watercolourists in England; his works are in the collection of the Royal Academy. The Duc d'Aiguillon copied music for the opera; the Comte de Marin was a famous and much-praised violinist and harp-player. Porcelain false teeth had been invented in France in 1774, and they were introduced to England by Nicolas de Chémant, becoming popular despite their high cost. Doctor Solander sold 'the most powerful restorative ever known for all forms of nervous illness'.[24] The Comte de Loitte, who had looked after the accounts of Louis XIV, was the originator of the international auditing and accounting firm founded in London in 1845 by his grandson William Welch Deloitte.

In the world of show-business, Madame Tussaud exhibited her waxwork collection in London and throughout England. M. Maillardet opened a museum of automatons at 101 St Martin's Lane. The journalist J. B. Peltier put on a cruel but extremely popular show of animals being put to death with a miniature guillotine. Newspapers of the time were full of advertisements by French people offering their services as teachers or editors.

The education of children in this foreign land became a major source of anxiety for noble émigrés. The wealthiest were able to place them in English schools, but several French schools were soon created for them. These were mostly run by priests and placed on the outskirts of the city, offering pupils a healthier atmosphere. M. de Saint-Quentin opened a school for girls in Chelsea and the Abbé Carron directed two others, one for boys and one for girls, in Somers Town. At the height of their success these schools also attracted children from numerous English families. Two girls' schools were established at Hammersmith, and the most privileged attended the Abbé de Broglie's fee-paying school in Kensington.

Since teaching was their only source of revenue, the clergy became deeply involved in the establishing and running of French schools. The writer and journalist Edmund Burke, an ardent advocate of the restoration of the French monarchy, was deeply moved by the plight of the orphans of the participants in the disastrous Quiberon expedition (see below) – for them he opened the Penn School, with the Comte d'Artois as its president.

The white cockade regiments

Like the Huguenots of the previous century, many émigrés joined the British army. Officers managed to convince Prime Minister William Pitt and war minister William Windham to create special regiments to combat the French republican troops. Eight 'white cockade' regiments were formed under French officers – they bore the names of their commanders, like the Hector regiment, or were given more obvious names, like Royal Louis or Loyal Emigrant. However, they were mostly made up of volunteers and acquired a reputation for lack of discipline.

The most important operation was the one led in 1795 by the Comte d'Artois in Quiberon in Brittany. The plan was to land in force, join the Chouans in the Vendée region, defeat the Revolutionary forces and re-establish the monarchy. The expedition was a disaster because of the diverging opinions and conflicting interests of the principal players. The Comte d'Artois never set foot on French soil; there were heavy losses; large numbers of émigrés were taken prisoner and shot for having borne arms against France, and the survivors accused the English of betrayal for not sending the promised reinforcements.

This was followed a few months later by a raid on the Ile d'Yeu, also in Brittany and also led by the Comte d'Artois, which had equally disastrous results. The families of those killed in these expeditions were reduced to extreme poverty, and émigré morale was at its lowest. Following these two setbacks most of the émigré regiments were dissolved, the last ones following the Peace of Amiens in 1802, which allowed émigrés to return to France.

Differing political aims

The refugees from the Revolution were divided among themselves by their various political allegiances. The ultra-Royalists wanted a complete return to the *ancien régime*, while the constitutionalists wanted reform; they were regarded as traitors by the ultras and as subversives by the Tory government in London.

The exiles voiced their disagreements about what kind of monarchy to re-establish, writing in the many French journals that were published in London and distributed in the countries that neighboured France in Europe. The Abbé de Calonne, brother of Louis XVI's ex-minister of finance, edited the *Courrier de l'Europe*, in which he mainly translated the debates in the English parliament. The journal was then renamed the *Courrier de Londres* and taken over by the Comte de Monlosier, who had been a deputy for the nobility at the constituent assembly. He used a network of correspondents in other European countries. He was a constitutionalist, and in 1796 published his *Vues sommaires sur les moyens de paix pour la France, pour l'Europe, pour les émigrés* in which he analysed the complexity of the relationships among the émigrés, and the political gulf that separated them from republican France. The journalist Jean-Baptiste Peltier edited the satirical journal *l'Ambigu* between performances with his mini-guillotine; he joined the ultras despite being attracted by the theories of the constitutionalists. The Genevan Jacques Mallet du Pan, also a constitutionalist, denounced the Directoire in his *Mercure Britannique*.

These papers were filled with the views of intellectuals, politicians and writers on the Revolution, the fate of the émigrés, and politics both in England and other European countries. Gerard de Lally Tollendal, who as a reformist was not popular in ultra-Royalist circles, did none the less become a champion of the exiles' cause with his *Défense des Émigrés*, in which he denounced the revolutionaries' anti-émigré laws, and accused the republican government of attacking them without allowing them any right to reply. Pierre-Victor Malouet, then a deputy of the third estate, had sent his *Défense de Louis XVI* to the Convention. As an émigré in London, he took part in all the political debates discussed in the newspapers. Chateaubriand, during his exile in London, published his *Essai historique, politique et moral sur les Révolutions anciennes et modernes*. Although he was mostly on the side of the constitutionalists, his *Génie du Christianisme* places him alongside the ultras.

The revolutionary violence taking place in France provoked extreme reactions among the English. Edmund Burke, in 1790, published his *Reflections on the French Revolution*, an anti-revolutionary diatribe to which the pamphleteer Thomas Paine responded vigorously the following year with *The Rights of Man*. This became a bestseller, proving once again the great interest taken by the English in the French Revolution.

The English had mixed feelings about the émigrés. The aristocrats were, on the whole, welcomed by their British counterparts. However, ordinary English people resented the arrival of foreigners who might disrupt their everyday lives; they feared competition for jobs and did not want their daily habits interfered with. Anti-French sentiments are illustrated in the many cartoons of the time, which became tools for political propaganda. The government for its part feared infiltration by spies and political agitators arriving under cover of political asylum. A farcical incident took place in 1797, when French soldiers attempted an invasion by landing in four ships near Fishguard in South Wales: the 'invaders', who were clearly drunk, fled after they took local women dressed in their traditional red cloaks for English soldiers.

The Alien Act, passed in 1793, strengthened controls on the immigrants and their movements, forcing them to register their arrival, supply an address and obtain permission for any move. The law of *habeas corpus*, which forbade arbitrary arrest, was suspended between 1794 and 1801, and the censorship of newspapers became draconian.

Emigré memoirs

Writing has always provided a form of therapy in stressful times, and a huge number of memoirs and works on the subject of emigration were published in London, since censorship forbade their publication in France. The Huguenot publishing houses and bookshops lent themselves perfectly to this purpose, and their number increased during the Revolution, the most well-known being the Dulau and de Boffe bookshops in Soho. The English printers Cox and Baily became specialists in French books. Many of the diarists describe the difficulties of daily life, such as the Marquise de la Tour du Pin in her *Journal d'une femme de cinquante ans,* and the Comtesse de Boigne in her memoirs. The Comte de Montlosier in his *Souvenirs d'un émigré* gives us his personal impressions of English public opinion. Chateaubriand evokes his memories of emigration in his *Mémoires d'Outretombe,* in which he poignantly describes the contrast between his poverty at that time with his return to London in luxury as ambassador many years later. Jean-Baptiste Cléry, Louis XVI's faithful valet, gave public readings of his *Journal de ce qui c'est passé à la Tour du Temple,* an account of the King's last moments which moved the most hardened of listeners to tears. The Abbé Barruel praised the welcome he had received from the English in his *Histoire du clergé pendant la Révolution.* The Abbé Baston wrote his memoirs and the Abbé de Lubersac produced his *Journal historique et religieux de l'émigration et déportation du clergé de France en Angleterre.* The Abbé Tardy, author of *Dictionnaire de prononciation française à l'usage des Anglais,* also published, in 1800, a *Manuel du voyageur à Londres ou recueil de toutes les instructions nécessaires aux étrangers qui arrivent dans cette capitale, précédé du grand Plan de Londres.*

Artists, too, described their lives in exile: the painter Henri-Pierre Danloux, in his diary, paints a vivid picture of Soho, and of his contacts with both émigré and English society. Elisabeth Vigée-Lebrun, in her *Souvenirs*, describes her émigré friends from Versailles, the royal family in exile and her travels in the English countryside.

Others wrote novels: Madame de Flahaut, forced to find a way of supporting herself and her son by Talleyrand, made a fortune with her *Adèle de Sénange*, which she followed with a dozen other novels. Madame de Genlis published an epistolary novel, while Madame de Stael depicted the emotions of an émigré in *Corinne*, a story that enabled indirect criticism of the French political regime. The Abbé Delille was the poet of emigration with his *Le Malheur et la Pitié*.

Many English authors, too, were inspired by the theme of escape from the guillotine. Fanny Burney, who was married to the émigré General d'Arblay, was well placed to observe refugee circles. She described them in her diaries and in her novel *The Wanderer*. Charles Dickens, in *The Old Curiosity Shop*, was directly inspired by Madame Tussaud's adventures in England. Several stereotype émigrés appear in *A Tale of Two Cities*; the name of the Telfson bank is curiously similar to that of Peter Thellusson, a French émigré banker who looked after émigré interests. The story of his will was the inspiration for another Dickens novel, *Bleak House*. Later, Thomas Carlyle wrote his magisterial *History of the French Revolution*. He left the manuscript at a friend's house, where an illiterate housemaid threw it on the fire. He rewrote it, and finally published it, to great acclaim, in 1837.

In the wake of the Huguenots

Parts of London had become marked by the influx of Huguenots during the previous two centuries. Aristocrats, bourgeois and tradesmen mingled in Soho, in the centre of town. French was spoken and many Huguenot artisans set up shops. Despite being Catholic, the new arrivals were welcomed by the old ones. The painter Henri-Pierre Danloux lived there, as did the Comtesse de

Flahaut, Rose Bertin and a horde of journalists, politicians and writers. Bookshops, such as Dulau at 11 Wardour Streeet and De Boffe at 7 Gerrard Street, became meeting places for émigrés starved of news. Madame Vigée-Lebrun finally found lodgings in Maddox Street on the edge of Marylebone, while the instrument-maker Sébastien Érard's shop moved several times before finally establishing itself permanently in Great Portland Street. The draughtsman Augustus Charles Pugin opened a drawing school in Great Russell Street in Bloomsbury.

St Patrick's, in Sutton Street, was the first Catholic church to be built in London since the Reformation. This, in the context of English history, was an extraordinary event. The church was consecrated in 1792 and three years later the Chapel of the Holy Cross was built at 10 Dudley Court. However, life in Soho was too expensive for most of the émigrés, especially the clergy, and they moved on to settle in areas more appropriate to their means and contacts.

The Huguenots had created 'French gardens' in Marylebone; following in their footsteps, the refugees from the Revolution concentrated themselves around Manchester Square and Portman Square. This community was mainly ultra-Royalist, composed of the highest aristocracy and members of the French royal family. The Comte d'Artois and the Duc de Berry went there in 1799, and the Prince de Condé in 1802. The constitutionalists, although they did not get along with the Royalists, also came to this area, where there were also several Creole families. The French royal chapel, now destroyed, was built in King Street (Portman Square). Often the refugees grouped together according to the regions they came from. Normandy was well represented, and the principal pub in the area was the Rose of Normandy. Chateaubriand, penniless at that time, lodged not far away: 'My friends found me a room more suited to my dwindling means . . . they installed me near Mary-Le-Bone Street, in a garret, whose skylight gave on to a cemetery.'[25] In 1835 Madame Tussaud opened her first waxwork museum at 58 Baker Street before settling definitively in the Marylebone Road.

A little to the north the village of Hampstead, with its splendid views over London and the surrounding countryside, was also very popular with the aristocrats. Turned in upon themselves, they lived there in a state described by the Duchesse de Saulx-Tavannes as one of 'extreme dejection'.[26] There appear to have been around two hundred émigrés living in Hampstead. The Abbé Jean-Jacques Morel led the community, which built St Mary's church in 1816. Also to the north, émigrés lived in Tottenham, where the future Cardinal Chevereux inaugurated a chapel in Queen Street in 1793, in which about a hundred worshippers could gather.

In Kensington, not far from the Albert Hall, the Jesuit Father de Broglie opened a fee-paying school for the sons of the richer émigrés. He then founded a parish which was forced to move several times as the number of its worshippers grew. This parish, Our Lady of Victories, is now in Kensington High Street.

Chelsea, then expanding rapidly, offered an alternative to a small number of émigrés. Rents there were lower, the country was within sight and the Ranelagh Gardens, with their entertainments, were very popular with the French. But the main reason for the installation of a French community in this area was the foundation of the parish of Saint Mary's Chelsea by the Abbé Voyaux de Franous. He had been Louis XVI's almoner and became that of the veterans at the Royal Hospital in Chelsea and of the soldiers in the neighbouring barracks when he arrived in 1793. A charismatic man, he drew the crowds and built the church of St Mary's in Cadogan Street. He was offered several bishoprics in France after the Restoration, but he preferred to remain in his London parish until his death in 1840. The church was enlarged and transformed several times: Edward Welby Pugin, son of the émigré architect Augustus Welby Pugin, helped with the new constructions. Madame Tussaud is buried there.

In Hammersmith the Benedictines from Dunkirk led by the Abbess Prujean installed themselves in an existing convent in 1795. These nuns came from English Catholic communities which had been settled in France since the Reformation. They founded a girls' school which was much used by the French émigrés.

Many of the richer aristocrats, appreciating the beauty and calm of Richmond, chose to settle there, particularly around the Green. The first to arrive were Madame de Boufflers and the Princesse d'Henin, who recreated their Parisian salons. Lally-Tollendal was a tolerated guest, despite being a constitutionalist, since he was the Princess's lover. The first president of the Paris Parliament, M. d'Aligre, owned a house on the Green and there are many French graves in the Vineyard Burial Ground, the Richmond cemetery.

In Twickenham, the Duc d'Orléans, the future Louis-Philippe, and his two brothers the Duc de Montpensier and the Comte de Beaujolais, lived at High Shot House in Crown Street from 1800 to 1808, an unpretentious house which was demolished in 1927. When they returned into exile between 1815 and 1817 during the Hundred Days, the Duc d'Orléans and his family occupied a house known henceforth as Orleans House. In a letter to an ex-émigré friend, the master of the house wrote with relief: 'I bless the heavens, day and night, that I am in my peaceful house in this old Twick.'[27]

Some of the constitutionalists decided to live together in the country in Juniper Hall, a fine house near Dorking in Surrey. Most of them came from great aristocratic families: the Comte de Narbonne, ex-minister of war; the Comtesse de la Châtre; François de Jaucourt, a member of the legislative assembly; General Alexandre d'Arblay, ex-aide-de-camp to Lafayette; the Duc de Montmorency and a few others. Madame de Staël, mistress of the Comte de Narbonne, raised some of the money necessary for the move; her dynamism attracted in her wake Talleyrand, the Marquis de Lally-Tollendal and his mistress the Princesse d'Henin. It was at Juniper Hall that General d'Arblay met the author Fanny Burney, who would become his wife. However, the lease came to an end during 1793 and the inhabitants dispersed.

The less prosperous émigrés, families of soldiers or the clergy, were drawn to the south and east of London, where rents were lower: 'The image of the emigration was gloomier and more austere in Southwark and Somers Town; this was no longer the world of the court, but that of the provinces, far less light-hearted and cheerful.'[28]

The émigrés in St Pancras would gather in Old Church, an Anglican church that had been placed at their disposal; many of them are buried in the neighbouring cemetery, which appears to contain the greatest number of French émigrés. M. Vial de Saint-Bel opened nearby the first veterinary school in England, which exists to this day.

The Somers Town district also offered a refuge to those of modest means, mainly members of the clergy. About 350 émigrés repatriated from Jersey joined them in 1796. The charismatic Abbé Carron, who had already shown himself to be extremely efficient in Jersey, soon established a network of self-help organisations for the refugees. He created pharmacies and hospices, libraries and seminaries for the priests, as well as opening two schools, one for boys and one for girls at 1 and 2 Phoenix Street (now Phoenix Road).

Portraits of emigrés

Among the hordes of impoverished émigrés flooding into London were two illustrious characters who would return years later under very different circumstances. François-René de Chateaubriand (1768–1848) had joined the émigré army and been gravely wounded. He had taken refuge, almost dead, on the island of Jersey, and from there had travelled to England. He settled in London in May 1793 and remained until May 1800. On arrival he found himself with diminishing resources living in a state of complete indigence. He wrote a book comparing revolutions, *Essai sur les Révolutions*, published in London by Baylis in 1797, and survived by translating. His friend Pelletier then suggested that he work outside London, in Suffolk, on deciphering twelfth-century French manuscripts. Afflicted by the deaths of his mother and sister, he threw himself into a work of apologetics, *Le Génie du Christianisme*, which was a great success. Chateaubriand returned to France, deeply marked by his stay in England, and confessed: 'I always retained, deep in my heart, regretful memories of England

. . . I had become English in manners, tastes and, to a certain extent, thought.'[29] He returned to London in 1822, by the front door this time, as ambassador.

In January 1792, Charles-Maurice de Talleyrand-Périgord (1754–1838) was sent to London by Louis XVI in order to negotiate an eventual alliance with England. This short mission did not bear fruit but, throughout his life, all his diplomatic activity was to be founded on the necessity for such an alliance. At the time of the September 1792 massacres, he asked Danton to send him to London as a diplomat so as not to appear on the list of émigrés and thus ensure his safe return to France. His official job was to open negotiations for the eventual adoption of a universal system of weights and measures in Europe. His arrival in London was briefly announced in the press and the welcome he received from the royalist émigrés was anything but enthusiastic. Talleyrand was a non-conformist: he did not wear a wig but gathered his hair on the nape of his neck in the Jacobin style. He had hardly arrived when a warrant for his arrest was issued by the Convention and he lost his job at the French embassy. He then found himself with no means of support and with the status of émigré, with the English government, ever fearful of revolutionary contagion, setting up a close watch on all his activities. Talleyrand's house, in Woodstock Street in Marylebone, became a gathering place for his old acquaintances who had fled the Terror. Among them were the Comte de Narbonne, the Comte de Montmorency, Madame de Genlis, Madame de la Châtre, as well as his ex-mistress Madame de Flahaut with whom he had had a son, Charles de Flahaut, who took English citizenship and married an English-woman. Talleyrand was a regular visitor to Juniper Hall, where he met Madame de Staël and his constitutionalist friends. He used this enforced leisure to write, keeping a journal as material for his future memoirs; he also wrote a biography of the Duc d'Orléans, *Philippe-Égalité*. Close to penury, he was forced to move to a smaller house in Kensington Square, selling his library in order to survive but continuing none the less to welcome his émigré friends.

In 1793 the English government launched a campaign against the constitutionalists, and Talleyrand was forced to leave London in a hurry. He embarked on 15 February 1794 on the *William Penn,* due to sail to America. The weather was so bad that the ship remained docked in the Thames for two weeks; refusing offers of lodging from friends, Talleyrand remained on board until the ship sailed. Like Chateaubriand, he returned to London later as ambassador.

A great many artists continued to arrive in London. Some were fleeing the Revolution and the ensuing chaos which had created difficult conditions for creative talent. Henri-Pierre Danloux (1753–1809) was an orphan brought up by an uncle who was an architect. He had lived in Rome for ten years, and then worked as a portrait painter in France. He was popular with the aristocracy, and was commissioned to paint portraits of the royal family in 1789. A convinced royalist, he emigrated to London in 1792 and settled in Soho, where he hoped to become a rival to Reynolds by undercutting his fees. He did not make a fortune, but was able to live comfortably. He kept a journal of observations of London life, with a mass of details on the comings and goings of both French émigrés and his English clients; he travelled up to Edinburgh several times in order to paint the French royal family in exile. One famous painting, *The Skater,* until now attributed to the Scottish painter Henry Raeburn and considered by many to be a symbol of Scotland, is now thought to be the work of Henri-Pierre Danloux. He was influenced by English painters, especially George Romney, and specialised in group portraits. His anglicised style, however, did not go down well when he returned to France.

Elisabeth Vigée-Lebrun (1755–1842), daughter of the portrait painter Louis Vigée, showed her promise at an early age: she became a success at fifteen thanks to her talent, combined with her beauty and intelligence. She married the painter and art dealer J. B. Lebrun, with whom she had a daughter. A great many of her paintings were of women, painted in a natural manner, without make-up and with simple hairstyles. She made her first portrait of Marie-Antoinette in 1779, and they became friends; she eventually painted more than thirty pictures of the Queen and her children. Being so close to the royal family she had to leave France in 1789. After twelve years of travelling around Europe, she decided to visit London in 1802, intending to stay a few months: she ended up remaining there for three years. She lived in Soho, and soon made friends in English high society, painting twenty portraits during her stay, including ones of King George IV and Lord Byron. In her lively and agreeably written *Souvenirs*, she paints an attractive picture of her life in London, and of the customs of English society, the climate and the countryside she loved to visit.

A small minority of the new arrivals chose to leave the chaos of French society, not to escape the guillotine but for economic reasons. Some succeeded so well in England that they remained permanently; one such was Madame Tussaud (1761–1850). Probably the most well-known of the French refugees settled in London during the Revolutionary period, Marie Grosholz was born in Strasbourg in 1761 and learned her waxwork skills in Paris from the doctor Philippe Curtius, the owner of a 'wax cabinet'. She was an able pupil, and at the age of seventeen she made masks of Voltaire and Benjamin Constant which can still be seen in her museum. When she returned to Paris in 1789, she helped Philippe Curtius make death masks of those who had died on the guillotine, including those of Louis XVI and Marie Antoinette. She was an invaluable witness to the upheavals of the Revolution, reproducing the scene of Marat's assassination and making a death mask of Robespierre.

When Philippe Curtius died in 1794 she inherited his collection of waxworks. A year later, at thirty-four, she married François Tussaud, with whom she had three children. As her business was not viable in France in the years following the Revolution, Marie travelled to England in 1802 with her eldest son, who was four, to show her collection to a new public, eager to observe the important players of the French Revolution. She brought with her about thirty waxworks, which she exhibited at the Lyceum in the Strand. Stuck in England after the failure of the Treaty of Amiens, she mounted an itinerant display with which she travelled

throughout England. With great courage and enterprise, she travelled the roads for thirty years. She was the victim of a shipwreck
on a trip to Ireland and lost almost all her collection, but was not
discouraged and built it up again. The character of Mrs Jarley in
The Old Curiosity Shop by Charles Dickens is clearly inspired by
Madame Tussaud, with her 'prodigious collection of effigies of
famous people'.[30]

To characters from the Revolution and Napoleon, she added
other portraits of politicians and sovereigns, including in 1809
George III and Queen Charlotte, as well as murderers and their
victims. One of her greatest successes is the Chamber of Horrors,
which fascinates the public to this day. By 1819 her collection
amounted to eighty-six pieces, three times the number she had
brought over from France. At the age of seventy-four she finally
established herself at 58 Baker Street, opening her first museum,
the Baker Street Bazaar. In 1884, her grandson moved the museum
to Marylebone Road, where it remains to this day. At eighty-one
she made a self-portrait in wax which still welcomes visitors to
her museum. She died in 1850 after publishing her memoirs,
leaving her sons a business which she had run with an iron hand
until the very end.

Another creative entrepreneur was the instrument-maker
Sébastien Érard (1752–1831), who made the first piano with
pedals. The son of a cabinet-maker, he was noticed by Louis XVI
and authorised to work exclusively for him, and he designed a
'piano-organ' for Marie-Antoinette. He then opened his own
piano and harp factory, and once that was established he joined
forces with his brother-in-law Jean-Baptiste. Their factory was
destroyed during the Revolution and he was forced to leave Paris
for London, where he had already opened an instrument shop in
1786. He opened another in 1792 in Great Marlborough Street in
Soho. Sebastien Érard took out several patents for his pianos, but
his real passion was for harps. The first concert harp, which he
created in 1810, brought immediate success, and he made the huge
sum of £25,000 pounds in its first year. After his death in 1831 his
nephew Pierre took over the business and won the gold medal at

the Great Exhibition of 1851. Érard instruments continued to be much appreciated by all the great musicians: Franz Liszt made a triumphal tour of England in 1824, playing his pianos. The Soho shop closed in 1890 and the Érard name was taken over by the German manufacturer Schimmel in 1971.

In another field the two Pugins, father and son, made an important contribution to the architectural movement known as the Gothic Revival. Augustus Charles Pugin (1762–1832) left France at the Revolution to come to London, where he entered the Royal Academy School. After working for John Nash, he decided to make a career as a draughtsman; he specialised in watercolour and book illustration, and became famous for his remarkably detailed views of Westminster, London, and other English towns, notably Oxford and Cambridge. In 1821 he published *Specimens of Gothic Architecture* and founded a school of drawing in his house at 106 Great Russell Street in the heart of Bloomsbury.

His son Augustus Welby Northmore Pugin (1812–52) was born in London, and contributed to the success of the neo-Gothic style as much through his writing as through his works. His influence on Victorian architecture, John Ruskin and the Arts and Crafts Movement was seminal; he defined the new style as a cohesive whole, combining interior decoration with exterior building. His most important work was the Westminster Parliament of 1840, rebuilt after the fire of 1834 in association with the architect Sir Charles Barry, for which he designed the entire interior decoration. Brought up Protestant by his mother, he converted to Catholicism at twenty-one after a series of tragedies. Deeply religious, he built many churches in an attempt to encourage a Catholic revival with his Gothic-inspired style; in recognition of his work the Pope awarded him a gold medal in 1847. In London he built St George's Catholic cathedral in Southwark, St Thomas of Canterbury in Fulham and the convent of St Joseph in Chelsea (now altered). He was charged with building the medieval court in the Crystal Palace for the 1851 Great Exhibition. He was married three times, widowed twice and had eight children; he became more and more difficult and was committed to an asylum, dying soon afterwards at the age of forty.

Among the great inventors of the nineteenth-century industrial revolution in England were two French engineers, the Brunels, father and son. Mark Isambard Brunel (1769–1849), a convinced royalist, was born into a family of prosperous farmers, but showed an early interest in mechanics; he travelled to New York in 1793, where he became chief engineer of the city. Arriving in England in 1799 he married an Englishwoman, Sophie Kingdom, and presented to the government a device he had invented to mechanise the fabrication of the wooden pulleys used in their hundreds by the Navy – one of the first examples of mass production. In 1809 he invented machines that could make leather boots in nine different sizes: by 1812 he was supplying boots to the entire British Army, until his factory was forced to close at the end of the Napoleonic wars. He was a brilliant inventor but a hopeless businessman, and was imprisoned for debt in 1821. The Duke of Wellington had him freed and a few months later he was charged with the construction of a tunnel under the Thames, between Rotherhithe and Wapping. In order to prevent the sandy and unstable ground from collapsing during the building, he devised a metal shield to protect the workers as they progressed, a system still in use worldwide. He was knighted and admitted to the Royal Society.

He eventually handed the supervision of the tunnel construction to his son Isambard Kingdom Brunel (1809–59), who was then twenty. The works, which had begun in 1825, had been delayed by two accidents. In 1827 water came into the tunnel and a worker was killed; the following year six others died and Isambard was severely hurt. The works were halted and only begun again seven years later. The Herculean difficulties of the project attracted public attention, and people came to visit the site, paying a shilling each. A concert was even held there as the acoustics were excellent, and Isambard held a great party there to celebrate his twenty-first birthday. The tunnel, known as 'the eighth wonder of the world', was inaugurated with great pomp and ceremony in

1843. It remained a foot tunnel for fifty years, accessible by a stair-case. In 1869 it was used by the East London Railway, and then incorporated into the Underground system in 1948.

I. K. Brunel became a great engineer. As well as the tunnel, he contributed to many projects: the Great Western Railway, great steamships such as the *Great Western* and the *Great Eastern*, and many bridges such as the Clifton Suspension Bridge in Bristol. In response to an appeal from Florence Nightingale he designed a prefabricated hospital for the wounded of the Crimean War. Like his father he was elected to the Royal Society, in 1830. Both men are buried in Kensal Green cemetery.

Places to visit

THE ROYAL FAMILY IN EXILE

Blue plaque

72 South Audley Street W1

The Comte d'Artois, the future Charles X, lived at this address from 1805 until 1814, until his return to France after the fall of Napoleon.

Westminster Abbey

Tomb of the Duke de Montpensier

He is shown crowned and draped in a coat decorated with fleurs de lys. The marble tomb was made by sculptor Richard Westmacott in 1830.

Hartwell House

Oxford Road, Aylesbury, Buckinghamshire

This very ancient property appears in the Domesday Book. Now a luxurious hotel, it was the home of the Comte de Provence, the future Louis XVIII, and the royal family in exile, from 1808 until 1814. The royalists in his court kept chickens and rabbits on the roof, and the émigrés opened little shops in the outbuildings. There are still portraits of Louis XVIII, his wife the Comtesse de Lille and other members of the court hanging in the saloons.

ÉMIGRÉ CLERGY

Five of the parishes formed by the French émigré clergy still exist, some rebuilt. These French parishes contributed to the renewal of Catholicism in London in the nineteenth century.

St Mary's

4 Holly Place, Hampstead NW3

The first Catholic chapel in Hampstead since the Reformation, modelled on the church at Verneuil in Normandy, birthplace of its founder, abbé Jean-Jacques Morel. His tomb is in the entrance, beneath a black marble slab. A monument in Caen stone was added in 1857. General de Gaulle was a parishioner here during his stay in Hampstead.

St Francis de Sales

729 High Road, Tottenham N17

Founded in 1793 by Père Chevereux, the original chapel has been rebuilt and now serves the local Catholic population.

Our Lady of Victories

16 Abingdon Road W8

On the left-hand wall is a plaque with a list of the French priests who looked after the parish. The first was the abbé de Broglie, from 1794 until 1806; the school he opened at Kensington House, near the Albert Hall, is also mentioned.

St Mary's

Cadogan Street SW3

The church has been rebuilt and contains a full-length statue of the abbé de Voyaux de Franous as well as a memorial plaque to Madame Tussaud and her family.

St Aloysius

20 Phoenix Road, Camden NW1

Now rebuilt, the parish was founded in 1799. Vestiges of the old building can be seen in a small chapel to the right of the altar. Panels inscribed with the history of the parish and of its founder, the abbé Carron, whose bust can be seen on a shelf; text celebrating his virtues on a tombstone.

Catholic schools

- **Phoenix Road NW1**
  Two Catholic schools still occupy the site of those founded by the abbé Carron beside St Aloysius church.

Sacred Heart Convent

212 Hammersmith Road W6

Benedictines of English origin who had been established in France since the Reformation returned to England during the Revolution and founded a school in Hammersmith, later taken over by the Order of the Sacred Heart.

Middlesex Hospital
Mortimer Street W1
Founded in 1747 for the poor, this hospital welcomed émigré priests during the French Revolution. Closed in 2005, it was partly demolished in 2008. The few remaining buildings are still used by the NHS.

ÉMIGRÉ DISTRICTS

Soho

There are very few traces of the refugees from the Revolution in Soho. But one can imagine them: as with the Huguenots, the émigrés' presence still echoes in the old streets, in which several eighteenth-century houses have escaped the developers.

- **Manette Street.** Named after a character in Charles Dickens's *A Tale of Two Cities*, set in Paris and London during the Revolution. Dr Manette is a French émigré who takes refuge in Soho with his daughter. The name Manette, a diminutive of Marie-Antoinette, is particularly appropriate to the period of the novel.

- **Darblay Street.** Named after General d'Arblay, a constitutionalist émigré married to the English novelist Fanny Burney.

- **St Patrick's**
  Sutton Row W1
  In the past, this Irish Catholic church served the French community as well.

- **Middlesex Hospital.** See page above.

- **Commemorative plaque**
  Paddington Street Gardens
  Paddington Street W1
  Chateaubriand lived at this address from 1793 until 1800, in great poverty. He survived by giving French lessons and translating.

St Pancras

- **St Pancras Old Church.** Because of urban developments, the tombs in the churchyard have been transferred to the East Finchley cemetery. Several of them had French names.

- **Burdett-Coutts Sundial.** In the St Pancras churchyard, commemorative monument with names of famous émigrés: Monsignor de la March; General Comte Joseph de Puisaye from Vendée and the Comte d'Hervilly, both participants in the Quiberon expedition; Comtesse de Polastron, mistress of the Comte d'Artois; Comte de Gramont; Marquise de Tourville; Marquis de Bonneval; Charles de Broglie.

- **Royal Veterinary College**
  Royal College Street NW1
  On the staircase, full-length statue of Monsieur Vial de Saint Bel, founder of the college.

Richmond

- **Vineyard Burial Ground**
  VIneyard Passage TW10
  Consecrated in 1790, this small cemetery was closed in 1874. Constitutional journa - list Jacques Mallet du Pan was buried there in 1800 and is on the list of recorded tombs. The tomb of the Vicomtesse de Cambis, another émigrée, has recently been restored.

- **St Elisabeth's Church**
  The Vineyard TW10
  This Catholic church not far from the cemetery was built on the site of a chapel built by the French émigrés of the area.

Wimbledon

- **Southside House**, on the edge of the Common. There are no traces of émigrés in Wimbledon but there is a pearl necklace in a case in Southside House which, according to rumour, belonged to Marie-Antoinette. John Pennington, owner of the house, was working in the British Embassy in Paris at the time of the Revolution, and was able to save several aristocrats from the guillotine. Marie-Antoinette was allegedly wearing the necklace on the day of her execution and the executioner picked it up. According to the story, the governor of the Bastille, Barras, took back the necklace and gave it to Josephine de Beauharnais, for whom he had a soft spot. She then gave it to the young John Pennington to thank him for helping several French nobles to escape to England. Consisting of a single row of pearls, the necklace was said orignally to have had several rows; according to the story, the imprisoned queen would detach one pearl and give it to her jailer each time she was allowed to see her son crossing the courtyard. It is more likely that what John Pennington received as a mark of gratitude were two solid gold candlesticks in the same case, part of a set of eighteen given by the city of Paris to Marie-Antoinette on her marriage.

Juniper Hall
Old London Road, Mickleham
Dorking, Surrey

The home of a group of high-ranking constitutionalist émigrés. On the gate, a plaque recalls their presence: 'In 1792, this house was the refuge for a group of progressive French aristocrats who had fled to England to escape the worst excesses of the French Revolution. The group included the Princesse de Hénin, the Comtesse de la Châtre, Madame de Stael, Jaucourt, Louis de Narbonne, Lally Tollendal, Alexandre d'Arblay and Talleyrand. It was here that Fanny Burney, the novelist, visiting her sister Susanna Phillips of Mickleham, met Alexandre d'Arblay to whom she was subsequently married at Mickleham Church.' The old drawing-room retains its eighteenth-century decor. In a stained-glass window on the staircase are portraits of some of the émigrés of Juniper Hall – Madame de Stael, Talleyrand, General D'Arblay – surrounding Fanny Burney. The house now belongs to the National Trust and is used by the Field Studies Council.

Fishguard, Pembrokeshire, Wales
A tapestry in Fishguard Town Hall, modelled on the Bayeux Tapestry and entitled 'The Last Invasion', is a comic account of the last invasion of British soil, by French troops sent by the Directory in 1797, which ended with a French surrender.

FAMOUS ÉMIGRÉS

Chateaubriand
Commemorative plaque. See page 115, col. 1.

Talleyrand

- **Madame Tussaud's**. Wax figure.

- **Inscription**
  11 Kensington Square
  Talleyrand, impoverished by his years in exile, moved from Marylebone to a smaller house at this address from 1792 until 1798, where he continued to receive and help his fellow émigrés.

- **Blue plaque**
  21 Hanover Square, W1
  Later, when he returned as ambassador, Talleyrand lived here (1830–34).

- **Juniper Hall**
  See left. Talleyrand figures on the stained-glass window at Juniper Hall, where he came to see his constitutionalist friends.

Henri-Pierre Danloux
The National Gallery, National Portrait Gallery, Royal Academy, National Maritime Museum and Royal College of Music all contain works by Danloux.

Elisabeth Vigée-Lebrun
Works in the National Gallery and the Wallace Collection.

Sébastien Érard
Horniman Museum
100 London Road SE23
Érard harp with pedals.

Madame Tussaud
Madame Tussaud's
Madame Tussaud's waxwork collection moved to Marylebone Road in 1835. Since its creation, the waxwork museum has represented many iconic French historical figures such as Joan of Arc, Voltaire, Victor Hugo, Sarah Bernhardt, General de Gaulle, Brigitte Bardot, Gérard Depardieu . . . The collection changes with the times, and a model of Madame Tus-

saud herself stands at the entrance. There is also a medallion of Madame Tussaud on the east face of the building.

- **St Mary's**
  Cadogan Street SW3
  Plaque mentioned above (page 114, col. 2), listing Madame Tussaud and several members of her family buried there.

- **St Mary's Catholic Cemetery**
  Harrow Road, Kensal Green W10
  Plaque in memory of François Tussaud, grandson of Madame Tussaud.

- **Blue plaque**
  24 Wellington Road, St John's Wood NW8
  Madame Tussaud lived here in 1838/1839.

Augustus Welby Northmore Pugin

- **Palace of Westminster.** Augustus Pugin carried out all the interior decoration of Parliament. The Pugin Room is a bar and tea-room in the House of Commons, named after Pugin in 1978. A portrait on the wall of him by the painter J. R. Herbert is in a frame designed by Pugin himself.

- **Catholic Cathedral**
  St George's Southwark
  St George's Road SE1
  In 1848, Pugin built the first Catholic cathedral since the Reformation. Heavily damaged by bombs in 1941, it was restored and reopened in 1958. Pope John Paul II celebrated a Mass for the sick there in 1982.

- **St Thomas of Canterbury**
  60 Rylston Road SW6
  Restored several times, this is the only Pugin church in London which has remained intact. The adjoining presbytery has remained as it was when it was built.

- **Albert Memorial.** Portrait of Augustus Pugin on the north panel of the frieze, in the architects' section.

- **Victoria & Albert Museum**
  British Museum
  Several objects, both secular and religious, also furniture, designed by Pugin in the British galleries of both museums.

- **National Portrait Gallery**
  Portrait of Augustus Pugin (1840).

Marc and Isambard Brunel

- **Thames Tunnel**
  Rotherhithe Station (East London line)
  This 406-metre long tunnel is made up of two parallel tubes communicating in the middle. The entrance is between Rotherhithe and Wapping stations. It was the first tunnel dug under a navigable river, thanks to its tunnelling shield. Fourteen million passengers travel through it every year.

- **Brunel Museum**
  Railway Avenue, Rotherhithe
  Previously called the Brunel Engine House, dedicated to Marc and Isambard Brunel and the construction of the tunnel.

- **Paddington Station.** The station was built in 1854 by Isambard Kingdom Brunel, in collaboration with Matthew Digby Wyatt, to house his Great Western Railway. On a wall on Platform 1 is a 1954 plaque showing Brunel in his top hat. Further along the same platform is a statue of him sitting on a chair.

- **Victoria Embankment.** Bronze statue of Isambard Kingdom Brunel by the sculptor Marochetti (1877), of Brunel holding a set square.

- **National Portrait Gallery.** Portraits of Marc Brunel by Samuel Drummond (1835) and of Isambard Brunel by Callcott Horsley (1857)

- **Brunel University**
  Kingston Lane, Uxbridge, Middlesex
  The Brunel College of Technology started in Acton in 1928, but moved to Uxbridge in 1966–67. Originally specialising in technology and science, it now offers a wide

choice of subjects. On the campus, a bronze full-length statue of Isambard Brunel.

- **£2 coin**. To celebrate the bicentenary of his birth, a portrait of Isambard Brunel was struck on the £2 coin in 2006.

- **Commemorative plaques**

  98 Cheyne Walk SW10
  Sir Marc Isambard Brunel lived at this address from 1808 until 1825 with his wife and his son Isambard Kingdom.

  262 West Ferry Road E14
  Plaque in memory of the launch in 1858 of Isambard Brunel's *Great Eastern*, the largest ship ever built.

- **Kensal Green Cemetery**
  Harrow Road, Kensal Green W10
  Modelled on the Père Lachaise cemetery in Paris, there are many tombs of nineteenth-century personalities, including the Brunel family vault.

7

NAPOLEON,
THE MORTAL ENEMY
FROM TRAUMA TO TRIUMPH

*'England is an extraordinary country. They are completely mad!
Here all the streets are called after victories: Wagram, Austerlitz
. . . But there: Trafalgar Square, Waterloo Place . . . They've
only chosen names of defeats!'*

ALPHONSE ALLAIS

With British-style irony, Alphonse Allais made his inimitable comments on the long Anglo-French war which left a whole string of names of victories in the toponymy of both countries. The conflict began during the Revolution, in 1793, intensified with the rise of the First Consul, and only ended at the battle of Waterloo in 1815. However, Napoleon was no more able to invade England than Hitler would be in the next century. He was the mortal enemy but, unlike the other, he was admired as well, and still remains a powerful and legendary figure in the land he never conquered.

Napoleon versus Nelson: Trafalgar
The trial of strength began when General Bonaparte was sent to Egypt by the Directory in 1798 to cut off the route to the Indies which was so vital to the English. In August 1798 the French fleet was destroyed near Aboukir by Nelson. When the French army in

Egypt capitulated in 1801, the English demanded that the antiquities obtained by French archaeologists should be handed over,
thus acquiring the Rosetta Stone. The first consul, forced to abandon his Eastern dream, began to plan the invasion of England
instead.

Ever since two expeditions in 1796 and 1797 which had
planned landings via Ireland, Boulogne-sur-Mer became the base
for outfitting an invasion fleet; the English on the other side of the
Channel reinforced their coastal defences and recruited volunteers. Nelson, in command of naval operations, attacked the port
of Boulogne in August 1801; the English were repelled and forced
to negotiate, signing the Treaty of Amiens in March 1802, which
was greeted with joy and relief on both sides of the Channel. The
French regained their old colonies and King George III
renounced the title 'King of France' which his predecessors had
used since 1342. And the émigrés from the Revolution were
finally allowed to return to France.

However, the hostilities resumed as early as 1803. Bonaparte
had been First Consul for life since the previous year, and he
made use of an extremely efficient secret service both in France
and England, where many opponents of his regime had gathered.
His spies now infiltrated the French community in London, mingling with eminent figures and journalist émigrés who refused to
return to France while planning to restore the Bourbons to the
throne.

The English also had informants working in this shadowy
world – people such as Méhée de la Touche and Fauche-Borel.
Most feared by all was the mysterious Comte d'Antraigues, who
worked for Russia, Austria, Spain, Louis XVI and finally for the
Comte de Provence, the future Louis XVIII, who employed him
but also feared him. Pursued by Napoleon, he spent the last six
years of his life in exile in London, where he remained in close
contact with the English government and the Duc d'Orléans. He
was married to a famous opera singer, and both were murdered
by their butler in 1812. The motive for the crime remains a
mystery.

Several French newspapers in London were openly critical of Napoleon's despotism. Some of them, notably *l'Ambigu*, edited by Peltier, and Mallet du Pin's *Mercure britannique*, were read throughout Europe. In 1800 the first bomb attack against Napoleon, the *machine infernale*, failed. It had been planned in London by the Royalists and the Comte d'Artois. After the collapse of the Treaty of Amiens the English government decided to provide financial and material support for another plot against the First Consul in 1804, still with the collaboration of the Comte d'Artois. The French police, tipped off by the double agent Méhée de la Touche, arrested the three chief plotters, generals Pichegru, Moreau and Cadoudal. This conspiracy led to the execution, after a show trial, of the Duc d'Enghien, Louis-Philippe's cousin, who had been kidnapped on foreign soil, although his implication in the plot was never proved.

Napoleon, who had become Emperor in May 1804, had swept all obstacles aside in his land campaigns but still dreamt of gaining supremacy at sea from the English, who controlled the lucrative trade with the colonies and stood in the way of his totalitarian plans. He built an invasion fleet at Boulogne in record time, without worrying about technical constraints: the whole of France was called upon to finance the venture, and various unconventional means of invasion were planned by his engineers – balloons, a tunnel, even submarines . . . Success seemed to be guaranteed with an army of 130,000 men and a 'national flotilla' of around 2,300 flat barges. Napoleon proceeded to hand out Légion d'Honneur crosses and had a special medal struck with the words 'Fall of England, 1804'.

This huge project had the desired intimidating effect and the English were effectively alarmed by the swarming of this warlike ant-heap. Madame Vigée-Lebrun, on a visit to Brighton, remarked: 'When I was there, the English feared the arrival of the French; generals were constantly reviewing the National Guard, which was in constant movement, beating drums and making an infernal racket.'[31] Posters were put up all over the country calling on men to sign up at hastily opened recruitment offices, sometimes even in pubs. A raid on Boulogne to destroy the flotilla was a failure.

Napoleon, in order to ensure the success of his Channel cross-ing, needed the protection of his fleet, but this was blockaded in the Mediterranean and Atlantic ports by the English fleet; led by Nelson, it had been carefully deployed at strategic points along the coast. In order to break the deadlock, Napoleon dreamt up a com-plicated plan: he ordered Admiral de Villeneuve to draw Nelson away by heading towards the Antilles, and then turn back towards Brest. Villeneuve, pursued by Nelson, took shelter at Cadiz and then decided to face him off Cape Trafalgar. On 21 October 1805, the English fleet, better at manoeuvres, broke through the French line and won the battle. But it cost them dear: a French sailor called Robert Guillemard, perched in the rigging of the *Redou-table*, shot Nelson, who died a few hours later. Lieutenant John Richard de Lapenotière, a descendant of Huguenots, was charged with announcing the news in London. He landed in Cornwall off the schooner *Pickle* on 4 November and, changing horses 21 times, rode flat out to reach London 37 hours later. The news spread like wildfire, and England celebrated its victory in mourn-ing. Napoleon affected indifference in the face of this disaster. He was in Austria and his victory at Austerlitz in December 1805 con-firmed France's supremacy on land. Admiral de Villeneuve, aban-doned by his master, was captured and taken to Reading; there were by this time 3,000–4,000 French prisoners in English jails.

Nelson's ship took five weeks to return to England, carrying the admiral's body preserved in a barrel of rum. At the naval head-quarters in Greenwich, he was placed in a coffin made of wood from the French ship *L'Orient* from which Napoleon had con-quered Egypt, and which had been destroyed at the Battle of the Nile. A huge funeral took place on 9 January 1806 for the man who was henceforth regarded as one of England's greatest heroes. And to forestall any renewed invasion plans, the English set about building, right up until 1812, a series of 103 Martello towers, named after a tower in Corsica which was part of a coastal defence system. These watchtowers were never used.

THE
TRAFALGAR WAY

KENSINGTON

On Monday 21st October 1805 the Royal Navy decisively defeated a combined
French and Spanish fleet off Cape Trafalgar on the south west coast of Spain.
This victory permanently removed the threat of invasion of England
by the armies of Napoleon Bonaparte.

The first official dispatches with the momentous news of the victory, and the
death in action of Vice Admiral Lord Nelson, were carried to England
on board H. M. Schooner PICKLE by her captain,
Lieutenant John Richards Lapenotiere.

Lapenotiere landed at Falmouth on Monday 4th November 1805 and set out
"express by post-chaise" for London. He took some 37 hours on the 271 mile journey,
changing horses 21 times, one of these being very late on 5th November at Hounslow.
His orders were to lose no time in reaching the Admiralty so, as the horses were
not yet spent, he made what speed he could through Kensington
in a dense fog towards his final destination.

Over the following four weeks other important messages arrived from the fleet
with further details of the victory and anxiously awaited information on casualties.
All the dispatches were landed at Falmouth and their couriers took the same
route through Kensington, where horses and hospitality were available
from the inns to all travellers on what is now The Trafalgar Way.

Erected by the Council of the Royal Borough of Kensington and Chelsea
on 8th September 2005
to inaugurate The Trafalgar Way from Falmouth to London and
to honour the men of Kensington and Chelsea
who fought for their country at Trafalgar.

*The Trafalgar Way, Kensington. Plaque relating the journey made
on Monday 4 November 1805 by the Huguenot Lieutenant John
Richard Lapenotiere from Falmouth to the Admiralty in London to
bring the news of the victory at Trafalgar and the death of Nelson. It
took him 37 hours to travel 271 miles, changing horses 21 times.*

Napoleon versus Wellington: Waterloo

Between 1808 and 1814, England allied itself to Portugal and to
the Spanish people, who had risen against King Joseph who had
been imposed upon them by Napoleon. In 1813, after their victory
at Vittoria, the English forces under General Wellesley pursued the
French as far as Toulouse. To mark his gratitude to the victorious
general, the King made him Duke of Wellington. The new Duke,
who spoke perfect French, became the British ambassador in Paris
after Napoleon abdicated in April 1814. Later, when Napoleon
escaped from exile on Elba, Wellington returned to the army and
fought and won the Battle of Waterloo on Belgian soil. It appears
that on the morning of the battle, Napoleon misguidedly
remarked to Marechal Soult that victory would be 'won by
lunchtime'.[32]

Napoleon's and Wellington's paths only crossed at Waterloo, but
the Englishman was so fascinated by his adversary that he arranged
for his government to buy Napoleon's sister Pauline Borghese's
house in Paris, which is the British embassy to this day. The two
men had other things in common: they shared two mistresses, the
singer Giuseppina Grassine and the actress Josephine Weimar,
better known under her stage name Mademoiselle George. The
latter, when asked one day to compare her famous lovers, replied:
'Monsieur le Duc was by far the strongest lover!' And finally,
Wellington saved Napoleon's life twice: first when he stopped a
soldier from taking aim at him at Waterloo, and later when he
argued against the Prussian Marshal Blücher who wanted to have
him shot.

The Duke, on his return to London, was showered with
honours, money and praise; he bought Apsley House and transformed it into a Waterloo museum filled with objects linked to
Napoleon and his last battle. He gave a dinner each year for the
generals who had been with him on the great day. When he died
in 1852, after a long life spent in the forefront of political life, his
coffin was placed on a triumphal gun carriage made of metal from
the cannons captured at Waterloo, and there followed a period of

national mourning equal to the one that had followed the death of Nelson.

A large number of prisoners were taken during the Napoleonic wars. In all, about 122,000 men were held in England during the Empire, notably in the Norman Cross prison at Peterborough, in Porchester Castle in Portsmouth and at Dartmoor. At the beginning they were crowded into ports, on pontoons or prison hulks, but later the authorities moved them away from the coast and built prisons further inland. They were decimated by cold, hunger and disease. Later they were helped by émigré priests, and allowed to take up occupations according to their skills: Jean Pons Guillaume Viennet, a politician and poet, wrote and performed plays, while Ambroise-Louis Garneray was such a successful painter of ships that he received commissions from British officers.

French officers were quite decently treated. General Cambronne, who was wounded and taken prisoner at Waterloo, spent several months in England, and married Mary Osburn, a Scottish nurse who had looked after him while he was in captivity. Lucien Bonaparte, who was captured by the English trying to sail to America, remained a prisoner, in relative comfort, until 1814.

After Waterloo, Napoleon abdicated in favour of his son, the King of Rome, on 22 June 1815, and then set off for Rochefort in Charente-Maritime on the Atlantic coast, urged by his brother Joseph to sail to America. He hesitated and then decided to go to England to 'sit, like Themistocles, at the enemy's door', and with that intention he embarked on the *Bellerophon*, which the British government had sent to capture him. The captain, without making any promises, greeted him respectfully, but the fallen emperor felt he had been duped when Admiral Lord Keith announced that he would be sent into exile on St Helena. On 4 August 1815, on board the ship, he wrote: 'I appeal to History. She will say that an enemy who waged war on the English people for twenty years came freely, in his misfortune, to seek shelter under its laws. What greater proof could he give of his esteem and his trust? But how did England respond to such magnanimity? She pretended to extend a hospitable hand to this enemy, and when he gave himself up in good faith, she destroyed him!'[33] The *Bellerophon* remained at anchor for several days off Torbay on the south coast, but such was the curiosity she aroused that she had to be moved to a larger and better protected anchorage at Plymouth.

The Napoleonic legend

Napoleon never set foot on English soil but, as soon as he was no longer to be feared, his legend began to grow. The Bonaparte myth, sprung from the original fear of invasion, exerted a deep fascination. The accounts published by the scholars who had accompanied General Bonaparte to Egypt had aroused as much interest in him as in the land of the Pharaohs. In 1810 the naturalist William Bullock had an Egyptian Hall built in Piccadilly; in 1816 he exhibited various objects connected to Napoleon, notably the campaign carriage he used at Waterloo. The exhibition was visited by 200,000 people. Madame Tussaud, on her tours of England, joined the Napoleon craze, adding objects connected to the emperor to her waxwork collection, including his death mask. George IV used the coronation of Napoleon as a model for his own in 1821, just after Napoleon's death. In his *Mémoires d'outre-tombe*, Chateaubriand, who became ambassador in London in 1822, expressed astonishment at this infatuation of the English, who 'had passed from denigration of Nic[34] to stupid enthusiasm'. Today, in London, Trafalgar Square and Waterloo Station are reminders of England's victory over the most feared enemy in her history. His thirst for conquest had inspired caricaturists such as James Gillray, Thomas Rowlandson and George Cruikshank, who portrayed William Pitt and the French emperor carving up the world between them, and John Bull sitting at his table enjoying the English victories over the French. Gillray, in one very popular series, placed Napoleon in the context of Swift's *Gulliver's Travels*.

Fear of the 'Corsican ogre' crops up even in children's nursery rhymes. Some of them allude to 'Boney', the nickname for Napoleon. Boney became Bogey, or the Bogeyman, as in the threat mothers would make: 'the Bogeyman will get you,' or more elaborately as in the nursery rhyme:

> *Baby, baby, naughty baby,*
> *Hush, you squalling thing, I say,*
> *Peace this moment, peace, or maybe*
> *Bonaparte will pass this way.*
>
> *[. . .]*
>
> *Baby, baby, he's a giant,*
> *Tall and black as Rouen steeple,*
> *And he breakfasts, dines, rely on't,*
> *Every day on naughty people.*
>
> *[. . .]*
>
> *And he'll beat you, beat you, beat you,*
> *And he'll beat you all to pap,*
> *And he'll eat you, eat you, eat you,*
> *Every morsel snap, snap, snap.*

In the nineteenth century, with the rise of the historical novel, romantic literature introduced a cult of Napoleon. In England, poets such as Sir Walter Scott, Lord Byron, Wordsworth and Coleridge sang his praises while disapproving of his thirst for conquest. The memoirs of those who had known him or accompanied him to St Helena were avidly read. Such was the curious afterlife of the Frenchman who had caused such terror to the normally unruffled English.

Places to visit

BATTLE OF TRAFALGAR

Nelson's column
Trafalgar Square WC2

Trafalgar Square was built between 1829 and 1841 to commemorate the 1805 battle. At the centre is a 44-metre high column surmounted by a statue of Nelson, erected between 1839 and 1842. The four panels at the base of the column, made from melted-down French cannons, depict Nelson's battles.

Holland Park
Kensington High Street W8

At the entrance is a plaque showing the stages of Lieutenant Lapenotière's route from Falmouth to London bringing the news of Trafalgar and the death of Nelson. In 2005, to celebrate the bicentenary of the battle, a rider retraced his steps along the Trafalgar Way. The Ordnance Survey produced a map of the route he followed.

St Paul's Cathedral. In the crypt is Nelson's tomb. His coffin was made from a piece of wood from a French ship captured by the English.

The Trafalgar Tavern
Park Row, Greenwich SE10

Built in 1837 beside the Thames to commemorate Admiral Nelson and the famous battle, this establishment looks more like a fine house than a pub. Very popular at the end of the nineteenth century, it is once more elegant and popular after a refurbishment in the 1960s.

National Maritime Museum. The museum buildings, linked by a colonnade to the Queen's House, were constructed in 1807 to commemorate the Battle of Trafalgar, to which one section is devoted; Nelson's uniform and blood-soaked socks are on display. Among the war booty is the prow of the English ship *Polyphemus*, previously a French ship called *Fortune*. Captured by the English in 1799, she took part in the Battle of Trafalgar on the Eng-

lish side. Another prow and back part of the *Implacable* was once part of the French ship *Dugay-Trouin*, captured at Trafalgar; above it, a French flag.

Portsmouth, Hampshire

The *Victory*, Nelson's flagship, in which he died during the Battle of Trafalgar, has been restored and is open to the public.

Windsor Castle. In the armoury is the French musket ball that killed Nelson, as well as objects that belonged to Napoleon.

BATTLE OF WATERLOO

Apsley House
149 Piccadilly W1

Bought by the Duke of Wellington, this house, also known as 'Number One, London', contains the largest collection of Napoleonic memorabilia in London. Among them are his sword, left in his carriage at Waterloo, and several standards representing different departments in France, presented to the Duke in 1815 when Paris was taken. At the foot of the stairs, a fine statue of Napoleon in Carrara marble, commissioned by Bonaparte from the sculptor Canova when he was First Consul and showing him as a naked Roman emperor holding a small winged Victory in his right hand. When the sculpture arrived in Paris, Napoleon had become Emperor. Somewhat embarrassed, he sent it to the Louvre. After Waterloo, the British government bought it to give to the Duke of Wellington. A painting by David Wilkie shows a rider bringing the tidings of Waterloo to Chelsea pensioners eagerly awaiting the news. The Waterloo gallery contains superb paintings by the greatest painters: Goya, Velazquez, Ribera, Murillo, Caravaggio, Van Dyck, Rubens, Correggio . . . These were taken by Joseph Bonaparte, Napoleon's brother and King of Spain, and were found in his luggage after Wellington's victory over Napoleon's troops in 1813. The Duke of Wellington wanted to return the paintings to Spain, but King Ferdinand VII gave them to him in gratitude for defeating the French. In the basement, death masks of Napoleon and Wellington share a case. Born in the same year (1769), Napoleon died at 52, and Wellington at 83. Close to Apsley House, a monument and two statues of the Duke of Wellington, in memory of his victory over Napoleon.

Wellington Arch (Constution Arch). Erected in 1826 to celebrate Wellington's victories over Napoleon, the arch is open to the public.

Two statues of Wellington. Equestrian statue of Arthur Wellesley, Duke of Wellington, and one of Achilles symbolising him, cast from metal from French cannons.

Waterloo Bridge. The first bridge was opened on 18 June 1817, the second anniversary of the Battle of Waterloo. It was demolished in the mid-1930s and replaced in 1945 by the present bridge.

Waterloo Station
Waterloo Place SE1
Opened in 1848.

'Waterloo' churches. An act of Parliament was passed in 1818, granting a large sum for the construction of churches to be built in gratitude for the victory. Thirty-eight were built in London between 1818 and 1828, among them St John Waterloo, near the station; Holy Trinity Marylebone, and St Peter's Hammersmith.

National Army Museum. Model of the Battle of Waterloo, containing all the troops involved, as well as a collection of objects found on the battlefield. Also Napoleonic memorabilia, most notably the skeleton of his horse, Marengo.

The Queen's House, Greenwich. Two paintings showing Napoleon as a prisoner on board the *Bellerophon* in the port of Plymouth, waiting to set off for St Helena in July 1815. One is a portrait of the Emperor by Sir Charles Eastlake, the only portrait from life of Napoleon by an Englishman. The other, by Jean-Jacques

Chalon, shows a small silhouette of Napoleon on the *Bellerophon*, as he appeared on the deck every day at six o'clock. He became a great attraction, and crowds of people came out on small boats to look at him.

Windsor Castle

- **Great Hall.** In a glass case, among other trophies of war, the red coat Napoleon wore at Waterloo.

- **Waterloo Chamber.** Gallery created by George IV to commemorate the victory at Waterloo. He commissioned Sir Thomas Lawrence to paint portraits of soldiers and politicians who had contributed to the fall of Napoleon. His portrait of Wellington dominates the room.

- **Guard Room.** Above the busts of the Dukes of Marlborough and Wellington, two French flags, one with the arms of the King of France, the other a tricolor, which are renewed each year. They are given by the descendants of the two dukes as a symbolic rent for the estates given to their ancestors in recognition of their respective victories against the French.

OTHER SOUVENIRS OF THE NAPOLEONIC ERA

Cleopatra's Needle
Victoria Embankment WC2
The obelisk, Cleopatra's Needle, was given to England by the Sultan of Egypt in commemoration of Nelson's victories over Bonaparte at Aboukir Bay (1798) and that of Sir Ralph Abercrombie at Alexandria (1801).

Dalmeny House
South Queensferry, Edinburgh
Lord Rosebery, owner of the house and Prime Minister at the end of the nineteenth century, was fascinated by Napoleon. He wrote a biography, *Napoleon: The Last Phase*, and collected several works of art which had belonged to the emperor. This 'Napoleon' collection is one of the most important outside France. The house

also contains French furniture, and fine porcelain from Vincennes and Sèvres. It is open to the public for a few weeks in summer.

Martello towers. Along the south and east coast of England a hundred massive towers equipped with cannons were built between 1805 and 1812 in case of a French invasion. Copied from a fortified tower at Martello in Corsica which had held out against the English in 1794, twenty-five of them can still be seen on the south coast.

French prisoners of war
Norman Cross Eagle Memorial
A1, Peterborough, Cambridgeshire
In 1796, the first prison camp was built in a hurry at Norman Cross. It held 7,000 prisoners, of whom around 1,700 are buried in the camp cemetery. In 1914, the Entente Cordiale Society erected a monument in their memory, a column surmounted by a bronze eagle, near the site of the prison.

Peterborough Museum
Priestgate, Peterborough, Cambridgeshire
Important collection of artefacts made by the French prisoners at Norman Cross, one of which is a guillotine in perfect working order.

Dartmoor Prison Museum
HMP Dartmoor, Princetown, Devon
Several objects relating to the history of the prison, particularly from the Napoleonic period.

NAPOLEON IN LONDON MUSEUMS

British Museum. After the 1801 Treaty of Alexandria was signed following Napoleon's defeat in Egypt, the conquered French handed the English, among other antiquities, the Rosetta Stone which had been discovered by a French officer in July 1799. It is one of the most important possessions of the British Museum, where it has been on display since 1802.

National Army Museum. Among the many objects relating to the Napoleonic wars, a jug commemorating the Treaty of Amiens and a 1795 recruitment poster for the 6th Warwickshire Regiment. Also Napoleon's gold watch, given by Sir Hudson Law whose petty behaviour made Napoleon's exile miserable.

Victoria & Albert Museum. Objects from the Napoleonic era: Empire furniture, which was fashionable throughout Europe until about 1830; two marble busts of Napoleon and Josephine.

Tate Britain. Turner's *The Field of Waterloo* (1818) is part of a series of drawings made on the Waterloo battlefield in 1817. Other paintings show the Battle of Trafalgar.

National Portrait Gallery. Portraits of Napoleon.

Wallace Collection. Miniatures of Napoleon's family; paintings by different artists of his military campaigns.

Soane Museum
13 Lincoln's Inn Fields, Holborn WC2
The first portrait of Napoleon to come to England, *Napoleon as a Young Man* (1797), was acquired by Sir John Soane, who greatly admired him.

Madame Tussaud's. Wax effigy of Napoleon on his deathbed.

Cartoon Museum
35 Little Russell Street WC1
Numerous caricatures from the Napoleonic wars in this museum devoted to the history of caricature and cartoons in England.

Other museums
Apsley House
National Maritime Museum
The Queen's House, Greenwich

1. William, Duke of Normandy, with his half-brothers Odo of Bayeux and Robert of Mortain on the day of the landing in England. From the Bayeux Tapestry.

2. *Above: the tombs of Eleanor of Aquitaine and Henry II,*
Royal Abbey of Fontevraud, Anjou.

3. *Opposite: Charles of Orleans in the Tower of London.*
By an unknown medieval artist.

Es nouuelles dalbyon
Si vous en plaist escouter
Mon frere z mon compaignon
Sachiez qua mon retourner
Ay este deca la mer
Et en a ioyeuse chiere

4. Henrietta-Maria, Queen of England.
After Anthony Van Dyck, c. 1632–35.

5. *Louise de Keroualle, Duchess of Portsmouth and mistress of King Charles II, who is represented by the King Charles spaniel cradled in her left arm. By Henri Gascar, c. 1670.*

6. Roubillac at work on his bust of Garrick.
By Andrea Soldi, 1757.

7. *The Chevalier d'Eon.*
By Thomas Stewart, after Jean Laurent Mosnier, 1892.

8. Above: Madame de Stael and Talleyrand, Fanny Burney and General d'Arblay. Painted glass window at Juniper Hall, Surrey.

9. Right: commemorative plaques in London.

10. Opposite: Augustus Pugin on the architects' corner of the Albert Memorial, Kensington Gardens.

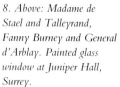

11. *Above: Napoleon Bonaparte.*
By Benjamin Robert Haydon, 1830.

12. *Opposite, top: Orleans House, Twickenham, where*
the French King Louis-Philippe lived in exile in from 1815
to 1817. He visited the house when he returned in 1844.
By Edouard Pingret, 1844.

13. *Opposite, below: Napoleon III, Empress Eugénie*
and the Prince Imperial living in exile
at Camden Place, Chislehurst.
By an unknown photographer, 1872.

14. *Above: Painters' corner on the Albert Memorial, Kensington Gardens, featuring Delacroix, Delaroche, Géricault and others.*

15. *Below and opposite: some French restaurants and cafés still open in London.*

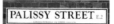

16. *Top: Court of Honour at the Franco-British Exhibition,*
after which the area was called the 'White City'.

17. *Above: French-influenced London street names.*

18. *Opposite, above: Michelin House.*

19. *Opposite, below: Rodin's* The Burghers of Calais.

20. *Left: Free French sailor and soldier put up a poster in London after de Gaulle's BBC appeal on 18 June 1940.*

21. *Centre: Free French banknote designed by Edmund Dulac.*

22. *Bottom: Churchill and de Gaulle on the Champs Élysées, 11 November 1944.*

8

LONDON, A SANCTUARY FOR THE POLITICALLY PERSECUTED
FROM FALLEN SOVEREIGNS TO HUNTED COMMUNARDS

'Between you and me, the only thing I have to fear by going to England is the over-warm welcome'[35]

LOUIS–PHILIPPE to VICTOR HUGO

The scale of the Napoleonic wars forced both countries to understand that an entente between them would be the only guarantee of peace in Europe. The four sovereigns who succeeded each other in Paris after the fall of Napoleon – Louis XVIII, Charles X, Louis-Philippe and Napoleon III – were all awarded the prestigious Order of the Garter by the reigning English monarch, such was his anxiety to make a striking display of his desire for a cloudless relationship between the two countries. England continued, too, with its tradition of offering shelter to French deposed sovereigns and their families, who eventually all went into exile on English soil.

England, refuge of the last kings of France
So it was that the Comte de Provence settled at Hartwell House in Oxfordshire, surrounded by his court. His émigré compatriots shared their loyalty between him, his brother the Comte d'Artois

and the Duc d'Orléans. The two competing aspirants to the throne, Bourbon and Orleans, were closely watched by the British authorities. The Comte de Provence, as the older, was supported by the Prince Regent, the future George IV. The English government authorised the Comte d'Artois to travel to France to announce the imminent return of the King, Louis XVIII, and one fine morning a carriage covered in white rosettes arrived at Hartwell: the Prince Regent had sent his aide-de-camp to tell the Comte de Provence that he had been recalled to the French throne. He set off for London on 20 April 1814, where he was cheered by the crowds, singing a song in fashion at the time: 'England, no more your foe, will bring you aid / When France shall welcome home the White Cockade.'[36] He then joyfully received émigrés and envoys from the British government. He awarded the Prince Regent the Order of the Holy Spirit, the most prestigious decoration of the *ancien régime*, while expressing his immense gratitude: 'After God, it is to the Prince Regent that I owe my crown.'[37] In return he was given the Order of the Garter.

A few days later he was escorted to Dover by the Prince Regent, cheered by the crowds, and set sail for France on an English ship. There was an enormous sense of relief in the country, as the return of the Bourbons meant, above all, victory over Napoleon. A huge popular festival was organised in Hyde Park, with a re-enactment of the Battle of Trafalgar on the Serpentine: French ships went down in flames to the tune of the English national anthem. As soon as the monarchy was re-installed in the Tuileries after an absence of a quarter of a century, 'thousands of oddly dressed English flocked to Paris'.[38] Captain Gronow (1794–1865) had fought in Spain and at Waterloo under Wellington. He spent a large part of his life in France and his second wife was French. His memoirs provide a lively description of the events of his life and the characters he came across. The Duchesse d'Angoulême had to 'renounce this foreign dress on the day she returned to Paris' because 'the long separation between the British Isles and the continent had led to a great difference in costume'.[39] There was now a wave of anglomania in France, with many cultural exchanges and mixed marriages: Vigny, Lamartine, Tocqueville and Prince Jules de Polignac were among many who married Englishwomen.

At the death of Louis XVIII in 1824, his brother the Comte d'Artois succeeded him under the name of Charles X. Surrounded by ultras, he soon alienated the French with his autocratic style of government: 'I would rather saw wood than reign in the manner of the King of England,' he said.[40] He was forced to abdicate at the July revolution in 1830 and he returned into exile, where he lived under the name of Comte de Ponthieu first at Lulworth Castle in Dorset, and then at Holyrood in Edinburgh. He spent two years there before moving to Prague and then Slovenia, where he died in 1836.

After the monarchy had been restored in France, the Duc d'Orléans, the future Louis-Philippe, had also been forced into exile for having plotted against King Louis XVIII. Remembering his happy, peaceful days at 'Twick', he returned to Twickenham with his wife and children, to the house which was later called Orleans House. He lived there from 1815 to 1817 in some comfort, with a large entourage. When he became King of France after the abdication of Charles X in 1830, he made Talleyrand ambassador to London. The embassy, thanks to the Talleyrand's niece the ambitious Duchesse de Dino, became a glittering and prestigious address, first at 50 Portland Place, and then at 21 Hanover Square.

Three of Louis-Philippe's children married members of the Saxe-Coburg family who were related to Queen Victoria, and the goodwill between the two royal houses led to an exchange of state visits. In 1843, Queen Victoria and Prince Albert were received with great pomp at the Château d'Eu in Normandy, and the following year Louis-Philippe was received at Windsor, and awarded the Order of the Garter. In France, with the rise in socialism, radicalisation brought about the 1848 Revolution and the King and his wife were forced to flee across the Channel disguised as 'Mr and Mrs Smith'. Louis-Philippe shaved off his moustache, wrapped himself in a huge coat and wore a cap and large glasses. The English consul was able to bring the fugitives safely to

Newhaven with nothing more than the clothes they were wearing.

Queen Victoria, despite their deep friendship, wrote: 'we cannot make *cause commune* with them and cannot take a hostile position opposite to the new state of things in France.'[41] The deposed King and his family settled at Claremont, near Esher, under the name of Comte and Comtesse de Neuilly. The old King died there only two years after his arrival, at the age of seventy-seven; Queen Marie-Amélie remained there until her death in 1866. One of their sons, the Duc d'Aumale, bought back Orleans House, where he spent twenty-two years until 1870, campaigning against the Second Empire and controlling several European papers, such as the *Continental Review* which was published in London. Orleans House became the rallying point for the French in exile and the Orleans family remained in the area until the beginning of the twentieth century. In 1886, after the 'exile law' which forbade any previously reigning families from living in France, the Duc d'Aumale went back to London, where he lived in great style at Moncorvo House near Hyde Park.

England, last refuge of the empire

After the Restoration, all Bonapartes were forbidden to live in France. Napoleon I's nephew, Prince Louis-Napoleon, the future Napoleon III, came to London several times between 1831 and 1848, moving in to 1 Carlton Gardens in 1838. The French ambassador watched him closely, worried about his political intentions, and Paris attempted to get him expelled from England by sending over the extravagant Comte Leon, Napoleon's illegitimate son, to compromise him. In August 1840, Louis-Napoleon set off for Boulogne with a group of faithful followers to attempt a coup d'état in France. The operation was a fiasco and he was arrested and condemned to life imprisonment in the fortress of Ham in Picardy. He escaped after six years, disguised as a workman and, back in London, moved into a modest house at 3 King Street, near St James's. He found his friends again and assured the French ambassador that he was finished with politics.

Louis-Napoleon was intelligent and well informed; his charm and courtesy gained him the trust of those he met, but they concealed a steely determination to place his family back on the throne. He was a great seducer, and kept several mistresses in London: one in particular, a Miss Howard, became devoted to the Napoleonic cause and placed her fortune at his disposal. He later made her Comtesse de Beauregard. The moment to return to France was fast approaching: in February 1848, when Paris rose against Louis-Philippe, the agitation reached London, and Louis-Napoleon offered his services as a special constable to keep order at a large demonstration which the English government feared might set off a revolution.

Back in Paris in September 1848, he was elected Prince-President, and subsequently, as head of the short-lived Republic, he organised the coup d'état of 2 December 1852 which enabled him to restore the empire and become Emperor. At the beginning of his reign, the English were wary – memories of his uncle were still vivid in people's minds. When the French began to reinforce their fleet, Prime Minister Lord Palmerston started to build forts along the coast between Plymouth and Portsmouth; they became known as Palmerston's Follies and were never used. Despite these anxieties, England was the first country to recognise Emperor Napoleon III. The imperial couple, on an official visit in April 1855, travelled across London to loud cheers to Paddington, where they were greeted by the engineer Isambard Brunel at the station he had built. When they reached Windsor Castle, Empress Eugénie panicked before dinner, when the luggage containing her dresses and jewels, along with her hairdresser Felix, failed to arrive. She was forced to borrow a dress from one of her ladies-in-waiting and to decorate her hair with fresh flowers. The dinner was an immediate success and Napoleon III was, in his turn, awarded the Garter during his stay. They were acclaimed by the London crowds, but heavily guarded as there were a great many French refugees hostile to the imperial regime.

In August of the same year Napoleon III invited Queen Victoria to France for the inauguration of the Great Exhibition in

Paris. The two monarchs, during this visit, visited the tomb of Napoleon I: 'It was touching and pleasing in the extreme to see the alliance sealed so completely . . . and to see old enmities and rivalries wiped out over the tomb of Napoleon I, before whose coffin I stood . . . at the arm of Napoleon III now my nearest and dearest ally!' the Queen noted in her journal.[42]

In 1870 the Franco-Prussian war brought disaster: Napoleon III was taken prisoner at Sedan and the empire collapsed. In September, with a small group of followers, Empress Eugénie left France to take refuge in England. She rented Camden Place in Chislehurst, half an hour from London by train. Her son the Imperial Prince joined her there soon afterwards and the Emperor arrived after his release in March 1871, now ill and ageing. Queen Victoria visited them several times. When she saw the fallen Emperor she noted: 'it was a moving moment, when I thought of the last time he came here in '55, in perfect triumph . . . He seemed much depressed and had tears in his eyes, but he controlled himself and said: il y a bien longtemps que je n'ai vu votre Majesté . . .'[43] He kept a close eye on events in France and never lost hope of restoring his regime; he died on 9 January 1873 after an operation, and thousands of French and English people, including the Prince of Wales, paid their respects. He was buried first at St Mary's in Chislehurst, then in 1888 his body was moved to St Michael's Abbey at Farnborough, built by his widow.

Aged seventeen, his son the Imperial Prince was now the Bonapartist pretender. He was educated at the Royal Military Academy at Woolwich, at the same time leading an active social life, encouraged by his mother. He became great friends with Princess Beatrice, Queen Victoria's daughter, but he was bored and longed for glory, so he succeeded in joining British forces fighting the Zulus in South Africa. He wrote to his mother, who was horrified by his departure: 'Inaction is killing me. Do you want me to wither and die of boredom like the Duc de Reichstadt?'[44] He arrived in Cape Town in March 1879, but the commander of the British forces was conscious of his responsibility and did not allow him on any dangerous missions. Nevertheless, he was killed in an ambush while on a routine reconnaissance mission, at the age of twenty-three. His body was brought back to England and he was buried in his English uniform at Chislehurst in mid-July, beside his father. His death shocked the country and his funeral, attended by the Queen and her daughters, drew an enormous crowd. With his death the dream of a Bonapartist restoration disappeared forever.

Prostrated by the deaths of her husband and son, Eugénie wanted to build an imperial mausoleum for their tombs. She bought a large property at Farnborough in Hampshire, where she built a church and a monastery, St Michael's Abbey, and moved the bodies there. She settled at Farnborough Hill in 1881, and lived there until she died in 1901, dividing her life between good works and travel, always remaining close to Queen Victoria. She survived the Queen, lived to the age of ninety-four and was buried along-side her husband and son. Attempts to repatriate their bodies are periodically made, arousing much controversy in French political circles, but the Benedictine order which runs the abbey remains firmly opposed to any such plan.

London, shelter for political exiles and den of anarchists

Restrictions imposed on strangers by English laws were relaxed after the Napoleonic Wars. Waves of refugees from successive French regimes were drawn to London, where they could find relative freedom of expression: royalists, republicans, Bonapartists, socialists and communists arrived in succession. New ideologies arose with the Industrial Revolution, and workers' revolts became common: the greatest wave of refugees came after the suppression of the Commune – 3,500 people crossed the Channel, fleeing the ensuing repression. Alexandre Ledru-Rollin and Louis Blanc were the two major figures of French socialism exiled in London at that time. There were also idealists and utopians such as Etienne Cabet, Ernest Coeurderoy and Alphonse Esquiros.

From London, Louis-Napoleon had founded *Le Capitole*, a Parisian paper in which he tried to manipulate French public opinion in his favour, as he made attempts to overthrow Louis-Philippe. Once the empire had been re-established, London once again became a base for those now plotting against his regime. From now on political exiles began attempting to form international political parties. Nine Frenchmen were founder-members of the International, the pillar of which was Karl Marx, himself a refugee in London – Charles Longuet and Paul Lafargue married two of his daughters. The first became a professor at King's College London, and the second, one of the propagators of French Marxism, founded the French workers' party. The socialist journalist Prosper Lissagaray became engaged to Eleanor Marx's youngest daughter. Using eye-witness testimonies, he wrote *L'Histoire de la Commune de* 1871, which Eleanor translated into English.

These political exiles created societies such as the Society of Refugees from the Commune, and the Centre for Social Studies. They belonged to Masonic lodges, one of which, the Philadelphes, contained a majority of Frenchmen as members. These lodges placed them in contact with British political circles and gave them a better picture of the Industrial Revolution which was transforming England. Women, too, socialist and feminist militants such as Flora Tristan and Jeanne Deroin, exerted their influence and campaigned for the emancipation of women.

In 1881 an international anarchist congress was held in London. Some took action: in 1894 a Soho tailor, Martial Bourdin, killed himself trying to blow up the Greenwich Observatory.[45] Two Frenchmen were presumed guilty of a bomb attack on the house of an English judge. All these activities were closely watched by secret services from both countries. Thus, at the time of the Commune, a French network of agents and spies was sending thousands of reports to the French police in Paris.

By the end of the century, London had become a haven for foreign anarchists. In 1894, after the assassination of the French President Sadi Carnot, a wave of expatriates, less educated and more militant than their predecessors, arrived in London to a more hostile welcome than before.

During the Dreyfus affair, which shook French society to its roots, Emile Zola published his famous 'J'accuse!' in 1898; he was condemned to a year in prison, but preferred to go into exile in London. In the meantime, the man presumed guilty of treachery, Commandant Esterhazy, was acquitted in a closed trial. When Dreyfus was rehabilitated, the French government forced Esterhazy to 'retire' to England under the name of Comte Jean de Voilemont.

Soho remained, as it had been for previous generations, a rallying point for political exiles. The writer William Thackeray saw there 'a dingy modern France . . . There are French cafés, billiards, estaminets, waiters, markers, poor Frenchmen, and rich Frenchmen . . .'[46] They lodged at the Hotel de la Seine in King Street, met at the Café de La Sablonnière in Leicester Square, ate at Chez Victor in Old Compton Street: most of the businesses in the quarter were run by French people. The first patisserie in London, Maison Bertaux, was started by a Communard and is still open today. The French Chamber of Commerce was established in 1883 to further the interests of French entrepreneurs such as Emile-Justin Menier, who opened a chocolate factory in Southwark in 1870. An illiterate mason from the Creuse managed to become a teacher at the military preparatory school in Wimbledon. The caricaturist Pilotell earned a living with his satirical drawings.

Most of these exiles came from the new working classes and suffered great poverty. Already in 1842, the Comte d'Orsay had founded the Société Française de Bienfaisance to help the French in need. The chef Alexis Soyer was moved by their plight to set up soup kitchens. In 1865 the church of Notre Dame de France was built for French Catholics, with an adjoining school which survived until shortly after the Second World War. A French hospital with a dispensary opened in Shaftesbury Avenue in 1867. The majority of French exiles no longer had any links with the church or the monarchy: in 1870, the songwriter Eugene Pottier expressed his hopes in the words of his anthem: 'Arise, damned of the earth! Let us gather together and tomorrow the Internationale will be the human race . . .'

Places to visit

THE LAST KINGS OF FRANCE

Apsley House. Magnificent set of Sèvres porcelain with an Egyptian theme, given to the Duke of Wellington by Louis XVIII to thank him for his victory over Napoleon. On the first floor, portraits by Gérard of Louis XVIII and Charles X.

Travellers Club
106 Pall Mall SW1
Talleyrand, when he returned to London as French ambassador under Louis-Philippe, was a member of the Travellers Club; they raised the bannister on the staircase so that he could hold on, as he had a club foot. The bannister is still there.

Blue plaque
21 Hanover Square W1
See Talleyrand, page 116, col. 2.

Moncorvo Close SW7. This street name is the only trace of Moncorvo House, built in 1879 in Ennismore Gardens and demolished in 1964. The Duke d'Aumale, Louis-Philippe's son, lived there from 1886 until 1890.

Wallace Collection. Miniatures of Louis XVIII, Charles X and their families, by French artists.

Hartwell House. See page 114, col. 1.

Orleans House
Riverside, Twickenham TW1
The Duke d'Orleans, the future Louis-Philippe, back in exile in London in 1815, settled in Twickenham with his wife and children. His house became known as Orleans House. His son the Duke d'Aumale transformed it into a prestigious art gallery, which he agreed to open to the public during the Great Exhibition of 1862. When he returned to France in 1871, he moved the collection to the Chateau de Chantilly, which had been returned to him. Later Orleans House was partially demolished but since 1972 it has again been an art gallery. The stables and wings escaped demolition, as

well as the Octagon Room in the grounds, where there is a medallion portrait of Louis-Philippe placed there by his son.

Claremont House
Claremont Drive, Esher, Surrey
King Leopold of Belgium, Queen Victoria's uncle and owner of this house, placed it at the disposal of Louis-Philippe and his family when they went into exile in 1848. They remained there until 1866. The house is now a school.

Windsor Castle

• **St George's Chapel**
Coats of arms of members of the Order of the Garter on choir stalls. Close to that of Charles the Bold are those of the nineteenth-century French kings: Louis XVIII (1814), Charles X (1825) and Louis-Philippe (1844).

NAPOLEON III

Blue plaque
1c King Street, St James's SW1
This was Louis Napoleon's last address during his years in exile before returning to take power in France in 1848. It was the first blue plaque in London.

Foreign Office
King Charles Street SW1
Full-length portraits on the Muses Staircase of Napoleon III and the Empress Eugénie by Mélincourt, presented to the East India Company in gratitude for its contribution to the Universal Exhibition in Paris of 1855.

National Portrait Gallery. Collection of visiting-card photographs of Napoleon III and the Empress Eugénie.

Chislehurst

• **Camden Place House**
Camden Park Road
Built in 1717, the house was bought by francophile Nathaniel Strode who offered it

to the Empress Eugénie when they went into exile. Napoleon III died there in 1873. Plaque on the exterior facade, photos and documents framed in the downstairs gallery are reminders of the imperial family in exile. At the foot of the stairs, a marble bust of the empress. This elegant house now houses the Chislehurst Golf Club.

- **St Mary's Catholic Church**
  28 Crown Lane
  The Empress added a chapel to the left of the choir, built in 1854, to hold the tomb of Napoleon III. A paving stone shows where it was before it was moved. The tiles on the floor are engraved with an N and the imperial eagles. There is also an N on the wall at the entrance. In another chapel on the right of the choir, a marble funerary monument with an effigy of the Imperial Prince in British army uniform. In 1888 both bodies were transferred to the imperial crypt in Farnborough Abbey.

- **St Mary's churchyard**
  Several members of Napoleon III's entourage are buried here. One of them is Prince Joseph Poniatowski, a senator in the Second Empire, who followed Napoleon III into exile in Chislehurst.

- **Imperial Prince Memorial**
  Prince Imperial Road, Bromley
  Monument in a small clearing on the Common by Camden Place.

- **Street names**
  Prince Imperial Road
  Empress Drive
  Imperial Way
  Reminders of the presence of Napoleon III and his family at Chislehurst.

Farnborough
Aldershot, Hampshire

- **Farnborough Hill House.** The Empress Eugénie moved into this Victorian house in 1881, adding eighteen rooms to hold her vast collection of Napoleonic memorabilia.

The house is at the top of a hill, from which she could observe the progress of the building of the abbey she commissioned to hold the tombs of Napoleon III and the Imperial Prince. During the First World War, part of the house became a hospital for wounded officers, and she would employ young and pretty nurses to improve their morale and accelerate their recovery. Farnborough Hill House is now a school.

- **St Michael's Abbey** and the imperial crypt
  280 Farnborough Road
  The abbey was built in the Gothic style by the architect Gabriel Destailleur between 1883 and 1888. Gargoyles of dragons and monsters contrast with the grandeur and monastic austerity of the interior. Beside the abbey, Eugénie built a monastery for Benedictine monks from the abbey of Solesmes in France (it is now run by English Benedictines). The tombs of Napoleon III, the Imperial Prince, and Empress Eugénie lie in small chapels around the circular crypt. Those of Napoleon III and the Imperial Prince were given by Queen Victoria.

Aldershot Military Museum
Evelyn Woods Road, Aldershot
The museum contains some of the Empress's clothes; she had been a great fashion inspiration during her reign. Once in exile at Camden House, she used her Paris ballgowns to cover the armchairs. She also gave some of them, including her wedding dress, to the monks at Farnborough, who made them into clerical vestments.

Windsor Castle

- **State apartments.** In the King's State Bedchamber, the present bed was completely transformed for the state visit of Napoleon III and the Empress Eugénie in 1855, with draperies in the Emperor's colours, green and purple, embroidered with the monogram LN EI (Louis Napoleon and Eugénie Imperatores)

- **St George's Chapel.** Napoleon III's coat of arms is in the chapel (south stall 5), as he was a member of the Order of the Garter. In the nave, a tomb with white marble effigy of the Imperial Prince by the sculptor Boehm. On one side is a quotation from his will and on the other, in French, a prayer found in his prayer book.

Palmerston's Follies
Between Portsmouth and Plymouth
Seeing that Napoleon III was restoring his navy at the beginning of his reign, Lord Palmerston feared a French invasion. From 1860, he had sixty forts built along the south coast of England, added to the existing, but deteriorating, Martello towers built at the beginning of the century against an invasion by Napoleon I. The forts were larger, but not a single shot was ever fired from them. They were used, however, during the two world wars. All the coastal defences were decommissioned in 1956.

FRENCH INSTITUTIONS

French Embassy
Albert Gate, 58 Knightsbridge SW1
In 1853, Count Walewski, son of Marie Walewska, Napoleon I's Polish mistress, and therefore cousin of Napoleon III, was the first French ambassador to be installed at this address, where the embassy still is.

Notre Dame de France
5 Leicester Place WC2
The French Catholic Church in London was founded in Soho in 1865, thanks to Cardinal Wiseman, who authorised separate parishes for foreign communities. The French Marian order, already installed in Spitalfields, was given the task of setting it up, and the Empress Eugénie helped to finance it. A hospital, an orphanage and a school were added to the church. The church was built of iron and was famous for its original design; destroyed during the Second World War, it was rebuilt in the 1950s.

French Hospital and Dispensary. These have moved several times since they were opened. At the corner of 172–76 Shaftesbury Avenue and 10 Monmouth Street W1, the French Hospital was opened in 1867 for impoverished French people. It had a dispensary as well as an annexe in Brighton for convalescents. French-speaking English doctors worked pro bono, and the hospital was funded from private donations. The building is now the Covent Garden Hotel, but the facade still bears the words 'Hopital et Dispensaire Français'. Despite its closure, a grant from the French state as well as private donations have enabled the French Dispensary to continue to care for French-speaking patients since 2005 at 184 Hammersmith Road W6.

Société Française de Bienfaisance. Created in 1842 by the Comte d'Orsay, who was its first president, to help the poorest of the French community in London. The society exists to this day.

French Chamber of Commerce
21 Dartmouth Street SW1
The Chamber of Commerce was established in 1883 to help French companies set up in England.

The Menier Chocolate Factory
53 Southwark Street SE1
The Menier family opened a chocolate factory in 1870 which remained in business until the twentieth century. Abandoned in the 1980s, the building was reopened in 2004 as a complex of restaurant, gallery, avant-garde theatre and rehearsal rooms.

Maison Bertaux
28 Greek Street, Soho W1
The first French patisserie in London, founded by a Communard refugee in 1871. Still in business, the tea-room and the first-floor room retain their old-fashioned atmosphere.

9

ROMANTIC VISITORS

'LONDON WOULD NOT BE SUCH A BEAUTIFUL CITY WITHOUT ITS FOG'[47]

'But now, at the first tremors of the earthquakes that threaten to topple thrones on the continent, swarms of terrified artists rush from all points of the horizon to seek shelter here, just as seabirds take refuge on land when great storms are brewing. Will the British metropolis be able to provide sustenance for so many exiles?'

HECTOR BERLIOZ, Preface to his *Memoirs*, 1848

In the field of arts and literature London became a magnet for the 'swarms of terrified artists' described mockingly by Berlioz. The nineteenth century was indeed, like the preceding one, rich in fertile exchanges between both sides of the Channel. Shakespeare, Byron and Walter Scott were a great source of inspiration for the romantics, and since political instability was detrimental to art, the revolutions in France of 1830, 1848 and 1870 all encouraged an influx of artists to London in search of security and a clientele.

A proliferation of painters

French painters were already well known to the British public thanks to the regular exhibitions held in London galleries. Theodore Géricault (1791–1824) arrived in London in April 1820. He had been bitterly disappointed by the reception of his *Raft of the Medusa* in Paris, and hoped for more success in London. The painting was shown at the Egyptian Hall in Piccadilly, where it was seen by 40,000 visitors, paying a shilling each. Turner was inspired by it for his *A Disaster at Sea* (1833–35). While in London, Géricault painted a series of watercolours, *The English Suite*, which were then marketed as engravings, and a single oil painting, *The Derby at Epsom*.

Eugène Delacroix (1798–1863) stayed in England in 1825, where he visited museums and met the portrait painter Sir Thomas Lawrence. He took up watercolours and painted the suburbs of London, Greenwich in particular. He was inspired by English literature for many of his paintings and lithographs: *Hamlet and Horatio at the Graveyard* (1839), *The Death of Ophelia* (1843), *Othello and Desdemona*, *Lady Macbeth Sleepwalking* (1850) and *The Death of Sardanapalus* (1827).

Paul Delaroche (1797–1856), although he did not often go to London, was also inspired by British history. He was fascinated by the Tudors and the Stuarts, and liked to show the scenes that preceded violent actions. Thus, in his *Edward's Children*, the two princes sit on their bed, one thoughtful, the other anxious, and seem to await the arrival of their executioner, shown by a shadow at the door and a dog on the lookout. The scene clearly refers to the death of Louis XVII in the Temple. Other scenes echoing the fate of Louis XVI and Marie-Antoinette are in *Charles I Insulted by Cromwell's Men* (1837) and *The Execution of Lady Jane Grey* (1833). Delaroche was enormously popular and exhibited at the Royal Academy, but his historical paintings fell out of fashion until the recent rediscovery of the latter two paintings in England. *Lady Jane Grey* was found 'by chance' at the National Gallery in 1973, and *Charles I* in Scotland in 2009. Today the Wallace Collection holds the largest collection of his works outside France: its founder, Lord Hertford, was one of his patrons.

The realist Eugène-Louis Lami (1800–90) began his career as an engraver, but he also painted watercolours, and was an illustrator and decorator. In 1826 his love of English painting drew him to London, where he lived for a year. He brought back a book of twelve engravings, MEMORIES OF LONDON, and a series called *Voyage to England*, produced with his friend Henri Monnier. On his return to France he became official painter to Louis-Philippe, whom he followed into exile in London in 1848, where he remained until 1852 living in Onslow Square in South Kensington. He painted the domestic life of the French royal family, in particular at the Château d'Eu during Queen Victoria's official visit, and she later took him under her wing. Lami painted political events, entertainments, London streets, and the uniforms of the British army, which fascinated him. He exhibited at the Royal Academy and took part in the preparations for the 1851 Great Exhibition in London, where he painted a series of watercolours of the foreign exhibits. As well as his work for English high society, he helped the Duc d'Aumale to curate his collection at Orleans House, and painted motifs for fans made by Duvelleroy in London. Napoleon III commissioned him to paint two large watercolours for Queen Victoria to commemorate her official visit to Paris in 1855.

Alphonse Legros (1837–1911) studied art in France with the sculptors Rodin and Dalou. He was a painter, sculptor and engraver, and he arrived in England in 1863, where he married an Englishwoman; he took British nationality in 1881. He was professor of engraving at the South Kensington School of Arts, and then taught fine art at the Slade, where he remained for seventeen years. He refused to speak English and used an interpreter to comment on his pupils' work. Legros was one of the founders of the Society of Painters and Engravers in 1881 and, reviving a lost art, the Society of Medal Makers four years later. He produced many portraits, including ones of Berlioz, Rodin and many famous Englishmen, often in the form of medallions, as well as various sculptures. He lived at 57 Brook Green and died in 1911 at the age of seventy-four.

Gustave Doré (1832–83) was mostly famous for his engravings. His illustrated Bible was a great success in London, and his publisher Grant & Co. commissioned a series of 180 engravings entitled *London: a Pilgrimage*. He came to London for three months a year five years running to complete this project. Most of his engravings illustrated the terrible poverty to be found at that time in the city. He was such a success that a Doré Gallery opened at 35 New Bond Street from 1869 until 1892 to exhibit his large religious paintings.

A form of miniature painting, the decoration of fans was a delicate operation in a very constricted format. This skill flourished in the nineteenth century thanks to the patronage of royal families and international exhibitions, and painters transformed it into an art. Jean-Pierre Duvelleroy, who founded his fan factory in Paris in 1827, won first prize at the 1851 Great Exhibition. He became the official supplier to Queen Victoria and in 1861 opened a shop at 167 Regent Street. During the Belle Epoque the fan, as well as being a useful portable air-cooler, was an invaluable accessory to flirtatious conversations. Maison Duvelleroy brought out a *Language of Fans*: held open before the cheek it meant 'I love you'; twirled in the right hand it meant 'I love another'. At the beginning of the twentieth century, Queen Mary, the wife of King George V, collected fans and the links between the makers and the royal family were closer than ever. In 1947 two fans signed by Duvelleroy were among the wedding presents given to the future Queen Elizabeth II. Fans eventually fell into disuse as accessories and the London branch of Duvelleroy closed down during the 1960s.

Fascination for London life, the Thames and the London fog

In Paris many painters' studios were ransacked at the time of the Paris Commune in 1871. Impressionists such as Monet, Pissarro and Sisley came to join other refugees in London, such as the landscape painter Charles Daubigny and the art dealer Paul Durand-Ruel. All were drawn by the London mists and were fascinated by the Thames.

Daubigny (1817–78) painted the river and St Paul's Cathedral, but probably only completed these canvases on his return to France.

Camille Pissarro (1830–1903) arrived in London in 1870 and settled near the Crystal Palace in Norwood in the southern suburbs. These were now linked to the centre by rail – a theme he often returned to with *Lordship Lane Station, Dulwich* (1871) and *The Train, Bedford Park* (1897). He was particularly inspired by the streets around his home, and the village-like atmosphere of the Crystal Palace, Dulwich, Norwood and Sydenham. Turned down by the Royal Academy, he exhibited, without much success, at the Durand-Ruel Gallery in New Bond Street. He married his companion Julie, who had followed him to England, at Croydon Town Hall, and they returned to France in June 1871. He returned to London three times during the 1890s, to visit his three sons Lucien, Georges and Felix, who lived to the west of the capital. As before, he painted local scenes, but now they were of Kew, Chiswick, Bedford Park and Stamford Brook Common. He also painted the Thames with *Old Chelsea Bridge* and *Charing Cross Bridge*. Lucien, for his part, continued to pursue an honourable career as a painter, and above all an engraver, of London scenes; his descendants still run a Pissarro Gallery.

Claude Monet (1840–1926) arrived in London in September 1870 with his wife and son. He was penniless and settled in Arundel Street near Leicester Square, then made contact with Daubigny who introduced him to the picture dealer Paul Durand-Ruel. During this first stay he painted a series of canvases depicting the Thames and the London parks. *Parliament and the Thames*, now in the National Gallery, foreshadowed the great series of paintings of the river that he would produce thirty years later. As with Pissarro, his paintings were turned down by the Royal Academy. Monet said later: 'England did not want our paintings. It was tough!'[48] After this stay he returned to London in 1887 for a short visit to his friend Whistler.

Monet had been drawn to London and its particular light, and said that he would like to depict 'some effects of fog on the Thames'.[49] He set out to complete this project over the course of three visits devoted entirely to the Thames. By then rich and famous, in September 1899 he and his wife stayed at the Savoy

Hotel, which had just opened by the river. They occupied Room
641, which had an unrestricted view of Parliament and Waterloo
and Charing Cross bridges. He made dozens of sketches which he
then worked on on his return to his house at Giverny. 'Without
the fog,' he observed, 'London would not be such a beautiful city.
It is the fog which gives it such a magnificent scale. Its massive
regular buildings become grandiose under this mantle of mystery.'[50] By the beginning of 1900, Monet was back in the Savoy
for two months, taking up the sketches from his previous visit and
working feverishly on several canvases at once. He determinedly
returned for one last visit in 1901. He left about a hundred views
of the Thames, mostly reworked at Giverny. Finally, in 1904 he
gave thirty-seven canvases to Durand-Ruel: the exhibition was a
huge success.

Jacques Tissot (1836–1902) was an extremely anglophile political refugee – he even changed his name to James. He was a successful painter both in Paris and London, where he mostly painted
high society. At first he lived in Hyde Park Gate with his friend
Thomas Bowles, a journalist at *Vanity Fair*, who introduced him
to many English painters. He then moved to Grove End Road in
St John's Wood with his dazzling mistress, Mrs Kathleen Newton,
who sat for almost all his English paintings. James Tissot was both
a painter and a businessman; visitors to his studio in Grove End
Road were always sure to find champagne on ice, and he greeted
them dressed as a dandy. He sold his works for a great deal of
money and lived in comfort. He often used waterside settings as
a background for his elegant subjects – the Thames, seaports or
boats – as well as Trafalgar Square, Kew Gardens or the Lord
Mayor's Show. In 1874 he painted the Empress Eugénie and the
Imperial Prince at Chislehurst. Tissot cast a detached eye on
English society and his paintings provide a valuable portrait of
Victorian high life. When Kathleen Newton died in 1882, James
Tissot returned to France, devastated.

Sculptors and musicians
In the field of sculpture, the French became extremely influential
in England, largely thanks to Alphonse Legros and Jules Dalou

who both taught in London. Baron Charles de Marochetti (1805–67), an Italian-born Frenchman, began his career as sculptor at the court of Louis-Philippe, whom he followed into exile. He remained in London, where he was popular with the royal family, although his English rivals, jealous of his success, criticised his flamboyant style. His best-known sculptures are the equestrian statue of Richard the Lionheart outside the Houses of Parliament and the tomb of Queen Victoria and Prince Albert at Frogmore House near Windsor. He exhibited several times at the Royal Academy, of which he became a member in 1867, the year of his death.

Baron Henri de Triqueti (1804–74), who made the bronze doors of the Madeleine church in Paris, worked for the Orleans family in France. Wounded on the barricades in 1848, he too followed Louis-Philippe to London where he was quickly introduced into society and married an Englishwoman, Emily Foster. His romantic style was much admired by Queen Victoria who commissioned several sculptures from him, the best-known being Prince Albert's cenotaph in the Albert Memorial Chapel in St George's Chapel at Windsor, which he worked on for ten years.

Jean-Baptiste Carpeaux (1827–75) was the favourite sculptor of the Second Empire; he took refuge in England in 1871 to escape the Commune. When he went to pay his respects to the emperor in Chislehurst he was commissioned to make a bust of him, which he only completed after Napoleon III's death, in 1874.

The sculptor Jules Dalou (1838–1902), a pupil of Carpeaux, took refuge in London as well in 1871 with his wife and child. On his arrival he lodged with his friend Alphonse Legros. He exhibited at the Royal Academy, and also at the Dudley and Grosvenor galleries. He was much admired and left numerous portrait-busts of, among others, the Duke of Westminster, Lord Leighton, the Duchesse de Gramont and the Countess of Carlisle. When he became professor at the National Art Training School (later the Royal College of Art) he knew only two words of English; to make himself understood by his pupils, he would model the clay in front of them, repeating: 'Like that! Like that!' He preferred working with clay rather than marble and produced very original compositions. In London he chose to depict intimate domestic scenes and represented women in many different poses, reading or looking after their children, as in *French Peasant Feeding her Child* of 1873.

Finally, musicians also play an important role in this procession of French artists. Now forgotten, the composer and conductor Louis Antoine Jullien (1812–60) left Paris in 1838 to escape his debtors and established himself in London. He organised grandiose and popular concert-shows with large numbers of musicians, sometimes even including military bands. These promenade concerts held in parks and gardens were the precursors of today's Proms, which are now the highlight of the summer music season in London. Jullien composed a great deal for these concerts; he was a flamboyant character, conducting with a jewel-encrusted baton with his back to the orchestra. His eccentricities were a gift to the cartoonists of *Punch* in England and *Charivari* in France. He became director of the Theatre Royal in Drury Lane and brought Berlioz to London. Permanently bankrupt, he left England for America in 1853 in the hope of making his fortune. He returned to London the following year and finally went back to France in 1859, where he died a year later, still in debt, in an asylum.

Hector Berlioz (1803–69) was in search of a position which would allow him to play his own music, which is what Jullien offered him in London in 1847. He was then forty-four and he crossed the Channel alone, leaving his wife Harriet Smithson in Paris. In London he lived with Jullien in Harley Street. His contract was for six years, but since he was not paid he left after eight months. During his stay he gave a series of concerts, some including his own compositions, which were greatly admired. He began writing his memoirs at the end of this first stay. He returned to London in 1851, and was a member of the jury judging musical instruments at the 1851 Great Exhibition. In 1853, Queen Victoria and Prince Albert attended the premiere of his *Benvenuto Cellini* at the Theatre Royal Covent Garden (now the Royal Opera House). Although much admired by the public, the opera was not to the Queen's taste, as she wrote in her journal: 'We saw and heard one of the most unattractive and absurd Operas, I suppose anyone could ever have composed . . .'[51] During his many stays in London, Berlioz, who spoke quite good English, stayed around Oxford Circus. He loved the city, and discovered all its many musical societies.

Charles Gounod (1818–93) arrived in London with his family in 1870 to escape the Prussian invasion. His operas *Faust* and *Romeo and Juliet* had been a great success in France. When his family returned to France in July 1871, he lodged with Harry and Georgina Weldon at Tavistock House, where Charles Dickens had lived. He was captivated by the soprano Georgina Weldon who persuaded him to compose music for the choir she had just formed at the Albert Hall, in which she was the soloist. Under her influence he was forever sueing his publishers and he finally returned to France in a state of nervous exhaustion in July 1874, leaving his manuscripts in London, notably that of his opera *Polyeucte*. Georgina refused to give them back, and he was forced to rewrite the opera completely, from memory. Furious at his departure, she even embarked on a court case against him!

Museums, art galleries and collections

Several London art galleries and museums have French origins. The Prince Regent, the future George IV, obtained a number of French works of art and pieces of furniture that had escaped the ravages of the French Revolution. The aristocracy followed his lead, and the opening of museums made these objects accessible to all.

In 1811, the first art gallery open to the public was inaugurated at Dulwich, thanks to a legacy of 314 paintings. A French art dealer, Noel Desenfans, was the originator of this collection. In 1790 he had joined forces with his Swiss friend Sir Francis Bourgeois, a painter and member of the Royal Academy. They were charged by the King of Poland with assembling an art collection, but when the kingdom disappeared in 1795 the two men decided to find a site to house the collection and place it at the disposal of the public. After the death of Noel Desenfans, Francis Bourgeois left it to Dulwich College, which already possessed a small collection of paintings. He commissioned his friend Sir John Soane to design a building to house it, the Dulwich Picture Gallery.

The Hertford family, founders of another private museum, was already in possession of a major art collection when the 4th Lord Hertford set out to enlarge it further. He lived mostly in Paris in the Villa Bagatelle, but had several properties in England including Manchester House, which became Hertford House, the present home of the Wallace Collection. Richard Wallace, his refined and cultured but illegitimate son, married Julie Castelnau, a saleswoman in a fashionable perfumery in Paris, and they had a son. He was a philanthropist who founded the Hertford British Hospital in Paris (still in existence) and gave the city fifty 'Wallace fountains'. After the destruction of the Tuileries during the Commune, Richard Wallace decided to send his whole collection to Hertford House and live there with his wife. After his death in 1890, Lady Wallace lived there as a recluse. In accordance with the wishes of her husband, she left the entire collection to the nation, on the express condition that it should be 'kept intact, without addition or mix and that it should bear the name of the departed.'[52] The Wallace Collection was opened to the public in 1900.

On the commercial front, French painting, particularly that of the Impressionists, was introduced to the British public by several galleries and art dealers who had settled in London during the nineteenth century and who enabled exiled French artists to earn a living. Ernest Gambart (1814–1902) was one of the first, in 1854, to open a commercial art gallery, the French Gallery at 121 Pall Mall. He alternated a winter exhibition of English paintings with a French one in spring, in which he showed works by Delacroix, Gérôme, Fantin-Latour, Gustave Doré and many others. In 1870, Gambart handed his gallery over to his nephew Leon Lefèvre, who moved it to 30 Bruton Street and renamed it the Lefèvre Gallery.

After the French defeat in the Franco-Prussian war in 1870, the famous Parisian art dealer Paul Durand-Ruel (1831–1922) evacuated a large part of his collection to safety in London. He opened a gallery at 168 New Bond Street and held the first of ten exhibitions in London under the name of the Society of French Artists. A great promoter of the Impressionists, he organised the first exhibition of their works in 1872. The Goupil Gallery, a competitor of Durand-Ruel in Paris, had opened a branch in London during the 1860s. It moved several times before finally settling at 5 Regent Street in 1893. It showed painters such as Theodore Rousseau, Ernest Meissonier and Ary Scheffer. Van Gogh worked there during 1873. The gallery was taken over in 1901 by William Stephen Marchant and destroyed by a bomb in 1941.

'London is a feast for sensitive souls'[53]

Since London was the largest and richest metropolis in the world during the nineteenth century, it is not surprising that the majority of French intellectuals and men of letters spent at least some time there in their lives, whether as visitors or exiles. Writers who admired and emulated Shakespeare, Byron and Walter Scott often chose themes from English history and literature and used London as a background for their novels. Thus in *Les Mystères de Londres* by Paul Feval (1844), inspired by Eugene Sue's *Mystères de Paris*, police intrigues were played out in the London fog. The works of Jules Verne were full of allusions to London and its inhabitants. His most famous character, Phileas Fogg, was 'calm, phlegmatic, with a clear eye and a steady brow [. . .], the essence of the composed Englishman'.[54]

Poets, too, were equally drawn to the city. Lamartine (1790–1869), when he was attaché at the embassy in Naples in 1821, had married a young Englishwoman, Mary-Ann Birch. He came to London in 1822 to meet his in-laws. He was fascinated by Byron and by his epic *Childe Harold*, and wrote *Le Dernier Chant du pèlerinage d'Harold* which was published in 1825. Alfred de Vigny (1797–1863) also married an Englishwoman, Lydia Bunbury, and made several trips to London, in 1836 and again in 1838 and 1839. He was deeply inspired by English literature, which he read in the original, translated *Romeo and Juliet* in 1827, and wrote an adaptation of *Othello* in 1829, entitled *Le More de Venise*. In 1835, his *Chatterton*, a tragedy loosely based on the life of the poet, opened to great acclaim.

Stephane Mallarmé (1842–98) arrived in London in 1862 with his companion Marie Gerhard, in order to study English since he had decided to become an English teacher. He lived at first, meagrely, at Panton Square in Soho, and got married at the London Oratory in Brompton Road in August 1863. Like many other visitors he was struck by the hushed atmosphere of the city, which he described in a letter to a friend: 'Here is the fog again, without which I would again have been idle today. But it is so beautiful, so gray, so yellow that I have just come home with Marie, swearing that we would never again face the loneliness of Hyde Park in such a fog.'[55] He returned to London in 1871 and paid a visit to Napoleon III in exile. From 1875 onwards he wrote regularly for the English magazine *The Athenaeum* in order to encourage a literary dialogue between the two countries. As a teacher he published *Les Mots anglais* in 1878, and as a poet ran a literary salon in Paris, regularly visited by English artists and writers, such as Oscar Wilde, Whistler, George Moore, Arthur Symons, Aubrey Beardsley and others. His abstract avant-garde poetry was influential in both France and England.

Paul Verlaine (1844–96) and Arthur Rimbaud (1854–91) arrived in London as a famous and scandalous couple in September 1872. Verlaine had abandoned his wife and child for his long escapade with the adolescent genius, which was interspersed with trips to France and Belgium. They lived at first at 34 Howland Street, north of Soho, mingling with the artists and refugees gathered around Leicester Square and spending their days in the Café de la Sablonnière in Leicester Square and the Reading Room at the British Museum. After a brief return to France, they lived at 8 Great College Street in Camden Town, giving French lessons in order to survive, although Rimbaud spent most of his time wandering around the docks and the slums.

Verlaine wrote several poems about London such as *Londres*:

Un dimanche d'été, quand le soleil s'en mêle,
Londres forme un régal offert aux délicats:
Les arbres forts et ronds sur la verdure frêle,
Vert tendre, ont l'air bien loin des brumes et des gaz,

Tant ils semblent plantés en terre paysanne.
Un soleil clair, léger dans le ciel fin, bleuté
À peine. On est comme en un bain où se pavane
Le parfum d'une lente infusion de thé.[56]

Rimbaud, for his part, began to write *Illuminations* and *Une Saison en enfer*, but under the influence of drink the relationship between the two poets deteriorated. A weary Verlaine set off without luggage for Belgium, where he was joined by his young lover, whom he wounded with two pistol shots. He was sentenced to two years in prison. Rimbaud, back in London in March 1874, lived at 178 Stanford Street near Waterloo before finally leaving England for good in December. When Verlaine came out of prison he returned to England for a few years, from 1875 to 1877, and then in 1879, where he taught French in boarding schools in Lincolnshire, Bournemouth and Lymington; he was very popular and made many friends. During this time he wrote the poems that appeared in the *Sagesse* collection. At the end of 1893 he made a last short visit to England in order to give a series of lectures in London and Oxford.

Verlaine and Rimbaud in London.
Drawing by Félix Régamey.

Another literary giant, Emile Zola (1840–1902), also spent time
in London. Despite Victorian England's disapproval of the realist
movement in literature, his novels were published there by 1888
and were a great success. His English publisher, Henry Vizetelly,
had to spend three months in prison on a charge of obscenity
when he published *La Terre*. After 'J'accuse!' Zola went into exile
in London in July 1898. He already knew the city, and in order
not to be recognised he stayed in different hotels under different
names. He was separated from his family, except for the occasional
visit, and found his year-long stay painful. He wrote a short story,
Angeline, which appeared in English in the *Star* magazine, and a
novel, *Fécondité*, as well as *Pages d'exil*, which would be published
after his death. He was a keen photographer and took many
photos of London.

England revealed: history, customs and social misery

The English were kept well-informed about contemporary
French works by literary magazines: *The Foreign Quarterly Review*,
The Athenaeum, *The Literary Gazette* and the *Westminster Review*.
Top French writers were among their contributors. Stendhal
(1783–1842), who came to London several times, submitted many
articles on French literature to the *Literary Gazette*, the *London
Magazine* and the *New Monthly Magazine*, which were later gathered in the *Chroniques pour l'Angleterre*, a series of entertaining
vignettes of French society.

Coming from the other direction were many chroniclers of
English life. The journalist Léon-Paul Blouet (1848–1903) was the
London correspondent for a Parisian paper during the 1870s. He
became a French teacher, working for eight years at St Paul's
School in the City. He was a mischievous observer and wrote and
published, under the pseudonym Max O'Rell, *John Bull et son île:
moeurs anglaises contemporaines*. It was an immediate success and
Blouet gave up teaching to concentrate on writing. His English
wife translated his books: *Les Filles de John Bull*, *Les Chers Voisins*,
Oh les Enfants! and *Souvenirs d'un ex-professeur de français en
Angleterre*.

The great anglophile François Guizot (1787–1874), ex-prime minister and ambassador to London under Louis-Philippe, wrote several studies of English history and literature before going into exile in London in 1848–49. He made use of his enforced leisure to finish his *Histoire de la Révolution d'Angleterre de Charles 1er a Charles II* and to begin his *Histoire de la République d'Angleterre et de Cromwell*.

Clémence Royer (1830–1902), a philosopher, scientist and feminist, spent a year teaching in England. She translated Darwin's *On the Origin of Species* into French.

Hippolyte Taine (1828–93), historian and philosopher, published a history of English literature in five volumes in 1863. He was offered a chair by Oxford University in 1871, and gave lectures on Corneille and Racine. In his *Notes sur l'Angleterre* (1872) he covers all sorts of subjects: social classes, customs, society, government, education, the conditions of the working classes and so on.

Many French people living in London were shocked by the nature and the scope of social inequality. In his journal, which he wrote during his stay in London in 1834, Jules Michelet (1798–1874) foretold the deep social repercussions of the Industrial Revolution.

Alexandre Ledru-Rollin (1807–74), a politician and supporter of republican causes, became a committed socialist. After the 1848 Revolution he lived in exile in London for twenty years. In 1850 he published *De la Décadence de l'Angleterre*, an anglophobic work contrasting the greatness of Britain with the misery in which so many Britons lived. He was shocked by the exploitation of the Irish and used to visit his compatriots, the Huguenot weavers, based for many generations in Spitalfields and by this time living in extreme poverty, victims of technological progress.

Louis Blanc (1811–82) was a socialist theorist in France who spent twenty-two years in London and published several works on the social and political problems of the English, as well as *Lettres sur l'Angleterre* (1866–67). The writer Jules Vallès (1807–85) took refuge in London for nine years, from 1871 to 1880. He too denounced proletarian misery in his sarcastic and highly coloured *La*

Rue à Londres. More a rebel than a revolutionary, Flora Tristan (1803–44) also took pity on the plight of the working classes and of women in particular. During her four visits to London between 1826 and 1839, she explored the London slums and delivered the result of her research in *Promenades dans Londres,* a sociological study published in London in 1840.

At the end of this great invasion, all these French visitors, whether they were historians, writers, journalists or politicians, were shocked at the reality of what they had discovered about English life. Almost all described their experiences in England as if they wished to warn France not to repeat the errors of the English Industrial Revolution.

Places to visit

ALBERT MEMORIAL
See page 58, col. 2.

PAINTERS
There are numerous works by French artists in London museums.

Theodore Géricault. National Gallery, British Museum, Royal Collection, Courtauld Gallery. Géricault is depicted on the painters' section of the frieze on the eastern panel of the Albert Memorial.

Eugène Delacroix. National Gallery, Victoria & Albert Museum, Wallace Collection, Courtauld Gallery.
Delacroix is depicted on the same eastern panel of the Albert Memorial as Géricault.

Paul Delaroche. National Gallery, Victoria & Albert Museum, Wallace Collection and Royal Collection. The architect of the Albert Memorial, inspired by Delaroche's great fresco at the Beaux Arts in Paris, did not forget to include him in his group of painters, where he is shown seated and surrounded by other French artists.

Eugène Lami. Wallace Collection, Courtauld Gallery, Victoria & Albert Museum, Royal Collection.

Alphonse Legros. Tate Britain, Victoria & Albert Museum, National Portrait Gallery.

Gustave Doré

- **Museum of London**

- **Sotheby's**
  34–35 New Bond Street W1
  The Galerie Doré was located at this address before Sotheby's.

Duvelleroy

- **Victoria & Albert Museum**

- **Fan Museum**
  12 Crooms Hill, Greenwich SE10

Charles Daubigny. National Gallery.

Camille and Lucien Pissarro

- **National Gallery, Tate Britain, Courtauld Gallery**

- **Stern Pissarro galleries**
  66 St James's Street SW1
  46 Ledbury Road W11
  These two galleries are run by descendants of Camille Pissarro, many of whom were and still are painters.

- **Blue plaques**

  77A Westow Hill, Upper Norwood SE19
  Camille Pissarro's address when he first lived in London in 1870–71.

  Kew Green, Kew TW9
  Pissarro lived in the house on the corner of Kew Green and Gloucester Road in 1892.

  27 Stamford Brook Road W6
  Lucien Pissarro, son of Camille, settled in London in 1890, and lived at this address for 34 years.

Claude Monet. National Gallery and Tate Britain. At the Savoy Hotel a suite is named after him: he spent six months there over three years.

Jacques Tissot. Tate Britain, National Portrait Gallery, Guildhall Art Gallery, National Maritime Museum.

SCULPTORS

Charles Marochetti

- **Palace of Westminster**. The statue of Richard the Lionheart is a bronze copy of the one displayed at the Great Exhibition of 1851.

- **Westminster Abbey**. Bust of Thackeray.

- **St Paul's Cathedral**. Monuments commemorating the Crimean War.

- **Waterloo Place**. Monument to Lord Clyde, general in the Indian Army.

- **Euston Station**. Statue of Robert Stephenson in front of the station.

- **Victoria Embankment** SW1. Statue of Isambard Kingdom Brunel

- **Blue plaque**
  34 Onslow Square SW7
  Marochetti lived at this address for about eighteen years. His studio was in the mews behind the house.

- **Trafalgar Square**. Marochetti collaborated with Sir Edwin Landseer to sculpt the lions in the square.

- **National Portrait Gallery.** Marble bust of Marochetti by Sir James Stephen and bronze statuette of Marochetti by Gabriele Ambrosio (1888).

- **Frogmore House**. In the garden, mausoleum covering a granite tomb with effigies of Prince Albert and Queen Victoria, with four angels, made by Marochetti after Prince Albert's death in 1861. The one of Queen Victoria was added to the tomb forty years later, at her death, in 1901.

Henri de Triqueti

- **University College**
  Gower Street WC1
  'Marmor Homericum' marble bas-reliefs with Homeric themes in the south cloister of the Wilkins building.

- **Windsor Castle**. In St George's Chapel, cenotaph to Prince Albert: effigy of prince and coloured marble panels on wall.

Jean-Baptiste Carpeaux. Victoria & Albert Museum

Jules Dalou

- **Royal Exchange** EC3. Fountain surmounted by bronze sculpture of a seated woman holding two babies, entitled 'Charity', his first public commission in London (1877).

- **National Portrait Gallery, Victoria & Albert Museum, Royal Collection**

- **Windsor Castle**. St George's Chapel: monument to one of Queen Victoria's grandchildren who died in infancy.

MUSICIANS

Louis-Antoine Jullien
Proms, Royal Albert Hall
Kensington Gore SW7
Jullien revived the glamour of the promenade concerts begun in the eighteenth century, transforming them into grandiose musical spectacles with vast orchestras, lights, flowers and animals. With these concerts, he wanted to bring music to a larger public by gradually introducing them to classical music and to great musicians.

Hector Berlioz
Blue plaque
58 Queen Anne Street W1
The house where Berlioz stayed during his second visit in 1851 was also the home of the Beethoven Quartet Society, whose rehearsals and concerts he enjoyed listening to. He was so overcome by the beauty and power of a choir of 6,500 children's voices at a concert in St Paul's that he added a children's chorus to his *Te Deum*.

Charles Gounod
Blue plaque
15 Morden Road, Blackheath SE3
Gounod moved into this house when he arrived in London with his family in 1870.

ART GALLERIES

Dulwich Picture Gallery. The founders of the collection, Frenchman Noel Desenfans and Sir Francis Bourgeois, are buried in the mausoleum beside the gallery. Of the French artists in the collection, Nicolas Poussin is well represented with nine paintings.

- **Desenfans Road**, Dulwich SE21
  This street close to the gallery commemorates one of its founders.

Wallace Collection. Superb collection of paintings and *objets d'art*, rich in French art of the eighteenth century. In the entrance, marble bust of Lady Wallace who left the collection to Great Britain. In the garden in front of the house, replica of a 'Wallace fountain', reminder of the fifty drinking fountains donated by Richard Wallace to the city of Paris at the time of the Commune.

Lefevre Fine Art Ltd
31 Burton Street W1
Although under new management, the Lefevre Gallery still exists.

WRITERS

Stéphane Mallarmé
Commemorative plaque
6 Brompton Square SW3
Brompton Oratory, where he was married on 10 August 1863, was close to his house.

Verlaine and Rimbaud
Commemorative plaque
8 Royal College Street, Camden NW1
The house, in very poor condition, was saved from destruction after a campaign led by French and English intellectuals.

Émile Zola
Commemorative plaque
Queen's Hotel, 122 Church Road
Crystal Palace, Upper Norwood SE19
Émile Zola wrote his novel *Angéline* in this hotel in a suburb of London.

Léon-Paul Blouet
(alias Max O'Rell, humorist)
National Portrait Gallery
Two portraits of the writer.

François Guizot
Commemorative plaque
21 Pelham Crescent SW7
Historian and Prime Minister under Louis-Philippe, François Guizot lived at this address for a year, 1848–49, when he went into exile.

10

THE GREAT INVASION OF THE NINETEENTH CENTURY
A FLOW OF FRENCH ARRIVALS, LED BY CHEFS AND NUNS

'London is francophile' VERLAINE

By the nineteenth century one could no longer count all the French who, from every walk of life, had come to settle in London. Leading this never-ending procession of peaceful invaders were the chefs; it was they who were greeted with the loudest applause from their hosts. They opened the majority of the early restaurants and hotels in London and enriched the vocabulary with many culinary terms: casserole, vinaigrette, soufflé, vol-au-vent, sauce, pièce montée, à la carte, menu . . . From the very beginning of the century it became the fashion for the great houses to have a French chef or maître d'hôtel.

An avalanche of French cooks and the beginnings of the hotel business

In London, traditional inns and taverns were gradually giving way to more luxurious establishments, while the more enterprising chefs opened 'hotels' (the word 'inns' was no longer used). Provincial aristocrats and visiting foreigners stayed in these, and clubs used by the gentry proliferated in London, several of them owing their reputation to their French chefs. A new middle-class clientèle also encouraged the opening of restaurants separate from the hotels to which they had originally been attached.

One of the most distinguished of these newcomers was Louis-Eustache Ude, who had been chef to Louis XVI. He emigrated to London, where he worked for Lord Sefton and the Duke of York, the Prince Regent's brother, before becoming maître d'hôtel at the United Service Club, founded for officers after Waterloo. In 1822 he published *The French Cook*, in English, which was a considerable success. His supremacy recognised, in 1827 he became chef of the new Crockford's Club at 50 St James's Street, which had the largest and most luxurious casino in Europe where fortunes were made and lost: 'Words cannot describe the splendour and animation of the first days of Crockford's . . . and the most delicious dinner, cooked by the great Ude.'[57] He was extremely vain and known for his poor temperament – members of the club would take pleasure in trying to make him fly off the handle. He left Crockford's after twelve years, in 1839, in a fit of pique.

The Prince Regent suggested to his French maître d'hôtel, Jean-Baptiste Watier, that he should open a club to rival White's and Brooks's, where members had been complaining about the poor fare. Watier recruited the Prince Regent's own French chef, Labourie, and started Watier's Club. It opened in Piccadilly in 1807 and soon became a popular rendezvous for dandies: 'The dinners were exquisite, the best Parisian chefs could not surpass Labourie,' wrote a contemporary.[58] This club was also a casino and several members of the high aristocracy ruined themselves there, which caused its closure in 1819.

Antonin Carême (1784–1833), the great celebrity of his profession, began working in a pâtisserie as a child. His passion for architecture, which he studied in his spare time, was reflected in his culinary creations: he attached great importance to the presentation of dishes and would create grandiose scaffoldings for his tiered cakes. Some of his innovations have become the norm in the present day: he introduced the Russian custom of producing dishes in a sequence instead of the French one of presenting everything at once. He also invented the high white chef's hat, still worn today. Carême was in the service of many of the great men of his time, from Napoleon, for whom he made a wedding cake, to Tsar Alexander and Talleyrand. He arrived in London in 1816 to be 'chef de cuisine' for the Prince Regent who, conscious of the effects of his greed on his health, once said: 'Carême, you will kill me from over-eating!' to which the master-chef replied: 'My lord, my great work is to arouse your appetite with the variety of my dishes, it is not my job to regulate it!'[59] He made a fortune publishing cookery books which were translated into English to great acclaim. After eighteen months in England he returned to Paris because, as he said 'my soul is completely French and can only live in France'.[60]

After working as chef for an English family, Alexandre Grillion opened one of the first luxury hotels in England in 1803, in a beautiful house in Albemarle Street near Piccadilly. The exiled French King Louis XVIII spent three nights at the Grillion before his return to France in 1814, receiving émigrés and English nobles who had come to congratulate him. After this, royal families passing through London would stay at the Grillion. The hotel was the precursor of the Grillion Club which exists to this day, started in 1812 by Members of Parliament from all parties who decided to gather every Wednesday to relax, the only rule being that they should not discuss current political affairs. A member of the family, Peter Grillion, took over the Clarendon Hotel next door, and the club used this for its meetings. Around 1820 another member of the dynasty, Francis Grillion, opened an annexe nearby, the Coburg Hotel. The Duchesse d'Angoulême stayed there in 1832, and received Queen Adelaide, wife of William IV. At the end of the First World War, the hotel changed its German name and became the Connaught Hotel in Carlos Place. Members of the Grillion Club now meet once a month at Brown's Hotel, the only survivor of the Albemarle Street hotels of the early nineteenth century.

Jacquier, another successful chef who had made a fortune in the service of Louis XVIII at Hartwell, opened the Clarendon

Hotel in New Bond Street, with a second entrance in Albemarle Street. His establishment was considered one of the best in town, and a group of collectors and bibliophiles founded the Roxburghe Club during a dinner there in June 1812. Members met there for an annual dinner until its closure, and their club still exists today. The hotel had been taken over by Peter Grillion in the years preceding its closure in 1872.

As for the chef Jacques Mivart, he transformed two houses in Brook Street in 1812 into a hotel which, thanks to its reputation, very soon attracted foreign royalty and diplomats. The hotel prospered and in 1838 he was able to buy five adjacent houses and enlarge the establishment. He sold the hotel to William Claridge in 1854, who retained the same clientele by maintaining the high quality of service and gastronomy which had made the Mivart Hotel so successful. The Empress Eugénie stayed there in 1860, and received Queen Victoria and Prince Albert. At the end of the nineteenth century, Claridge's was bought by the Savoy group, who enlarged and modernised it; it is still one of the most luxurious hotels in London.

Alexis Soyer arrived in London after the 1830 Revolution; he was in the service of several English aristocratic families before becoming in 1837 the head chef at the Reform Club, where he worked until 1850. He reorganised the kitchens, modernising their equipment with a refrigeration system and a variable temperature oven. On the day of Queen Victoria's coronation he served almost 2,000 breakfasts.

Soyer was much afflicted by the death in 1842 of his wife, an English artist, and began to devote himself to charitable causes. He organised soup kitchens in Ireland during the Great Famine of 1847. In 1850 he opened a French restaurant in South Kensington, Soyer's Gastronomic Universal Symposium, to cater for international visitors to the Great Exhibition in Hyde Park. He rented Gore House opposite the exhibition, which had just been vacated by Lady Blessington and the Comte d'Orsay, and transformed it into a themed restaurant. The decoration was luxurious and original: at the height of the summer, the walls of one of the rooms were covered with carved ice. However, the venture collapsed after three months.

During the Crimean War in the 1850s he collaborated with Florence Nightingale and on his return put his experience at the service of the army, advising it on the organisation of field kitchens and soldiers' rations. His influence and his inventions, such as the Soyer portable oven, were crucial and his recommendations on army catering were followed into the middle of the twentieth century. The last Soyer ovens were only destroyed in the Falklands war in 1982 when the ship they were in was bombed. Like many of the great chefs of his time, Alexis Soyer was practically illiterate. This did not prevent him from publishing his recipe books, often intended to supply the poor with recipes, such as one for Irish stew, so that they could be well fed at low prices. Soyer was a colourful character and an inspiration to the *Punch* cartoonists: his friend Thackeray made him into the comic French chef Alcide Mirobolant in his novel *Pendennis*. Soyer died in London at forty-eight. His grandson Nicolas followed in his footsteps and was a famous chef at Brooks's Club at the end of the nineteenth century.

Another great name in the history of London hotels was the wine merchant Daniel Nicolas Thévenon. He had been made bankrupt and had taken refuge in England, where he changed his name to Daniel Nicols. In 1865 he opened the Café Royal in Regent Street, a luxury establishment with eight floors, which had everything: grand decor, wine cellar, billiard room, grill room, café, restaurant and private rooms. It attracted a rich clientèle as well as famous artists and writers such as Sickert, Oscar Wilde and Whistler. In 1894 the happy atmosphere was overshadowed by the murder of the doorman by a killer who was never caught. After several renovations during the twentieth century, the Café Royal still retains its reputation as a luxurious establishment with an international following.

In 1867 Auguste Kettner, Napoleon III's chef, opened Kettner's in Soho, which became a restaurant with a champagne bar and private rooms upstairs. It had one particular attraction: it was linked to the neighbouring Palace Theatre by an underground passage. Among its regular customers were Edward VII and Oscar Wilde, who wrote and entertained friends in his favourite corner. In 1877 Kettner published a cookery book, *Book of the Table: a Manual of Cookery*, in which he mingled recipes and anecdotes.

Other celebrities in the profession were the Swiss César Ritz and the Frenchman Auguste Escoffier, who in 1889 were invited to take over the direction of the new Savoy Hotel and its kitchen. The height of luxury and comfort, it was the first hotel to have a lift. One demanding client remarked: 'Ritz and Escoffier have made London a place worth living in.'[61] Already famous, Escoffier set about revolutionising kitchens with his innovations: he brought in lighter and simpler dishes, divided the staff into teams, improved hygiene and working conditions. He worked at changing employers' attitudes towards their workforces, starting from the principle that a worker who is treated with respect will work all the better. Pierre Hamp, one of the commis chefs at the Savoy, described this change in practice: 'I entered a new world where the worker was no longer in mud and hovels.'[62] In return, Escoffier expected an exhausting amount of work from his employees. He brought his ingredients from France and offered his demanding and elegant customers personalised dishes, which he would dedicate to them: Peach Melba, for example, was invented for the Australian singer Nellie Melba.

With his success at the Savoy behind him and his revolutionary ideas introduced, in 1899 Escoffier joined the Carlton Hotel, where he was to spend twenty-five years. He continued to name his recipes after famous people, helping to make them immortal: 'Consommé à la Talleyrand', 'Timbale du Maréchal Foch' and 'Fraises Sarah Bernhardt'. He was the author of many collections of recipes and in 1912 he created the Ligue des Gourmands to serve the same menu, conceived by him, on the same day in several different towns.

As for Ritz, he continued to pursue his career, opening prestigious hotels in several large European cities. In London he participated in the opening of the Carlton and the Hyde Park Hotel.

His most famous one is the Ritz in Piccadilly, opened in 1906, built by the Alsatian Charles Mewès who had just finished the Ritz in Paris. César Ritz was already very ill when the London hotel opened, and he never directed it.

English Catholicism renewed in the French style

In a great flurry of wimples, hundreds of French nuns crossed the Channel in the nineteenth century and at the beginning of the twentieth, a time when Anglo-Catholicism was experiencing an unprecedented revival. Under pressure from Irish Catholics, the government had passed the Catholic Emancipation Act in 1829, returning civil and political liberty to Catholics. In 1850 Pope Pius IX reestablished an ecclesiastical hierarchy by naming the first English cardinal since the Reformation, Monsignor Wiseman.

In France in the same time French nuns were founding new orders in the face of mounting anti-clericalism. They were encouraged by the English Catholic authorities to establish themselves in England, and many did so, although few of them could speak English. Devoid of means and often facing great hostility, they managed to open hospitals, retirement homes, schools and orphanages in many different towns. One of the first to settle in London was Madeleine d'Houet, who had recently founded the Société des Fidèles Compagnes de Jésus. When she arrived in 1830, she was put in charge of the Catholic schools that had been opened for the children of French émigrés from the Revolution in Somers Town, Tottenham and Hampstead. She founded a boarding school for young women from the bourgeoisie and high society called Gumley House in the southern suburbs of London. Two of Louis-Philippe's granddaughters attended it.

In 1840 the order of Notre-Dame-de-Charité-du-Bon-Pasteur sent Jeanne-Marie Regaudiat to London where she founded an institution for helping prostitutes and a school for 'at risk' girls in Fulham Palace Road, on a site now occupied by the Peabody Trust. Madeleine-Sophie Barat, founder of the Société du Sacré-Coeur, opened a school at Berrymead (now Acton) in 1842 and another in Hammersmith in 1893. The Little Sisters of the Poor in Paris sent five nuns over, led by Victoire Larmenier, to found the Sisters of Nazareth in Hammersmith to look after the elderly and sick children. By her death in 1878, Victoire Larmenier had opened seven other establishments in England. Her order now runs forty all over the world.

The nursing sisters of the Bon Secours order cared for the poor free in their own homes. Mother Sainte-Béatrix and three other nuns opened a retirement home in Westbourne Grove in Notting Hill in 1870, while helping the poor in the area at the same time. Their doctor was A. J. Cronin, author of *The Citadel*. The order closed its London house in 2005. The Nuns of the Assumption, an order founded by Anne-Eugénie Milleret who was canonised in 2007, opened a convent and school in Kensington in 1857. The convent of the Carmelites of the Very Holy Trinity was founded in 1878 in Notting Hill by Madeleine Dupont, who inspired a great many vocations through her example and her devotion, until her death in 1942 at the age of ninety-two. She founded thirty-two Carmelite houses in Great Britain between 1907 and 1938. In around 1887 about two-thirds of Catholic convents in England were of French origin. They remained under the authority of their mother houses in France, but some of them broke off to create a new order in England, such as that of the Sisters of Nazareth. All these foundations, in England and in the rest of the world, retained a French influence in the way they were organised and in their religious practice.

Another nun, of Burgundian origin, followed in their wake. Marie-Adèle Garnier (1838–1924) had founded the Benedictine congregation of the Worshippers of the Sacred Heart of Jesus in Montmartre in 1898. Anticlerical pressures in France, which led eventually to the separation of church and state in 1905, drove Marie-Adèle, now Mother Marie de Saint-Pierre, to move to London. Helped by Cardinal Vaughan, head of the Catholic Church in England, she established her order in a large house close to the site of the Tyburn tree near Marble Arch: this was where the gibbet had stood since the Middle Ages and where many Catholics had been executed during the Reformation. Their co-religionists had for a long time wished to build a chapel in memory of their martyrdom. Mother Marie de Saint-Pierre built a convent dedicated to them and expanded the order, which now has eight houses scattered throughout the world. She died in 1927, is buried in the garden of the convent and is in the process of being canonised.

Pioneers of photography and
French in search of adventure

Some of the French in England distinguished themselves by their inventive spirit, their spectacular feats, and their bold pioneering. Louis-Jacques Mandé Daguerre (1787–1851), inventor of the daguerreotype process in photography, started as an architect specialising in theatrical scenery. He married an Englishwoman, Louise-Georgina Arrowsmith, whose brothers became partners in his London ventures. He drew crowds with his diorama, a precursor of film: landscapes and monuments painted on two vast canvases became alive under plays of light, with the public sitting on a revolving platform in specially adapted halls. Opening first in Paris in 1822, and then in several English cities, the diorama of London was a circular structure partly designed by Pugin and inaugurated in 1823 at 18 Park Square, south-west of Regent's Park. Despite its popularity, however, it was a commercial failure and closed in 1848.

One of Daguerre's pupils, originally from Lyon, established himself in London as a glazier in 1827 in High Holborn. In 1841 the new craze for photography and in particular for portraits led Antoine Claudet (1797–1867) to open a studio on the roof of the Adelaide Gallery behind St Martin in the Fields. Claudet took photography forwards by experimenting with different methods and inventing various new devices. Handling a daguerreotype was a very complex process and the camera, which was very expensive, only produced one image. So Claudet perfected a calotype which produced images on paper from a negative, thus allowing an unlimited number of copies. He was the first to photograph his clients with accessories posing against a painted background, thus producing a more animated image. In 1851 he moved his studio to 107 Regent Street, baptising it 'The Temple of Photography'. He was elected to the Royal Society and became official photographer to Queen Victoria in 1853. A large part of his work was destroyed when the Temple of Photography burnt down in 1867.

Camille Silvy (1834–1910) decided to abandon a diplomatic career and concentrate on photography, settling in London in 1859. He began by making portraits of actors and actresses, and then started a fashion for photographic visiting cards. His reputation grew and he became the photographer to high society, to the Orleans family and to the British royal family, although he never photographed his patron, Queen Victoria. His success was such that at one time there were said to be a million of his photographs in circulation in London. Working in his studio at 38 Porchester Terrace in Bayswater, he took enormous trouble with his portraits, some of which were true works of art. He did not simply limit himself to visiting cards and portraits of the gentry either, but was interested in all social classes and in everyday life, leaving us with a magnificent account of English society at the end of the nineteenth century. In 1860 he created a 'photographic library' containing facsimiles of illuminated manuscripts, as well as launching a magazine, the *London Photographic Review*. In 1868, when the photographic visiting card went out of fashion, Silvy closed his studio and, after a brief return to diplomacy, went back to France to fight the Prussians. He suffered from depression and spent the second half of his life, from 1874 to 1910, in psychiatric hospitals.

After the photographers, the adventurers: since the Montgolfier brothers' first hot-air balloon flight in 1783, many aeronauts put on highly popular public displays. Jean-Pierre Blanchard (1753–1809) made several ascents from the the the Royal Military Academy in Chelsea. On 7 January 1785, accompanied by the American Doctor Jefferies, he made the first balloon crossing of the Channel, from Dover to Calais, in less than two hours.

André-Jacques Garnerin (1769–1823), taken prisoner by the English in 1793, spent his eighteen months of captivity flirting with the idea of escaping by parachute. On his return to France he perfected a system elaborated by Blanchard, who planned to attach a parachute to his balloon as a safety device in case of accident. Garnerin's risky-looking contraption was shaped like an umbrella with a seven-metre diameter. In 1802, the year of the Peace of Amiens, he came to England to demonstrate his ascensions at the Ranelagh Gardens, the Vauxhall Gardens and at Lord's cricket ground. He was watched by an enthusiastic crowd, joined by all of high society. The Prince of Wales presented the aeronaut with a signed letter of recommendation for the owners of any property he should happen to land on. On 21 September 1802, Garnerin was the first man to jump with a parachute in England. He rose from Grosvenor Square in his balloon and, harnessed in his contraption, cut himself loose. After a descent enlivened by strong winds he landed safely in a field near St Pancras. His wife Jeanne followed his example and became the first female parachutist.

Just as flamboyant was Jean-François Gravelet (1824–97), better known as Charles Blondin, the most famous of all tightrope walkers. In 1859 he crossed the Niagara Falls on a 335-metre rope stretched 50 metres above the water. He repeated this exploit several times, varying his positions, balancing on a chair, or stopping halfway across to cook an omelette on a portable stove. The 'hero of the Niagara' made a fortune by putting on a series of displays in Europe. He finally settled in England, and in 1861 he performed at the Crystal Palace, making dangerous jumps, on stilts, on a rope stretched across the central transept of the huge building. He gave his last display in Belfast in 1896. He lived in Ealing and named his home Niagara House.

Originally from Rochefort, the sailor Joseph-René Bellot distinguished himself by participating in Anglo-French exploratory missions to Madagascar and Brazil. In 1851 and 1852, the French Navy authorised him to take part in two English expeditions sent to search for Sir John Franklin, who had disappeared several years before. Franklin had set out with several ships in 1845, to search for the North-West Passage in the Canadian Arctic. The many search parties sent after him opened up areas hitherto unknown.

Bellot is the only Frenchman to have given his name to a place in that region: the Bellot Straits lie at the northernmost point of the American continent. On his return he was admitted to the Royal Geographical Society in London. He disappeared during his second voyage, at the age of twenty-seven. He was respected and admired by all who had served with him, and a monument in his honour was erected by fellow members of the expedition at Greenwich. Jules Verne was inspired by this explorer in *Les aventures du capitaine Hatteras*: 'I suppose that, when M. Bellot went out [. . .] the wind carried him into the crevasse and [. . .] he was unable to swim to the surface. [. . .] He was mourned throughout England.'[63]

Unusual characters: a dandy, a Bonaparte and a chess player

One of the most fashionable Frenchmen in London during the first half of the nineteenth century was the Comte d'Orsay (1801–52). He was the young protégé of the very rich Lord and Lady Blessington, and their ménage à trois was a source of fascination and scandal in polite society. During his first stay in London in 1821, when he was just twenty-one, he met them at Lady Blessington's salon at 10 St James's Square. The following year the Blessingtons set off on a Grand Tour, taking young Alfred d'Orsay with them. They met Lord Byron at Genoa and lived for some time in Naples, where d'Orsay married their daughter Harriet, who was then fifteen. They then moved to Paris, where Lord Blessington died in 1829; Lady Blessington, d'Orsay and Harriet returned to London the following year. Lady Blessington started a literary salon in a magnificent house in Seymour Place opposite Hyde Park, which was frequented by all the great political, literary and artistic personalities of the time. In a setting of works of art chosen by him, the young count caused a sensation. When his wife Harriet, tired of being neglected, left him, he installed himself nearby at 22 Curzon Place. In 1834, Lady Blessington was forced by her extravagance to move her salon to a more modest house, Gore House, on the site of the present Royal Albert Hall.

The Comte d'Orsay, during his London years, was the arbiter of masculine fashion. He was probably bisexual, and dressed in the most refined manner, setting the tone in the same way as the great dandy Beau Brummel had done earlier in the century. He became a reference point for fashion, and for other activities such as interior decoration and horse-racing. He was an excellent rider and made a fine sight on his regular rides in Hyde Park. He gambled, too, mainly at Crockford's and White's. He was a friend of Disraeli, Tolstoy, Thackeray, Carlyle and Dickens, and was reunited with his childhood friend Alfred de Vigny in London in 1839. He wrote novels, frequented the world of theatre, and took an interest in politics: he became close to Louis-Napoleon and used his influence to get favourable articles written about him in the papers. Wanting to become an entrepreneur, he embarked on the creation of a hippodrome at Notting Hill, which was inaugurated with great splendour in June 1837, only to close four years later. By 1840 he was heavily in debt and decided to make use of his artistic talents and become a painter and sculptor. He acquired a certain renown and exhibited at the Royal Academy in 1843.

The Comte d'Orsay was a naturally generous man and was shocked by the poverty of some French refugees: to help them he created the Société Française de Bienfaisance, which still exists today. In 1849 he fled England under cover of darkness to evade his creditors, escaping to Paris. Lady Blessington, also heavily in debt, put the contents of Gore House up for sale and joined him in Paris a few weeks later, but died of a heart attack soon after her arrival. In London the Gore House sale was a great event – more than 20,000 people went to the viewing, which lasted for five days. In Paris the Comte d'Orsay was made director general of the Beaux-Arts by Napoleon III, but died soon afterwards in 1852.

Louis-Lucien Bonaparte was born in 1813 at Thorngrove House in Grimley, Worcestershire. He was the son of Lucien Bonaparte, Napoleon's youngest brother. Captured by the English in 1810 while on a ship heading for America, Lucien was held in England until 1814. He led a comfortable life at Thorngrove, where he wrote a long poem about Charlemagne. After the fall of

Napoleon, Louis-Lucien followed his parents to Italy, where he married an Italian woman. He studied comparative linguistics, an unexplored subject at the time, and in 1847 published his first book on European languages, *Specimen lexici comparativi*. At the beginning of the 1850s he settled in London to pursue his studies. Separated from his wife, he lived with Clémence Richard, whom he had met during one of his journeys to the Pays Basque and with whom he had a son. Louis-Lucien was mainly interested in the regional dialects of Italy, England and the Pays Basque. He created a classification system, and produced a number of important works, particularly on the Basque language, whose origins are unknown and which does not belong to any of the European language groups. Thanks to a grant from Napoleon III, he installed a printing press in his Bayswater house, where he had an important library, and was able to publish his own works and translations, particularly of the Bible. He was a member of the Philological Society and the Athenaeum. In 1854 Oxford University conferred on him an honorary degree in civil law. When the empire collapsed and he lost his pension, the English government conferred one on him in recognition of his studies of English dialects. He married Clémence in 1891, after the death of his first wife, and died three months later in Italy. His body was taken to London and he is buried in Kensal Green Cemetery.

Finally, we must mention a French chess player who, like Philidor before him, amazed the English. Louis de la Bourdonnais (1795–1840) learned the rudiments of the game at the College Henri IV in Paris, and then took lessons with the champion Alexandre Deschapelles, whom he managed to beat in 1821. He went to London for several tournaments, all of which he won. In the course of one of his visits, in 1825, he married an Englishwoman, Eliza Waller Gordon. After being ruined by property speculations, he decided to earn his living with his hobby, and published in 1833 his *Nouveau Traité du jeu des échecs*. There then began the longest rivalry in the history of chess, between de la Bourdonnais and the Irishman Alexander MacDonnell. They played a series of contests of eighty-five games over several months between 1834 and 1835. Each player spoke only his own language, and the only word they had in common was 'Check!' They played every day except Sunday and the match was sometimes inter-rupted by de la Bourdonnais making a quick trip to France. Mac-Donnell's death in 1835 put an end to the championship and de la Bourdonnais was declared the winner. In 1836 he produced the first magazine devoted to chess, *Le Palamède*. After more financial setbacks, he settled in London in 1840 and worked at Simpson's Divan Club, a well-known chess club in the Strand. He died a few months later and lies, like his adversary MacDonnell, in Kensal Green Cemetery.

Places to visit

CHEFS AND HOTELS

Louis-Eustache Ude

- **The Fifty Club**
  50 St James's Street SW1
  In 1966, The Fifty replaced Crockford's,
  where Ude worked for twelve years.

- **Crockford's Club**
  30 Curzon Street W1
  Crockford's new address. The club continues to offer an exclusive clientele a restaurant, casino and reception rooms in the
  heart of Mayfair.

- *The French Cook*
  Book published by Ude in 1813.

Alexandre Grillion

- **Hotel Grillion**
  7 Albemarle Street W1
  The building still exists. Now offices, the
  original structure, staircase and some of the
  decorative details remain intact.

- **The Grillion Club**
  The club, whose members used to meet in
  the Hotel Grillion, celebrated its bicentenary
  in 2012.

- **Connaught Hotel**
  Carlos Place, Mayfair W1
  François Grillion opened an annexe to the
  Grillion which became the Connaught,
  where General de Gaulle kept a suite during
  part of his stay in London during the Second World War.

Louis Jacquier

- **Cartier**
  175 New Bond St, W1
  The shop occupies the original site of
  the Clarendon Hotel, opened by Jacquier
  and taken over in its last years by Peter
  Grillion.

- **Roxburghe Club**
  Society of Antiquaries
  Burlington House, Piccadilly W1
  One of the last reminders of the Clarendon
  Hotel and its owner Jacquier, this biblio-
  philes' club was founded during a dinner at
  the hotel in 1812, and exists to this day.
  There are a few French names in the list of
  members since its foundation. One is the
  Duke d'Aumale who was its president dur-
  ing his exile in London after the death of
  Prince Albert. Another is Prince Gabriel de
  Broglie, Chancellor of the Institut de France,
  who was elected in 2003.

Jacques Mivart
Claridges Hotel
Brook Street, Mayfair W1
The Hotel Mivart became Claridges Hotel.

Alexis Soyer

- **Kensington Gore** and **Gore Hotel**
  190 Queen's Gate SW7
  Alexis Soyer rented Gore House which had
  previously been occupied by the Comte
  d'Orsay and Lady Blessington (1834–49).
  He turned it into a grand restaurant during
  the Great Exhibition of 1851. The house
  was demolished to make way for the Albert
  Hall, but the street name and the hotel
  recall its existence.

- **Kensal Green Cemetery**
  The tomb of Alexis and Emma Soyer is surmounted by a statue representing Faith. At
  the foot of the monument a portrait of
  Emma, who died in childbirth at the age of
  twenty-eight.

- **Florence Nightingale Museum**
  St Thomas's Hospital
  2 Lambeth Palace Road SE1
  Several documents concerning Alexis Soyer
  and his actions during the Crimean War.

- **National Portrait Gallery.** Painting by Jerry
  Barrett, *Nightingale Receiving the Wounded*

at Scutari (1857), depicts a scene from the Crimean War. Alexis Soyer stands on the left, holding an umbrella, in the group surrounding Florence Nightingale.

- **Commemorative plaque**
  28 Marlborough Place, St John's Wood NW8
  Alexis Soyer's house.

Daniel Nicolas Thévenon (alias Daniel Nicols)
The Café Royal
68 Regent Street W1
After its last renovation, the Café Royal is as luxurious as ever and remains an iconic establishment.

Auguste Kettner
Kettner's
29 Romilly Street W1
Brought under new management in the 1970s, with interior decoration preserved, with champagne bar, restaurants, cocktail bars and private rooms, on four floors. Celebrated its 104th anniversary in 2007. Portraits of Napoleon III in the bar.

César Ritz

- **Savoy Hotel**. Started by Ritz with Escoffier as chef, modernised several times. Most recently closed for a new renovation by French designer Pierre-Yves Rochon, reopened in 2010.

- **Ritz Hotel**
  Piccadilly W1
  Despite successive refurbishments, the ground-floor rooms keep their Louis XVI-style decor. Plaque on Piccadilly facade commemorates the opening of the hotel in 1906, with the names of the two architects, one of them Charles Mewès, of Alsatian origin.

Auguste Escoffier

- **Royal Opera Arcade**
  Pall Mall SW1
  Plaque relating the history of the arcade mentions the Carlton Hotel, destroyed by a bomb in the Second World War. Escoffier's cooking was an essential element for the

success of this luxury hotel. The site is now occupied by New Zealand House.

- **French Culinary Association**
  Westminster Kingsway College
  76 Vincent Square SW1
  Founded by Auguste Escoffier, with fellow chef Émile Fétu, in 1903 to help French cooks in difficulties. Now has more than a thousand members in Great Britain.

- **The Escoffier Challenge**. Annual competition run by the French Culinary Association for professional and apprentice chefs.

NUNS AND CONVENTS

Madeleine d'Houet

- **Maria Fidelis RC Convent School**
  North Gower Street and Phoenix Road, Somers Town NW1
  This Catholic school is descended from the one founded by abbé Carron during the French Revolution; it was taken over by the Order of the Faithful Companions of Jesus, created by Madeleine d'Houet, which still runs the school.

- **Gumley House Convent School**
  Isleworth, Middlesex TW7
  Madeleine d'Houet founded this school for the well-born young ladies who had come to live in this suburb of London. Her order still runs the school.

Madeleine-Sophie Barat

- **Sacred Heart High School**
  212 Hammersmith Road W6
  Taken over by the Order of the Sacred Heart in 1893 from the English Benedictines who founded it when they returned from France during the Revolution. One of the school buildings is called the Barat Building after its founder.

- **Woldingham School**
  Marden Park, Woldingham, Surrey
  New address of the Order of the Sacred Heart school.

Victoire Larmenier

- **Nazareth House**
  160–75 Hammersmith Road W6
  Founded by Victoire Larmenier, known as
  Mother Basile-Marie, now a care home for
  the elderly.

- **Larmenier and Sacred Heart**
  41a Brook Green, Hammersmith W6
  Sacred Heart primary school, supported by
  the neighbouring sisters of Nazareth House.

Anne-Eugénie Milleret

Convent of the Assumption
23 Kensington Square W8
Anne-Eugénie Milleret, known as Sister Marie-
Eugénie of Jesus, was one of the founders.
The original convent is still at the same
address. Above the door is written: 'The Religious of the Assumption were asked by Cardinal Wiseman, in 1857, to found a House of
Adoration in this diocese so that continuous
prayer would be offered for the acute problems of those times.'

Madeleine Dupont

Carmelite Monastery of the
Very Holy Trinity
87 St Charles Square W10
Occupies a large hidden area at the heart of
Notting Hill. Plaque relating the foundation of
the convent by Madeleine Dupont. Director
Michael Whyte, intrigued by the lives of these
nuns, spent ten years obtaining permission to
film them, resulting in the film *No Greater Love*
(2010)

Marie-Adèle Garnier

Tyburn Convent
Benedictine Adorers of the Sacred Heart
of Jesus of Montmartre
8 Hyde Park Place W2
Home to a community of Benedictines,
founded by Marie-Adèle Garnier. In the crypt,
an altar dedicated to the Tyburn Martyrs is
raised on a wooden structure like the ancient
gibbet. Photos of the founder in the nave and
her tomb in the garden. In wing adjacent to

chapel, exhibition relating the martyrdom of
Catholics during the Reformation. Also mentioned is Claude Duval, a French highwayman
hanged at Tyburn.

PHOTOGRAPHERS AND EXPLORERS

Louis-Jacques Mandé Daguerre
Diorama
18 Park Square East, Regent's Park NW1
Entrance to the Diorama with 'Diorama' sign
above the facade, behind which the circular
building is still standing.

Antoine Claudet

- **National Portrait Gallery**. Examples of his
  daguerreotypes.

- **Fox Talbot Museum**
  Lacock Abbey, Wiltshire
  The abbey, transformed into a private
  dwelling, belonged to William Fox Talbot,
  one of the pioneers of photography in
  England. He invented the calotype which
  was used by Antoine Claudet. Museum of
  photography with several of Claudet's
  daguerreotypes.

Camille Silvy
National Portrait Gallery. Twelve registration
books list the daily visitors to Camille Silvy's
studio in Bayswater, with a photo-contact for
each one; 17,000 were registered.

André-Jacques Garnerin
Science Museum. In the Flight Gallery, case
dedicated to the balloon mania that began
with the flight of the Montgolfier brothers in
France.

Charles Blondin

- **Kensal Green Cemetery**. Two medallion
  portraits, of the acrobat Blondin and his
  wife, on their tomb.

- **Blondin Street**, Tower Hamlets E3
  Street named after Blondin.

- **A Blondin**. An English building term describing a wooden basket used to transport

men and materials to inaccessible places such as quarries or buildings over water.

Joseph-René Bellot

- **National Portrait Gallery**. Portrait by Stephen Pearce (1851).

- **Old Royal Naval College**
  Greenwich SE10
  In front of the college, beside the Thames, granite obelisk by Philip Hardwich in memory of René Bellot, with the inscription: 'To the intrepid young Bellot of the French Navy who in the endeavour to rescue Franklin shared the fate and the glory of that illustrious navigator. From his British admirers, 1853.'

- **National Maritime Museum**. Section devoted to expeditions to the North Pole to search for Franklin, in which Bellot participated.

- **Bellot Street**, Greenwich SE10
  Named after the French explorer.

UNUSUAL CHARACTERS

Comte d'Orsay

- **White's Club**
  37–38 St James's Street SW1
  Collection of drawings and portraits by the Comte d'Orsay of a large number of celebrities of the time. Includes a version of the famous last portrait of an ageing Duke of Wellington, of which he was very fond.

- **Travellers Club**. Another version of the Duke of Wellington's portrait by d'Orsay.

- **Dickens House**
  48 Doughty Street WC1
  Two portraits of Dickens by d'Orsay (1841 and 1842) in Dickens's bedroom, plus one of Mrs Dickens, much admired at the time.

- **National Portrait Gallery**. Marble bust of the Comte d'Orsay by himself, and oil portrait of him by Sir George Hayter (1839).

Also, another version of his Wellington portrait and around a hundred drawings, portraits by d'Orsay of members of high society.

- **Victoria & Albert Museum**. Watercolour of Byron by d'Orsay.

- **Wallace Collection**. Portrait of Lady Blessington (d'Orsay's mistress) by Sir Thomas Lawrence. Lord Hertford added to the Wallace Collection, buying this painting at the sale of Gore House.

- **Madame Tussaud's**. Waxwork of the Comte d'Orsay (1845), at a time when he could not leave Gore House for fear of being arrested for debt. He went to the waxworks gallery incognito, Madame Tussaud recognised him, and suggested making a waxwork of him.

- **Hippodrome Mews** and **Hippodrome Place**
  Notting Hill W11
  These two streets and the circular design of some streets in Notting Hill recall the brief existence of the hippodrome in which d'Orsay invested money.

- **Kensington Gore** and **Gore Hotel**. See page 177, col. 2.

- **Société Française de Bienfaisance**. French charity founded by the Comte d'Orsay (see page 142, col. 2).

Louis-Lucien Napoleon

- **Kensal Green Cemetery**. Tomb in the Catholic section.

- **The Prince Bonaparte** (gastro-pub)
  90 Chepstow Road, Bayswater W2
  His house (now demolished) was close to this at 6–8 Norfolk Terrace, now 118–20 Westbourne Grove.

Louis-Charles de la Bourdonnais

- **Kensal Green Cemetery**. Tomb with inscription 'Celebrated chess player, died 13th of December 1840, at the age of 43.'

11

ALLIES AND BROTHERS-IN-ARMS

THE ENTENTE CORDIALE AND THE GREAT WAR

'I trust, in the future as in the past, England and France may be regarded as the champions and pioneers of peaceful progress and civilisation . . . There are no two countries in the world whose mutual prosperity is more dependent on each other.'

KING EDWARD VII[64]

Under Louis-Philippe, the French and English ministers François Guizot and Lord Aberdeen corresponded with one another about the common future of the two countries, and their wish for an *entente cordiale*, an expression that was then repeated in official speeches and dispatches. This wish was expressed by Queen Victoria after the French king's visit to Windsor in 1844. Napoleon III had understood the need for this rapprochement when, while still in exile and hoping to come to power, he wrote: 'Let us hope that the day will come when I will be able to unite the politics and interests of Great Britain and France in an indissoluble alliance.'[65] It was under his reign that, for the first time, the two nations fought alongside one another against Russia in 1853, in the Crimean War.

Entente Cordiale

By the end of the century, the Entente Cordiale was crucial in bringing to a close the tensions between London and Paris caused by colonial disputes which had culminated in the Fashoda crisis. England had dominated Egypt since 1882 and was a majority shareholder in the Suez Canal, which it wanted to protect at any price as it was the key to access to India, jewel of the empire. France, which had built the canal and had important interests in Egypt, did not take kindly to its neighbour carving out the lion's share of Africa. She therefore sent a military detachment to block the British advance on the land route from Cairo to the Cape. The Marchand mission, named after the officer commanding it, arrived first at Fashoda, in the Upper Nile, and planted a French flag there in July 1898, after months of hard travelling. Kitchener's forces arrived two months later and, in a climate of extreme Anglo-French tension, Marchand was horrified to receive a telegram from the new foreign minister Théophile Delcassé, informing him that 'in the general interests of France, the government has decided not to remain at Fashoda'.[66]

France certainly had other priorities in Europe, but it none the less felt humiliated by this climbdown. Delcassé admitted that his hair had turned grey in a few days at the height of the crisis. And there were other colonial rivalries opposing the two countries. Edward VII and President Loubet, fearing the worst, attempted a reconciliation and the dawn of the twentieth century saw their hopes fulfilled. The English king was anxious about William II's Germany, which was rapidly re-arming and threatening the balance of power in Europe. He was an enthusiastic francophile and he tried hard to be considerate: in 1902, he agreed, in a generous gesture, to attend a charity sale for the Société Française de Bienfaisance in London. In May of the following year, he decided on his own initiative to travel to Paris, where he at first received a cool reception from the Parisians despite the government's wish that the visit should be a success. However, he relaxed the hostile atmosphere with a friendly speech given in perfect French: 'Divine

providence has designed that France should be our near neighbour and, I hope, always our dear friend.'[67]

Two months later President Loubet made an official visit to
London, where he was received with great pomp by the King at
Buckingham Palace and the next day at the Guildhall by the Cor-
poration of the City of London. There was a long correspondence
before the visit between the two embassies on the subject of dress:
President Loubet and Foreign Minister Delcassé refused to wear
knickerbockers and silk stockings, which were *de rigueur* for audiences at court – they knew if they dressed like that they would be
laughing stocks in the French press. They were finally accorded a
dispensation and attended the audience in trousers. Their stay was
punctuated with other absurd incidents: banners in the street read:
'Vive le long président!' an odd translation of 'Long live the President!' At the palace banquet the President was invited to open the
ball with Queen Alexandra. He was a poor dancer and, for fear of
making a fool of himself, he asked his ambassador Paul Cambon
to take his place.

After intense diplomatic activity France and Great Britain concluded an accord – not in the form of a treaty, just a simple document settling their colonial disputes in a friendly manner. On
8 April 1904, this Entente Cordiale was signed by the indefatigable
French ambassador to London, Paul Cambon, and the British
foreign minister Lord Lansdowne, who, by an irony of history, was
the great-grandson of Talleyrand through his mother, née Emilie
de Flahaut. German re-armament had become the major preoc-
cupation of all European countries and the Entente Cordiale
became a Triple Entente between France, Great Britain and
Russia. There was increased cooperation between Paris and
London with a naval agreement in 1912: England would concentrate its fleets in the North Sea and the Channel, with France
doing the same in the Mediterranean. However, despite Paris's
demand to sign a proper accord, Great Britain did not supply a
firm engagement until 1914, on the brink of the war.

In the years following the Entente Cordiale, every kind of

exchange took place: visits from members of Parliament to Paris, and from deputies and senators to London, an official visit by Edward VII and Queen Alexandra to Paris in 1905, naval displays at Brest and Portsmouth, musical encounters, visits from British horticulturalists to Orleans, and municipal council meetings of Lyons held in London. The culmination of this rapprochement was the Franco-British Exhibition of 1908.

'The Franco'

Three years earlier, the French chamber of commerce had the idea of staging an international exhibition in which France and England could show off their progress and achievements in the fields of science, industry and the arts. Soon nicknamed 'the Franco', it was the first exhibition to be organised by two countries. Situated on sixty hectares to the north-west of Shepherd's Bush, it was a proper town consisting of twenty palaces and a hundred and twenty pavilions set around an artificial lake. It included a court of Honour, a court of the Arts, a court of Progress, the Elite Gardens, the Louis XV, Imperial and Royal Pavilions and much else, while domes and minarets lent an oriental atmosphere. Buildings coated in white stucco inspired the name 'the Great White City'. At night ten thousand lamps cast a magical light over the palaces.

England and France were the principal exhibitors, with their colonies also represented: palaces of music and decorative arts and halls of machinery stood alongside tea-houses from Ceylon and India, palaces from Australia, and villages from Senegal, Ceylon and Ireland. There were exhibitions on varied themes – education, engineering, navigation, women's work, sport – as well as numerous other attractions: a myriad of restaurants and cafés were scattered amid the parks and canals; an open-air theatre held three thousand spectators and showed acrobats, snake charmers and elephant drivers. Visitors could also amuse themselves at the music kiosks, the Canadian toboggan ride and the scenic railway. The highlight of these entertainments was the 'Flip-Flap', a ride on which two viewing cabins were suspended on long arms, each one holding fifty people; they passed each other at the highest point of their course, with views as far as Windsor Castle and the Crystal Palace.

Twelve thousand workers worked night and day on the construction of the White City. The commissioner for the exhibition, Imre Kiralfy, and the French and English architects Maurice Toudoire and John Belcher achieved the whole thing in seventeen months. A transport network was built which could bring 75,000 people per hour to the site. The underground line was extended and Wood Lane station was built by the entrance. There were 10,000 extra passengers per month on trains from France during the exhibition, which was opened in pouring rain on 14 May 1908.

When President Fallières made his official visit to the Franco, streets were decorated with tricolor posters marked RF (République Française) which the English took to stand for 'Real Friends'. In six months, the exhibition attracted more than eight million visitors.

The Olympic Games took place in the same year in London, and the buildings from the Franco were used for athletics in the White City stadium, which was at the time the largest in the world. It was during these games that the International Olympic Committee adopted the official marathon distance: 26.385 miles, or 42.195 km, the distance between Windsor Castle and the stadium.

In memory of the historic event, the Entente Cordiale Scholarships Trust was founded during the Franco-British summit of 1995 by Sir Christopher Mallaby, British ambassador to Paris, with the support of Maurice Druon from the Académie Française. The Trust distributes sholarships every year to twenty-five French and English students wishing to study for a year in each other's country. They are managed by the cultural department of the French Embassy in England, and by the British Council in France, and financed by private donations and charitable organisations.

Foch at the victory parade in London

On the eve of the First World War, the Franco was long forgotten as there were more pressing matters to worry about. France was not certain of British support until the very last moment. After intense negotiations, Foreign Secretary Sir Edward Grey wrote to his ambassador in Paris on 31 July 1914: 'M. Cambon repeated his question of whether we would help France if Germany made an attack on her. I said that I could only adhere to the answer that, so far as things had gone at present, we could not take any engagement.'[68]

Finally, on 4 August, Great Britain entered the war against Germany. Kitchener, the Secretary of State for War, appealed for volunteers in Britain and the Empire to augment insufficient numbers in the regular army. In 1916, Great Britain introduced obligatory military service. France had the same need to increase numbers, which were vastly inferior to those of the Germans, so President Raymond Poincaré increased the length of military service to three years starting in 1913. Aeroplanes were used for the first time in military combat. Louis Blériot's great exploit in July 1909, crossing the Channel by air, caused anxiety about security in Great Britain – it was no longer sufficient simply to protect the coastline. Germany possessed formidable airships, the Zeppelins, which dropped bombs on London and Paris while all nations developed planes inspired by Blériot's.

As soon as hostilities began, thousands of French and Belgian refugees came to England to escape the German troops. As in the past, the authorities set up mutual aid support systems. The French Institute opened the school that is now the London French Lycée.

After four years, in April 1918, the Allies set up a single command under General Foch. As Supreme Commander he then coordinated all the allied armies on the Western Front, including the British Army under Field Marshal Haig. Foch was able to communicate to his men his ferocious determination to win; under his command the Germans' advance was halted and they were forced to retreat. He was present at the signature of the armistice on 11 November 1918, having been made Marshal of France in August; he was considered to be the principal architect of the victory and was showered with honours both at home and in England, where he received the Order of the Bath. In July 1919 he rode at the head of a victory parade through the streets of London. King George V awarded him the highest rank in the British Army, that of Field Marshal, and the City of London presented him with the keys of the City and a sword of honour. After his death in 1929, the English erected a statue of him near Victoria Station.

The peace was signed in Paris in June 1919, but once victory had been achieved old grudges re-emerged. Language difficulties between the signatories caused suspicion and misunderstanding. Foch, deeply disappointed with the Treaty of Versailles, made a prophetic remark: 'This is not peace. It is a twenty-year armistice.'[69]

Players in the Entente Cordiale

There were a few exceptional French personalities who helped create the atmosphere which had led to the Entente. Paul Cambon (1843–1924), recently widowed, became the French ambassador to London on 1 December 1898, at the age of fifty-five; he remained in position for twenty-two years, an exceptionally long stay for a diplomatic posting. He did not speak English when he arrived, but was chosen by Delcassé for his conciliatory spirit and his exceptional political vision.

During his long stay in London he witnessed many important events, which he described with verve and humour in letters to his son or his brother, the French ambassador to Berlin. On the death of Queen Victoria in January 1901, he wrote: 'Chaos continues to surround the Queen's funeral arrangements. Nobody knows what they will do. The ceremony has to be organised by the Lord Chamberlain of the palace, and since it is the only time he has ever had anything to do, and that the occasion hasn't presented itself for sixty-three years, the confusion is total.'[70] And in May 1910, when King Edward VII, whom he knew well, died: 'I had seen the King the day before, and I had contemplated the moral misery of a well-meaning man faced with a huge burden.'[71]

During the ten years between the Entente Cordiale and the war, the ambassador worked tirelessly at cultivating the support and friendship of Great Britain. In 1907 he encouraged a rapprochement with Russia which led to the Triple Entente. All through July and August 1914 he pleaded ceaselessly with Foreign Secretary Lord Grey for British commitment to the looming war. During the conflict he continued to coordinate the actions of the two governments, making use of his deep knowledge of Great Britain. Like Marshal Foch, he was deeply disappointed by the Versailles Treaty. In 1921 he created the French committee for a tunnel under the Channel, and came to London for the last time in May 1922 to attend a banquet for the committee.

The most important French cultural institutions in London owe their existence to Marie d'Orliac (1891–1954). As a student in the capital she decided that she wished to introduce the English to contemporary French literature and art by bringing over representatives of the various disciplines from France. She explained her project to some English family friends, Lord and Lady Asquith, who provided her with generous financial backing. In 1910, at the age of nineteen, she opened the University of French Literature at Marble Arch House near Connaught Place. She very rapidly obtained support from intellectuals, academicians, politicians and men of letters who came from France to teach the language and literature, and to present French art to the English. Highly organised and energetic, Marie d'Orliac had the support of Paul Cambon, who said of her: 'She is not a woman, she is a flame.'[72]

In 1913, the Academy of Lille took the initiative and opened a French Institute in London, which was then merged with the University of French Literature, with Marie d'Orliac still at its head. The administrative committee included Lord and Lady Asquith, Princess Mary and such respected figures as the writer Rudyard Kipling and the politician Austen Chamberlain. During the First World War English post office workers, nurses and doctors took French lessons at the Institute to help with their contacts with the French and their work on the battlefields. A lycée was started in 1915 with the help of private donations, for the children of French and Belgian refugees; the school soon acquired an international reputation by accepting children from other foreign countries.

The Institute and the Lycée came under the same roof in 1919 at 1–7 Cromwell Gardens, opposite the Victoria & Albert Museum (now the Ismaili Centre). The French government, in order to maintain a good relationship between the two countries, made an annual grant to develop the activities of the Institute and to ensure the future of the school. Marie d'Orliac, who had become Marie Bohn on her marriage, directed the Institute and the school from 1910 to 1920. She was awarded the Légion d'Honneur in 1923.

In 1939 the two institutions expanded and moved to their new address between Cromwell Road and Harrington Road; the new buildings were inaugurated by President Lebrun. The Institute and the Lycée were separated in 1963 and in 1980 the latter was renamed the Lycée Français Charles de Gaulle. Since then more buildings have been added to accommodate the growing numbers of pupils. After the opening of new annexes in the 1990s, the whole complex celebrated its centenary in 2010 by opening two more schools.

At the beginning of the century, aviation had brought the two countries together in more ways than one. The *Daily Mail* offered a prize of £1,000 to the first aviator to cross the Channel. Louis Blériot (1872–1936), a French engineer, took up the challenge. He took off at 4.40 a.m. on 25 July 1909, despite a badly injured foot and a poor weather forecast. He made the crossing from Calais to Dover in thirty-seven minutes. The French destroyer *Escopette* was on hand to help him in case of problems, but Blériot very quickly overtook it, carried by the wind, saw the English coast and overshot Dover. Near the castle, a journalist from *Le Matin* waved a flag to show him where to land and, after several attempts were thwarted by the wind, he finally landed hard on the ground, damaging his aeroplane. He received a warm welcome, first in Dover, then at Victoria Station in London. The plane was exhibited at Selfridges, and thousands queued to see it. *The New York Times* found it 'so small it seems like a toy'. Indeed, the plane only measured 7.8 metres wide by 8 metres in length. Blériot received his *Daily Mail* prize from the hands of the British minister for war at a big lunch given in his honour at the Savoy. Everybody was conscious of the historic importance of his exploit, as well as what the consequences might be in the military field. A two-seater, the BE (Blériot Experimental) c2 was used by British aviators at the beginning of the First World War. Blériot also built planes for the French government. In 1910 he opened the first aviation school in England, the Blériot School of Flying, at Hendon aerodrome, and by 1912 there were no fewer than eight of them, all at Hendon. In 1916 the war ministry grouped them together into one school, the Royal Flying Corps Civilian School of Instruction. Hendon became a military airfield in both world wars.

Places to visit

THE ENTENTE CORDIALE

French Embassy. Two plaques on facade celebrate the Entente Cordiale.

THE FRANCO

White City W12

The site where palaces and pavilions of the Franco-British Exhibition stood was named 'White City' because of the whiteness of the buildings, which were re-used later for other international exhibitions. The army trained here during the First World War, and in the Second it was an evacuation centre for the wounded and a parachute factory. After this the palaces and pagodas were demolished. The stadium continued to be used for greyhound racing and boxing matches. It was demolished in the 1980s by the BBC to build its centre. Today all traces of the Exhibition have disappeared to make way for the Westfield shopping centre, opened in 2008.

Street names. India Way, Canada Way, Australia Road, South Africa Road, White City Road ... The names reflect the colonial presence at the Exhibition.

Wood Lane and White City underground stations
Specially built for the Exhibition.

Museum of London. Objects relating to the Exhibition.

FIRST WORLD WAR

Equestrian statue of Maréchal Foch
Grosvenor Gardens SW1
Statue by George Mallisard near Victoria Station, unveiled in 1930 by the Prince of Wales, with Foch's words inscribed on the pedestal: 'I am conscious of having served England as I served my own country.' The site acts as a war memorial for the French community in London. Every year, on 11 November, the French ambassador, accompanied by veterans, places a wreath on the monument.

Statue of 'La Délivrance'
Junction of Finchley Road and
North Circular Road NW2
Statue by French sculptor Guillaume Émile, unveiled by Lloyd George in 1927. A naked young girl holding a sword symbolises the joy of the Allied victory over the Germans at the Battle of the Marne. Smaller version at the Senate in Paris.

Westminster Abbey. Tomb of the Unknown Soldier unveiled on 11 November 1920 by King George V at the entrance to the abbey. He scattered a handful of French soil on to the coffin.

Royal British Legion Poppy Factory
20 Petersham Road, Richmond TW10
The Poppy Appeal takes place every year in the days leading up to 11 November, raising money for ex-servicemen and their families. The poppy is worn in memory of the flowers of the battlefields of the Somme.

Armistice Day. At 11 a.m. on 11 November (the eleventh hour of the eleventh day of the eleventh month) each year, the Armistice is remembered with a two-minute silence and a moving ceremony, the principal one being at the Cenotaph in the middle of Whitehall. Today the ceremony also commemorates the soldiers fallen in the Second World War and more recent wars.

Street names. Verdun Road SW13 and SE18, Marne Street W10, Mons Way, Bromley, and Arras Avenue, Morden, are all named after victories in the First World War.

Maison de L'Institut de France
8 Queen's Gate Terrace SW7
Not to be confused with the French Institute. After the war, Baron Edmond de Rothschild created a foundation in London to encourage

exchanges between English and French scholars. He gave the Institut de France a house in
Queen's Gate for visiting French academics to
stay in when researching in London. After it
was destroyed by a bomb in 1944, the Institut
was rehoused in a neighbouring street and still
welcomes French intellectuals.

Imperial War Museum
Lambeth Road SE1
Numerous relics of the First World War. Real-
istic recreation of the experience of trench
warfare.

PAUL CAMBON

French Embassy. Bronze bust in the entrance.

MARIE D'ORLIAC

French Institute
17 Queensberry Place SW7
Founded by Marie d'Orliac in 1910 during the
surge of optimism created by the signature of
the Entente Cordiale and the Franco-British
Exhibition. Cultural and linguistic activities,
library, media room, the Cinema Lumière and
café/restaurant. Bust and plaque to Marie
d'Orliac in the entrance.

Westminster Library
Buckingham Palace Road SW1
At the beginning of the war in 1914, Marie
d'Orliac opened a school for the children of
French and Belgian refugees. It held 120
pupils when it opened, became the Lycée, and
is now the Westminster Public Library.

Lycée Français Charles de Gaulle
35 Cromwell Road SW7
The successor to Marie d'Orliac's school now
holds more than 3,500 pupils of 48 different
nationalities. During the last twenty years the
Institut Français and the Lycée have opened
annexes to satisfy the needs of a growing
French population.

- **École Primaire de Wix**
  Wix's Lane, Clapham Common
  North Side SW4

- **École Primaire André Malraux**
  44 Laurie Road, Ealing W7

- **École Primaire Marie d'Orliac**
  60 Clancarty Road, Fulham SW6

LOUIS BLÉRIOT

Science Museum. Part of the fuselage of the
Blériot XI Monoplane in which he made the
first crossing of the Channel.

RAF Museum
Hendon NW9
On the site of the hangar where Louis Blériot
started his aviation school on 1 October 1910.
It became the London Aerodrome the following
year, used for the first aerial postal service and
for planes in the two world wars. Contains two
models of the XI Monoplane used by Blériot.

Imperial War Museum. Blériot's plane, the BE
c2, hangs in the entrance hall.

12

A SHARED MODERNITY

THE CONTINUING DIALOGUE
BETWEEN ARTISTS

*'Don't speak to me of singers, or pianists or artists of any
sort, I'm fed up with them. Packs of them arrive with
recommendations of every sort . . . Every senator or deputy
has some diva up his sleeve . . .'[73]*

PAUL CAMBON

In 1885, a group of English artists who had studied fine art in
Paris, then the artistic capital of the world, founded the New
English Art Club with the purpose of exhibiting the avant-garde
painters who had been rejected by the Royal Academy. These
artists, who had been inspired by Monet and Degas, included
Jacques-Émile Blanche, an anglophile French painter who became
their leader, and Walter Sickert, a great friend of Degas. London
galleries regularly exhibited the works of French painters, despite
Victorian England's reservations about promoting art from a
country with 'decadent' habits, exemplified by the passion shown
by these artists for prostitutes and Parisian night-life.

The struggle of the avant-garde
When, in 1898, the Goupil Gallery in London put on the largest
ever exhibition of the works of Toulouse-Lautrec in his lifetime,
his paintings were judged to be 'of a revolting ugliness' even

though Londoners were already familiar with his publicity posters in their streets. In 1905 *The Times* art critic wrote, 'On M. Cézanne, the still-life painter . . . we need not dwell.'[74] However, the modernists did not lose heart: in 1910 the art critic and great promoter of modern art in England, Roger Fry, organised an exhibition of French painters at the Grafton Gallery, which included Manet, Gauguin, Van Gogh and Cézanne, all assembled under the name 'Post-Impressionists'. The exhibition 'Manet and the Post-Impressionists' drew the crowds, and was such a success that another one was put on in 1912. Both made their mark on the London art world, and their influence can be traced in two art movements of the time: the Camden Town Group, created in 1911, with sixteen members including Sickert and Lucien Pissarro; and the Bloomsbury Group, with artists and avant-garde intellectuals including Roger Fry, Clive and Vanessa Bell and Duncan Grant.

The First World War interrupted the artistic dialogue between the two countries, but it started again as soon as hostilities ended. Abstract art, initially decried in England, began to be appreciated. Matisse, violently criticised at first, was praised to the skies in 1919 for his one-man show in London. Enlightened collectors left their Impressionist and Post-impressionist works to the National Gallery, which opened a French gallery. The industrialist Samuel Courtauld, of Huguenot descent, who had built up the largest private collection of these works in England, gave a large part of it to London University, which founded the Courtauld Gallery to hold them. He made a gift to the state in 1923 of the Courtauld Fund for the purchase of Impressionists and Post-Impressionists. His generosity allowed the National Gallery to acquire paintings at that time and to fill gaps in their French collection.

William Morris's Arts and Crafts Movement grew up at the beginning of the 1880s, in parallel with the work of French artists such as Hector Guimard (of the Paris Metro), Emile Gallé (ceramics, furniture and glass), and René Lalique (crystal) who had studied for two years at Sydenham Art College in London. All these applied their new style to their surroundings, from architecture to interior decoration, as well as painting, sculpture, jewellery,

furniture and textiles. They became known by selling their work
to tradesmen such as Arthur Liberty, founder of the famous
London department store. Toulouse-Lautrec bought Liberty materials for his apartment in Paris. In 1900, at the Exposition Uni-
verselle in Paris, these artists' style was christened Art Nouveau,
after the pavilion in which they exhibited.

The 1920s, known as the *années folles*, saw a surge of creativity,
and a new style known as Art Deco, from the Exposition internationale des arts décoratifs in Paris in 1925. In London a great many
public buildings were put up in that style, while the French
designers Marc Henri and Gaston Laverdet decorated luxury
houses, theatres and cinemas, using decorative details by Lalique
and the ironsmith Edgar Brandt. Two companies already well
established in France, Michelin and Cartier, opened branches in
London during the 1900s to represent French Art Nouveau and
Art Deco.

A parade of artists

There were so many French artists in London at this time that the
French ambassador Paul Cambon asked for some respite: 'They
swarm over,' he wrote, 'and put on exhibitions at every gallery in
London, which they solemnly ask me to open.'[75] The painter
Jacques-Emile Blanche (1861–1942) went to London almost every
year since his childhood, and considered himself an adoptive Englishman. His father, a well-known doctor and art-lover, had put
him in contact with the high society he frequented at Dieppe, a
popular seaside resort for the English. He numbered among his
friends almost all the notable writers and artists of his time, such
as Colette, Proust, Debussy, D. H. Lawrence, Virginia Woolf and
James Joyce, of whom he painted many portraits in a style that was
similar to that of Manet. He was particularly close to the painters
James Whistler and Walter Sickert. In a carriage adapted as a
mobile studio, he painted scenes from English life, regattas on the
Thames or the streets of London. In 1910, Paul Cambon commissioned him to do a series of paintings of the coronation of George
V for the embassy. These unfinished paintings, *Fêtes du couron-*

nement du roi George V d'Angleterre can be seen today in Manchester and Rouen. His portrait of the queen, *Alexandra épouse d'Edouard VII* (1905) hangs today in the British embassy in Paris.

By 1888, Jacques-Emile Blanche was involved with the New English Art Club and exhibiting in London galleries, as well as, after 1907, at the Royal Academy. In 1937 the Tooth Gallery in London showed fifty-four of his paintings, mostly views of London and the English countryside. He wrote in his spare time and left memoirs in French and English, having become so deeply integrated into English artistic life as to personify the Entente Cordiale, in this domain at least.

Monet's huge success in 1904 with the 'Views of London' exhibition encouraged the dealer Ambroise Vollard to send the young André Derain (1880–1954) to visit London three times, in 1905 and 1906, to paint views of the city. He managed the incredible feat of producing thirty paintings in this short time. Unlike Monet or Turner, he did not paint the fog in the capital, but rather its incessant activity, with the warm and luminous colours of the Fauvist movement. Regent Street, Hyde Park, Parliament by night and Westminster were all seen in a new light, while the Thames was portrayed as a bustling commercial hub with barges, bridges and warehouses. *Waterloo Bridge*, *The Thames and Tower Bridge*, *London Bridge (Charing Cross Bridge)*, *The Two Barges* and *Effects of Sun on Water, The Port of London* count as some of the masterpieces of Fauvism, a style that Derain gradually abandoned after 1907. In 1910 he exhibited at the Modern French Art Exhibition and then in 1913 at the Post-Impressionist and Futurist Exhibition. In 1919, he designed the scenery and costumes for *La Boutique Fantasque,* first performed by Diaghilev's Ballets Russes at the Alhambra Theatre in London, and later in 1947 for the ballet Mademoiselle Angot performed at Covent Garden. He also designed Oscar Wilde's play *Salomé.* In 2005 the Courtauld Gallery held a retrospective of Derain's London paintings, where twenty-nine of his thirty works were shown together for the first time.

The highly personal style of Raoul Dufy (1877–1953) with its bright colours was applied to the bridges over the Thames, to

Piccadilly and to St Paul's during his frequent visits in the 1930s. He was drawn to the rituals of English social life, and painted the Henley and Cowes regattas, the races at Epsom and Ascot, the changing of the guard at Saint James's and the coronation of George VI. He held a one-man exhibition in London in 1938. He also produced engravings on wood for textiles used in haute couture and interior design. The French restaurateur Marcel Boulestin used his 'Paris' motif for his London restaurant.

Edmond Dulac (1882–1953) gave up his law studies to devote himself to painting. In 1904, when he was twenty-four, his marriage broke up and he came to look for work in London. He very soon integrated into local life, and became an English citizen, changing the spelling of his first name to Edmund. The publisher Joseph Dent commissioned illustrations from him for a new edition of the works of the Bronte sisters. This job led to a long association with the Leicester Gallery and the publishers Hodder & Stoughton, for whom Dulac illustrated fables, fairy tales and poems for special gift editions. From the marvellous to the macabre, these tales inspired him to create a world full of fantasy and charm. The books, published one a year for several years running, were a great success, and are much sought after today. They include *The Thousand and One Nights, Shakespeare's Tempest, The Sleeping Beauty and other Tales, Hans Andersen's Fairy Tales* and *The Poems of Edgar Allan Poe*. Dulac was a member of the London Sketch Club and the St John's Art Club. Like Gustave Doré in the preceding generation, he became preeminent in the world of illustrators, who were all benefiting from the advances being made in colour printing techniques.

When the First World War broke out, Dulac participated in the war effort by illustrating fund-raising editions, such as *Edmund Dulac's Picture Book*, published for the benefit of the French Red Cross in 1915. The demand for luxury editions of illustrated books came to an end after the war and Dulac was forced to diversify his activities, producing portraits and caricatures for English and American journals, as well as designing sets and costumes for the theatre. He worked with Sir Thomas Beecham and W. B. Yeats, who dedicated his poem 'The Winding Stair' to him in 1933. He also designed postage stamps for the Royal Mail, and banknotes for the Free French government-in-exile during the Second World War. He died in London in 1953.

Charles Laborde (1886–1941) was already selling his drawings to French satirical journals at the age of fifteen. His caricatures of bourgeois life appeared in *Le Rire* and *L'Assiette au Beurre*, and during his many visits to London he discovered a particular affinity with the English and their way of life; he changed his name to Chas, a diminutive of Charles. After the war he became interested in engraving and made images of Parisians going about their daily business in *Rues et Visages de Paris*, the first of a series. In 1927, after a stay of several months, he produced *Rues et Visages de Londres*, which was accompanied by texts from contemporary writers such as Valéry Larbaud, Pierre Mac Orlan and Paul Morand.

Jean-Emile Laboureur (1877–1943), an interpreter with the English troops during the First World War, published a series of ten humorous engravings entitled *Petites Images de la Guerre*. He illustrated the works of both French and English writers, from André Maurois to Laurence Sterne, and he painted a circus-themed fresco in Marcel Boulestin's London restaurant.

The undisputed prince of sculptors, Auguste Rodin (1840–1917) went to London for the first time in August 1881, invited by his friend Alphonse Legros, and returned many times after that. In 1904 he became president of the London International Society of Sculptors, Painters and Engravers. In the same year his *Thinker* was exhibited in London and in 1907 he was awarded an honorary degree from Oxford. An insatiable womaniser, he had a liaison with Gwen John, a painter in Paris and sister of the painter Augustus John. She was the model for his *La Muse Whistler* (a monument to Whistler). Rodin returned to London in 1914 to install his *Burghers of Calais*, bought by the English, and to inaugurate an exhibition of contemporary French art at Grosvenor House which included nineteen of his works. Most of them were parts of his great project *The Gates of Hell*, destined for the Musée des Arts Décoratifs in Paris, which was never completed. When war was declared, he took refuge in London with his wife Rose; the couple lodged with Mrs Emily Grigsby at 80 Brook Street. His sculptures were stored at the Victoria & Albert Museum until the end of the war, but at Mrs Grigsby's suggestion Rodin decided to make a gift of eighteen out of the nineteen sculptures to the British nation to thank it for having fought alongside France.

Sarah Bernhardt (1844–1923) went to London for the first time in the summer of 1879 with the Comédie Française. Her performance was a staggering success and, for that first season, she rented a house at 77 Chester Street where she filled the garden with exotic animals – a baby leopard bought in Liverpool, three dogs, a monkey and a parrot. She also painted and sculpted and held an exhibition in a Piccadilly gallery which was visited by twelve hundred people, including the Prime Minister, Gladstone; almost all the works were sold. Back in London the following year, she acted in *Frou Frou* which, along with *La Dame aux Camélias*, became one of her most celebrated roles. In London, in April 1882, she married Jacques Damala, a mediocre actor of Greek origins. The marriage was celebrated at St Andrew's church in Soho and was attended by the Prince of Wales, who was rumoured to have been her lover.

All through her long career in the theatre, Sarah Bernhardt was adulated in London and it became one of her favourite cities. In 1892 Oscar Wilde wrote *Salome* for her, which was then banned by the censors for 'immorality'. She resided mainly at the Savoy, where a suite was kept for her, but she also stayed at the Carlton, where Escoffier created 'Fraises à la Sarah Bernhardt' and 'Le consommé favori de Sarah Bernhardt'. She only performed in French, but the public were none the less entranced by her charm and forceful personality. She continued to perform as Hamlet and Edmond Rostand's Aiglon until she was seventy-seven, even after her leg was amputated in 1915. Her last visit to London was in 1921, and after her death two years later a Requiem Mass was celebrated for her at Westminster Cathedral.

Explaining England to the French:
Bourget, Morand, Maurois and others

Writers who attempted to explain England to the French often found it hard to escape from the clichéd Victorian images of their youth: the notion of the gentleman, the institutions, the monarchy, Eton, Oxford and Cambridge, the English countryside, racing, cricket and regattas. Between the wars, French writers seemed to be constantly in search of this traditional England, perhaps seeking a reassuring familiarity after the upheavals of war.

Paul Bourget (1852–1936), a rigorous observer of Victorian life, travelled a great deal around England. His carefully analysed impressions in *Études et Portraits* (1888) were regarded as authoritative in France for a long time. After the First World War, they provided material for several novels, such as *L'Écuyère* (1921) and *Laurence Albani* (1934). Jacques-Emile Blanche, too, was a respected chronicler: he published his *Tableaux d'Angleterre* in 1931 and the autobiographical sketches *La pêche aux souvenirs* and *Portraits of a Lifetime*. He followed developments in literature and the arts, took an interest in the Bloomsbury Group and introduced Virginia Woolf to the French.

Pierre Bourillon, who took the pen name Pierre Hamp (1876–1962), was an apprentice under Escoffier at the Savoy. In *Mes Métiers* he describes life in the kitchens of a great London hotel. This menial work made him conscious of social inequalities and he devoted the rest of his life to defending the working classes. Unlike most of his compatriots, he set out to live like an Englishman: he learned the language, dressed like the English, and lodged with a poor family near Waterloo Bridge. His London experiences gave him a unique insight into English society, which he described, often ironically, in several works.

Paul Morand (1888–1976) became cultural attaché at the French embassy in 1913. A devoted anglophile, he returned every year. In 1933 he published *Londres*, and thirty years later *Londres revisité*, an exhaustive guide covering all aspects of the metropolis. For his part, Pierre Mac Orlan (1882–1970), author of *Quai des Brumes* (1927), was fascinated by the slums of the East End and the

River Thames. His intensely observed impressions portray a strange and sinister city, dark and mysterious as evoked in his song *La fille de Londres*, which was famous in its time. He published several reportages, such as *Images sur la Tamise* (1925), and *Rues et Visages de Londres*, illustrated by Chas Laborde (1928), which he continued with *Villes, Mémoires* (1929).

The poet, novelist and historian Hilaire Belloc (1870–1953), born in France, became a British citizen in 1902. However, he was just as interested in his country of birth as in his new one, and his works include histories (*History of England* and *The French Revolution*), biographies (*Cromwell, Charles II, Danton, Marie-Antoinette, Napoleon*) as well as books for children (*The Bad Child's Book of Beasts*), poetry, essays and fiction.

Louis Cazamian (1877–1965) was a professor of literature and English civilisation, and wrote many books on English literature, culture and humour, particularly that of Shakespeare. His *Histoire de la littérature anglaise*, written with Emile Legouis, was translated into English in 1926 and became a reference for several generations of English students.

Valéry Larbaud (1881–1957), author of *Fermina Marquez*, was a novelist and essayist whose fortune – he was one of the heirs to the Saint-Yorre mineral water business – allowed him to travel throughout Europe and devote his life to literature. He was a polyglot and extremely cultivated. He arrived in London for the first time in 1902, thereafter returning regularly and finally settling in Cheyne Walk in Chelsea, an area he described in his short novel *Beauté, mon beau souci*. He was welcomed into English Catholic literary circles and introduced the French to English literature with his translations of Coleridge, Conrad, Thomas Hardy, Samuel Butler and James Joyce, and his critiques in the *Revue de Paris*. A dissatisfied, spoilt young man, he acquired maturity through his experiences in England and developed his writing talents there. In *Le Journal intime d'A. O. Barnabooth* he evoked his London memories, and his conclusions about the country in *Le Coeur de l'Angleterre*.

André Maurois (1885–1967) was deeply attached to British

culture and acted throughout his life as an intermediary between the two countries, thanks to his many English friends. He worked as an interpreter with the British army in the First World War, and entertained himself by writing humorous vignettes about the various eccentric characters he came across. His first novel *Les Silences du colonel Bramble* was published in 1918; his friendly comments brought him success and encouraged him to write a sequel in 1922, *Les Discours du docteur O'Grady*. After the war he decided to devote himself to writing and he developed a new type of biography with *Ariel, or the Life of Shelley* (1924),[76] *Disraeli* (1927), *Byron* (1930) and *Le roi Edouard VII et son Temps* (1933). He also produced collections of essays such as *Les Anglais* (1926) and *Conseils à un jeune Français partant pour l'Angleterre* (1927), as well as book reviews for literary journals. In 1934 he moved to Pembroke Lodge in Richmond Park in order to work on his history of England, a magisterial work demonstrating his deep knowledge of British civilisation, which was published in 1937. He was awarded an honorary degree by the University of Oxford during this stay. He was sent again to London in 1940 to report on the dreadful plight of France and to encourage the British in their preparations for war; he then travelled to the United States to pursue the same campaign.

French gastronomy – always

Less well-known was Marcel Boulestin (1878–1943), theatre and music critic for a Parisian magazine who had many artist and writer friends, including Colette. He had been attracted to England since his youth and decided, after several visits, to settle in London around 1907. His humorous *Lettres de Londres* written for several different journals were gathered in one volume, *Tableaux de Londres,* in 1912. He worked as an interpreter in the British army during the war, returned to London in the 1920s and began to write books on French cookery. He then moved from theory to practice and opened the Restaurant Français in 1925, on the corner of Panton Street and Leicester Square, which was renamed Le Boulestin when it moved two years later to a basement at the corner of Southampton Street and Henrietta Street in Covent Garden. He decorated it in the Art Deco style, with murals by Marie Laurencin and Jean-Emile Laboureur on a circus theme, and textiles by Raoul Dufy. The French cuisine and general ambience ensured its immediate success. Boulestin continued to write books of French recipes for English cooks, and by the end of his career could boast of having sold more than 70,000 copies. He gave cookery lessons in London and the provinces, notably at Fortnum & Mason, and was the first to give cookery demonstrations on the small screen, broadcast live on the BBC – his *Cook's Night Out* was extremely popular. He died in 1943, but his restaurant continued until 1994.

There were other representatives of French gastronomy, some of them unusual such as L'Escargot, opened in Soho in 1927 by George Gaudin, who reared snails in the basement and was the first to dare to put them on the menu. The restaurant still exists, despite many changes of ownership and refurbishments, and has always been popular with celebrities from the world of the arts such as Laurence Olivier, Noël Coward, Ella Fitzgerald and Francis Bacon.

La Maison Prunier, a branch of the Paris Maison Prunier, famous for its caviar, opened at 72 St James's Street in 1934. At its inauguration a specially prepared caviar, 'Prunier Saint-James', was presented to the London branch by the mother house. Considered one of the best fish restaurants in London until its closure in 1976, Prunier re-opened in 2004 a little further up St James's Street.

In a very different category, Mon Plaisir, opened in 1943 by David and Jean Viala, offered French menus at accessible prices in a typical French atmosphere, with a map of the Parisian metro and show-business posters on the walls. At the end of the 1960s, the maitre d'hôtel Alain Lhermitte bought the restaurant, which still retains its unique charm.

Several other now prosperous establishments had modest origins in the early years of the twentieth century: Richoux in

Baker Street opened in 1909, Péchon's Patisserie Française in Kensington in 1925, and Madame Valerie's Patisserie Valerie in Soho in 1926.

It was hard to envisage the café-bar in England, where until recently the licensing laws controlled the pubs. But there was one exception, the French House. Victor Berlemont (Belgian, not French!), bought a pub in the heart of Soho in 1914 and opened a French café with pub opening hours. He was the first foreigner to be allowed to manage licensed premises in England. His thick moustache and convivial temperament attracted French customers as well as all the local intellectuals and artists, who felt as though they had crossed the Channel when they consumed their Pastis and Gauloises. The walls were covered with photographs of French music-hall artistes and sportsmen, such as Maurice Cheva-lier, Edith Piaf and the boxer Georges Carpentier. The last-named was a friend of Victor, who was a passionate boxing fan and had installed a boxing ring in the basement.

During the Second World War the many French soldiers in London made the café even more popular and it became Le Berlemont, surviving the destruction of its facade by a bomb. Victor's son Gaston was an interpreter for the RAF from 1940 until 1946 and took up the management of the pub on his return. After the war, an English clientele began to enjoy the French atmosphere of the establishment and artists, writers, journalists and television and film personalities would congregate there, including Francis Bacon, Lucian Freud and Dylan Thomas. The pub is now under new ownership,: again named The French House, it remains an integral part of the history of Soho.

Places to visit

POST-IMPRESSIONISTS

Courtauld Institute and National Gallery. Having built up the largest private collection in England of Impressionists and Post-Impressionists, Samuel Courtauld, an industrialist of Huguenot descent, gave the greater part of it to London University, which created the Courtauld Gallery to display it. He also established the Courtauld Fund for the purchase of Impressionist and Post-Impressionist paintings. His generosity enabled the National Gallery to acquire paintings of this period, thereby filling a gap in its collection of French art.

Tate Britain. Numerous French and English Post-Impressionists. Many great French painters represented: Cézanne, Seurat, Van Gogh, Gauguin. Also paintings by the Camden Town Group and the Bloomsbury Group.

British Museum. Post-Impressionist drawings and engravings.

ART NOUVEAU AND ART DECO

Michelin House
81 Fulham Road SW3
A listed building built by the Michelin tyre company in 1909. Designed by employee François Espinasse, the style is both Art Nouveau and Art Deco before its time. An example of the advertising of the time, the decoration is an imaginative glorification of Michelin tyres. The mascot, Bibendum, appears in various guises in the windows and the floor mosaics. On both the exterior and the interior, 32 decorative ceramic plaques illustrate the history of Michelin tyres used for horse-drawn carriages, bicycles, motorbikes and racing cars. One of them shows Edward VII, a keen motorist, and another shows a panel with the slogan: 'The Michelin tyre drinks up obstacles.' These panels were made by the French painter Édouard Montaut, who was devoted to the automobile. **Institut Français**. Opened in 1939, the Art Deco building was designed by French archi-tect Patrice Bonnet. On the facade ceramic plaques dedicated to Minerva, goddess of intelligence. Above, four medallions: the owl symbolising wisdom, the snake knowledge, the cock courage, and the olive branch peace. The interior of the building is sober; copy of Rodin's *Age of Bronze* and tapestry by Sonia Delaunay on staircase.

Cartier
175–77 New Bond Street W1
Official jeweller to the royal family thanks to the patronage of Edward VII, Jacques Cartier opened a shop in London in 1902, first at 4 Burlington Street. Adapting his creations to English tastes, Cartier's Art Deco Egyptian-themed creations were extremely popular. Cartier in London celebrated its centenary in 2002.

Victoria & Albert Museum, British Museum. Art Nouveau and Art Deco objects by French artists such as Lalique, Ruhlmann, Follot, Daum, Brandt and many others.

Museum of London. In the Art Deco section, interior of Selfridge's lift by French ironworker Edgar Brandt on the theme of Alsatian cranes.

Marc Henri and Gaston Laverdet
Many examples of their interior decorative work.

- **Theatres still open**

  The Piccadilly
  16 Denman Street W1

  The Prince Edward
  Old Compton Street W1
  Josephine Baker made her London debut here in 1933 with her banana dance.

  The Whitehall
  Whitehall SW1
  Now listed and restored, it has become the Trafalgar Studios.

  The Duchess
  Catherine Street W1

- **Cinemas**
Around 1930 the Astoria chain opened four luxurious cinemas, some of which are now listed buildings.

The Brixton
211 Stockwell Road SW9
Several times restored, now hosts pop concerts and is called the Carling Academy Brixton.

The Streatham
47–49 High Road SW16
The only one still a cinema; it has lost its Egyptian theme after a poor restoration.

The Finsbury Park
232–36 Seven Sisters Road N4
Transformed into a rock venue for young singers who eventually became the Beatles, Pink Floyd, Jimmy Hendricks, Eric Clapton . . . It is now a religious centre.

The Old Kent Road
Old Kent Road SE1
Inaugurated with a Maurice Chevalier film; demolished in 1984.

ARTISTS

Places and museums where one can see the works of French artists.

Jacques-Émile Blanche. National Portrait Gallery, Tate Britain, Garrick Club.

André Derain. Tate Britain, Courtauld Gallery

Raoul Dufy. Tate Britain, Courtauld Gallery, Royal Collection, Victoria & Albert Museum

Edmond Dulac, Chas Laborde and J. E. Laboureur
British Library
90 Euston Road, St Pancras NW1

Auguste Rodin

- **Victoria Tower Gardens**
Westminster SW1
In the gardens outside Parliament is a copy of *The Burghers of Calais*, the position of which was subject to much argument.

Rodin was displeased by the position given to the work in Calais in 1895. In 1913, he came to London to inspect several possible sites and to discuss the height of the plinth on which a translation of Froissart's account of the event would be engraved. This garden was finally chosen, to the satisfaction of the artist, and the sculpture was unveiled with little ceremony in 1915.

- **Victoria & Albert Museum**. Eighteen sculptures given by Rodin to England in gratitude for its alliance with France in the First World War. In the small sculpture gallery, four other works, including a portrait of Camille Claudel, his muse and mistress.

- **Tate Britain**. Seven works by Rodin, the best-known being *The Kiss*.

- **National Portrait Gallery**. Bronze bust of William Ernest Henley (1884–86).

- **Courtauld Gallery**. Several works and documents about the artist.

- **French Institute**. Plaster copy of *The Age of Bronze* in the hall.

Sarah Bernhardt
Most of the many theatres in which she performed are still in use.

- **Adelphi Theatre**
411–12 Strand WC2

- **Her Majesty's Theatre**
57 Haymarket SW1

- **Coliseum**
St Martin's Lane WC2
The biggest theatre in London at the time.

- **Garrick Club**
5 Garrick Street WC2
Several portraits of Sarah Bernhardt.

Hilaire Belloc
Blue Plaque
104 Cheyne Walk SW10
The writer lived here from 1900 to 1905.

FRENCH RESTAURANTS

The following restaurants, all still in business, opened at the beginning of the twentieth century.

L'Escargot
48 Greek Street, Soho W1

Caviar House & Prunier
161 Piccadilly W1

Mon Plaisir
Monmouth Street WC2

Richoux
41a South Audley Street, Mayfair W1
172 Piccadilly W1
86 Brompton Road, Knightsbridge SW3
3 Circus Road, St John's Wood NW8

After opening their patisserie, the Richouxs decided to serve their customers at any time of the day. So they opened a restaurant/tea-room with flexible opening hours. Behind the trademark red facade is good-quality cooking and service adapted to customers' timetables.

Patisserie Valerie
Many branches throughout London.

The French House
49 Dean Street, Soho W1
First French bar in London, founded by Victor Berlemont.

13

LONDON, CAPITAL
OF FREE FRANCE
THE FRENCH COMMUNITY
AND THE BLITZ

*'Perfidious Albion? That is easy to say; but one can rely on
England's cooperation once it has been given'*[77]

LOUIS CAZAMIAN

The advent of the worst danger that had ever befallen France
and England throughout their long history – that of enslave-
ment by a brutal dictator – proved conclusively, in the course of
the Second World War, the solidity and sincerity of an *entente* that
was not simply *cordial*, but henceforth vital. During the years
leading up to the conflict, the two countries drew together in the
face of the Nazi threat and King George VI and Queen Elizabeth,
only recently crowned, made their first foreign visit to Paris in July
1938. They were received by President Albert Lebrun who in turn
came to London the following spring. Germany invaded Poland
on 1 September 1939 and France and England declared war two
days later. There followed the nine-month 'phoney war' during
which the two sides watched each other without any significant
military activity. On 28 March 1940, England and France signed
an agreement not to negotiate any separate armistice with
Germany.

It's war!

This interlude came to an end on 10 May 1940 with the German invasion of Holland, Belgium, Luxembourg and France. The French army was quickly overwhelmed and the allied troops trapped on the beaches of Dunkirk. Great Britain requisitioned all available ships to bring them back to England during Operation Dynamo. Over nine days (26 May–4 June), 338,000 soldiers were evacuated, of whom 110,000 were French.

On 14 June, with the Germans entering Paris, the Queen addressed the women of France on the radio, in French, with a speech written with the help of André Maurois. She had been moved by her visit to the French wounded evacuees from Dunkirk, who had replied to her questions with 'Ça va,' and she spoke of better times ahead: 'It is this hope, which I owe to the courage of your wounded soldiers, that I would like to bring to you this evening.' The days that followed brought their share of disillusion and drama. The advance of the German army was so rapid that people were horrified by the unthinkable defeat. Demoralised, they turned to Marshal Pétain, putting their trust in the victor of Verdun. Paul Reynaud's government fled Paris in a chaotic exodus, and installed itself at Bordeaux. England sent the francophile Major-General Spears to join it and follow the developing situation, while Reynaud sent to Churchill an officer recently promoted to the rank of general, Charles de Gaulle. In mid-June de Gaulle made several journeys to London over a few days. He tried to obtain the help of the British government in establishing a French government in North Africa, to enable the French to continue the fight there. In their conversations, de Gaulle and Churchill envisaged a Franco-British fusion for the duration of the war: a common government, parliament, joint nationality and shared resources. Although they had no illusions about the difficulties of putting such a scheme into practice, they felt that it would have a powerful psychological effect on Germany. While de Gaulle was travelling back to Bordeaux with the official text for such an agreement, on 16 June Reynaud put the idea before his council of ministers, and they turned it down. The majority of them were deeply suspicious of British intentions.

Reynaud, in despair, asked the British government to agree to the separate armistice forbidden by the March agreement. Britain, fearing that the Germans would seize the French fleet, demanded that it should seek refuge in British ports. When the council refused this, Reynaud resigned. Marshal Pétain, who had become president of the council, then signed an armistice on 22 June, without consulting Britain.

De Gaulle learned of Reynaud's resignation on his arrival in Bordeaux on 16 June. Determined to pursue the struggle, he decided to return to England, with his aide-de-camp Geoffroy de Courcel and General Spears. He left with only 100,000 francs given to him from secret funds by Reynaud before his departure.

The Appeal of 18 June and the recruitment of volunteers

On his return to London on 17 June, General de Gaulle found himself unknown and almost completely isolated. His first broadcast on 18 June was a historic event, but was heard by very few people. The night before, Churchill had agreed to let him use the BBC. At 6 p.m. de Gaulle, alone in front of the microphone, spoke: 'I, General de Gaulle, now in London, invite French officers and soldiers on British soil, now or in the future, with or without their arms, I invite engineers and armament workers on British soil, now or in the future, to make contact with me [. . .] Whatever happens, the flame of resistance must not and shall not be extinguished.'[78]

In the confusion of the moment no recording was made of this first message, which was barely mentioned in *The Times* and the *Daily Express* the following morning. In France, few heard the broadcast because of power interruptions and because most people were listening to Radio-France which was giving news of the government in Bordeaux. The latter announced that General de Gaulle, being no longer a member of the government, had no authority whatsoever. De Gaulle made more announcements on

19 and 22 June; on 23rd he was stripped of his rank and condemned by a court martial to four years in prison. On 2 August
he was condemned to death *in absentia* for desertion, and on
8 December stripped of his French nationality.

On his arrival in London, de Gaulle had moved into a small
apartment at 7–8 Seymour Grove, near Hyde Park, and this was
where the volunteers who had heard his first BBC messages came
the very next day. His wife and children joined him on 20 June.
On 23 June, the British government put some space at his disposal
at St Stephen House on Victoria Embankment, where Sir Edward
Spears, now the British delegate to the Free French, had his office.
A month later they moved into permanent quarters at 4 Carlton
Gardens, near St James's Park.

In that summer of 1940, Churchill urged de Gaulle to make
himself better known and suggested he employ a public relations
consultant, Richard Temple. The British press then reported what
he told them about the leader of the Free French, presenting him
as a friend of Great Britain, an expert in armoured transport and
entirely trustworthy. De Gaulle posed for photographs designed
to present him in a more approachable light; Madame de Gaulle
appeared in some of these, but he refused to allow his children to
be shown. This two-month campaign achieved the desired result,
and de Gaulle became a well-known political figure in England.
But he still needed to convince the French in England to join
him, and in August 1940 he had posters put up on London walls
bearing the text of his 19 June broadcast, adding the words, which
have now entered history: 'France has lost a battle! But France has
not lost the war!' The text was in French and not dated, with an
English translation framed beneath it; slightly retouched, this text
was passed off as that of the 18 June appeal. Thus are legends born!

After the first wave, volunteers continued to arrive throughout
the war. But the more important functionaries and intellectuals of
the French community in London kept their distance: Paul
Morand, head of the economic mission at the embassy, returned
to Paris; Jean Monnet, president of the Franco-British coordina-
tion committee, took refuge in New York. André Maurois, who

had come to London to tell the British about the hopeless situation in France, also decided to go to America. Churchill was disappointed at this and said: 'We thought he was a friend; but he was merely a client.'[79] Some residents did, however, join the rebel general: Élisabeth de Miribel, great-granddaughter of Mac-Mahon, a friend of Geoffroy de Courcel and part of the embassy staff, volunteered as a typist; with two fingers she typed the appeal, becoming de Gaulle's personal assistant from the start. With the agreement of Pierre Cartier, M. Bellenger, director of the London branch of Cartier, placed his house, his office and his Rolls-Royce at the general's disposal during those first weeks.

The first Free French volunteers were often students and intellectuals from the north of France and Brittany, who arrived in London in often dramatic conditions. The lighthouse keeper of the Ile de Sein in Britanny heard the 18 June appeal and the whole island, led by its priest – 124 able-bodied men, the youngest only fourteen – rallied to de Gaulle. Every day de Gaulle received more offers of service. But those who arrived in London to join his cause, often at great personal risk, could be discouraged by his difficult personality. All volunteers were asked to sign an act of personal loyalty to de Gaulle, and some refused to do so. On the whole they were young and inexperienced, and few strong characters emerged. Those with any skill were immediately given important responsibilities. The journalist Maurice Schumann became the spokesman for Free France and the law professor René Cassin dealt with legal services. Newly-wed doctors André and Louise-Marie Lemanissier were posted to the Free French forces' infirmary in Gordon Street, near Euston Station. Charles Robet, alias Kerguelen, became the doctor at the headquarters in Carlton Gardens.

After the Germans moved into the Occupied Zone in 1943, more refugees arrived: parliamentarians such as Pierre Mendès-France, Vincent Auriol and Jean Pierre-Bloch, as well as intellectuals such as the writers Joseph Kessel and his nephew Maurice Druon, who arrived after a dramatic journey through Spain. Kessel wanted to fight but de Gaulle wanted him to use his pen

for the struggle: his articles for the paper *France* on the situation
in his country were taken up by the British press. He later published a shattering novel about his experiences in the Resistance,
L'Armée des Ombres, which was made into an equally moving film.
Among the later arrivals was the priest René de Naurois who
became chaplain to the Free French forces, and accompanied the
French commando Philippe Kieffer in the Normandy landings. A
female professor of philosophy drawn to mysticism, Simone Weil,
tried to persuade de Gaulle to train nurses to serve at the battle-
front. Weakened by the fast she had embarked upon in order to
share the sufferings of the French, she died in a sanatorium in
Ashford.

The first soldiers of the Free French Forces (FFL) were recruited from the ranks of French soldiers and sailors already in
Britain, and those who had escaped imprisonment in France and
had found their way to England by any means possible in order to
continue the fight. It is difficult to say precisely how many there
were; a little less than a quarter of the French expeditionary force
returning from Norway after its participation in the Narvik naval
operation joined up. They included Colonel André Dewavrin
who, under the pseudonym Colonel Passy, commanded the Free
French secret service. Of the French soldiers evacuated from
Dunkirk, estimated at between 100,000 and 120,000, only 2,000
went to London, the majority having been repatriated in May and
June 1940. Of the 2,700 wounded soldiers and officers convalesc-
ing in London, about 200 joined the Free French. A thousand
wounded were cared for in English hospitals; convalescents were
sent to White City in West London where the Franco–British
exhibition had been held in 1908. The French Medical Centre was
set up in 1940 at 14 Grosvenor Gardens for the Dunkirk evacuees.

About 130 French military and merchant ships took refuge in
British ports, mainly Portsmouth and Plymouth. A thousand officers and sailors from the merchant navy were put up at Crystal
Palace; it was a target for bombers, and they were later transferred
to safer quarters. The 6,500 officers and sailors from the navy were
sent to camps scattered around the country. About 200 French

airmen, of whom 150 were trainees, came to England at the beginning of July 1940. They were at first incorporated into the RAF, which was very short of pilots. After a short training period, they took part in the Battle of Britain. Later, exclusively French squadrons were formed and, by 1943, the Free French Air Force (FAFL) numbered 3,000 men. French soldiers in the camps were offered a choice: either be repatriated, incorporated into British army units, do war work in England, or join the Free French forces. On the whole, the British were not enthusiastic about the French joining their ranks; they thought there would be difficulties with integration, and they suspected them of lack of discipline.

Recruitment to the Free French forces was painfully slow, and at the end of June 1940 General de Gaulle had to go in person to the camps at Aintree, Haydock, Trenham Park and Arrowe Park to persuade men to join him. Those who did assembled at Olympia Exhibition Centre in west London; they slept on straw mattresses and, after medical checks and registration, were sent to camps at Camberley and Aldershot. De Gaulle put Admiral Muselier, who had joined him on 30 June 1940, in command of the Free French Naval Forces (FNFL) and, provisionally, of the Free French Air Force (FAFL) as well.

Some women responded immediately to the General's appeal. Simone Mathieu, 1938 and 1939 French tennis champion, was serving in the Women's Voluntary Service. She joined the Free French at once, and de Gaulle asked her to set up a women's corps on the British model. She was extremely energetic and recruited a hundred volunteers through classified advertisements in the papers. The first contingent was formed in November 1940. They were sent to Bournemouth for a three-week training session with the ATS, the women auxiliaries to the British army; they were given British uniforms on to which they sewed French insignia. The original name, Corps Féminin de la France Libre, gave rise to ribald comments, so their name was changed to Volontaires Féminines de la France Libre (VF). In 1941, after their barracks at 20 (now 42) Hill Street in Mayfair were destroyed by a bomb, they were transferred to Moncorvo House, near the Royal Albert Hall.

Simone Mathieu was soon replaced by Hélène Terré. She had come on a mission for the Red Cross in September 1941; wrongly suspected of espionage on her arrival, she was imprisoned in HMP Holloway. Freed a few weeks later, she took over the direction of the women volunteers, and ran them efficiently until the end of the war. There were about two hundred VFs, from all walks of society, aged between seventeen and fifty. After training they were sent to London to work for the three forces as secretaries, nurses, drivers or mechanics. After the war, their unit formed the basis of the Auxiliaires Féminines de l'Armée de Terre (AFAT). Like their male counterparts, they performed daily drills in Hyde Park or in the neighbouring streets. The female volunteers had their own song to the tune of the 'Gars de la Marine':

> *'We're the Free French women*
> *When we're in our khaki clothes*
> *We don't make any fuss.*
> *Everywhere in beautiful England*
> *We're received with open arms, we volunteers . . .*[80]

In June 1940, with the Germans advancing in the Finistère, some teenagers, mostly Bretons, were among those fleeing. They took advantage of the surrounding panic to head for England, determined to fight. They took enormous risks, some stowing away, others passing through Spain and spending months in Franco's prisons before reaching London. Among these brave volunteers, five boys of between fourteen and eighteen reached the English coast after a terrifying thirty-hour crossing on two canoes. In recognition of their exploit they were presented to de Gaulle and received by Mr and Mrs Churchill. When about 150 young men had regrouped at the Olympia recruitment centre, de Gaulle established a military school for Free French cadets. There they finished their studies and underwent military training to become officers. In the years that followed other young men came from France and the colonies, the school expanded and moved twice before settling permanently at Ribbesford Manor, near Bewdley in Worcestershire. Five successive promotions of cadets took part in all the battles fought by the Free French. Around a quarter of them were killed, among them Jérôme Saint-Denis, son of Michel Saint-Denis, alias Duchesne, director of the BBC programme *The French speak to the French*.

Between 3 and 6 July 1940 the French fleet, anchored at the Algerian naval base of Mers-el-Kebir, refused to sail to a British port. Their ships were then nearly all sunk on the orders of Churchill, to prevent their capture by the Germans. At the same time, French ships moored in English ports were occupied and their crews interned. The French were deeply offended and recruitment of volunteers slowed down, but de Gaulle was very painfully forced to support his ally. He launched new appeals for volunteers and recruitment began again, slowly. On 14 July he reviewed a parade of 3,000 Free French volunteers marching from Whitehall to the statue of Marshal Foch by Victoria Station. By the end of July the FFL numbered 7,000 men – very few, considering the number of French then living in Great Britain.

All volunteers were warned that they would be interrogated as soon as they landed in England. There was great anxiety that spies in the pay of the Germans would infiltrate the volunteers and refugees. 'Triage camps' were set up at the ports and in London, the main one for the French being at Olympia, where new arrivals were questioned by a committee of three.

The British government then opened its own interrogation centre, run by the Intelligence Service. From January 1941 until June 1945, rigorous interrogations were carried out at the Royal Victoria Patriotic School or London Reception Centre (RPC). The men were lodged in the Patriotic School, an imposing neo-Gothic building in Trinity Road in Wandsworth, and the women in a neighbouring school at 101 Nightingale Lane. The centre received refugees of all nationalities, many of them French, such as the two writers Joseph Kessel and his nephew Maurice Druon. The interrogations were polite but very severe and full of traps; they lasted for eight to ten hours a day, over a period of several days. A new arrival would be asked, for example, exactly where his

French school was, to give the names of his teachers, to describe
means of transport and other details. The answers would be carefully checked and analysed. All the new arrivals' possessions would
be minutely checked: bus tickets, cigarettes, makes of watch – all
could be clues. There were several cells in the basements and when
an enemy agent was uncovered he was transferred to Wandsworth
Prison across the road and hanged. Some were discovered too late.
One 'Frenchman' with too-perfect French, after a second interrogation by French intelligence, was found hanged – with a swastika
tattooed on his arm. Another was discovered to be a traitor after
he had been sent on a mission to France; it was arranged that his
parachute would fail to open. Some French people were imprisoned in ordinary prisons, often after false denunciations: this happened to Admiral Muselier who was sent to Pentonville, as well as
to Hélène Terré.

The Free French organisation
Churchill allowed de Gaulle to make the 18 June appeal against
the wishes of his ministers. Despite reservations about his guest's
surly manner, he continued unfailingly to support him. Only five
days after the armistice was signed by Pétain, he formally recognised him as the leader of the Free French. This recognition was
ratified by the signature of the statutes of Free France, drawn up
by René Cassin. Strengthened by this support, de Gaulle launched
a manifesto from Brazzaville on 27 October 1940, creating a
council for the defence of the empire and a provisional government which included the colonies. Free France became France
Combattante (Fighting France) in 1942, with assurance from Great
Britain of vital material and financial support.

When the building at Carlton Gardens became too small, its
various services were spread around London: the 'ministry' of the
interior moved to 17–19 Hill Street, while the secret services
(BCRA) were in Duke Street, near Oxford Street. The FAFL first
occupied the premises of the French Institute and Lycée, and then
moved to Stafford Mansions, near Buckingham Palace. The land
army was installed in Dolphin Square, by the Thames in Pimlico.

The Free French even created their own tribunals, with the agreement of Anthony Eden, the very francophile British foreign minister. On the financial side, a central fund for Free France was set up, with the help of the Bank of England, to receive loans from the British government as well as donations, mainly from the French colonies. It issued its own currency, with a rate of exchange against the pound that was fixed to the value of the pre-armistice franc. This currency could be used in those African countries which had rallied to the Free French cause.

Various symbols were adopted, both as a sign of gratitude and for their propaganda value. The cross of Lorraine, emblem given to the FNFL by Admiral Muselier, himself from Lorraine, became the official symbol of Free France in June 1941. Others, inspired by the French illustrator Edmund Dulac, now a British citizen, were the phoenix, symbolising national resurrection, and Marianne, who represented the Republic and liberty; they were printed on the stamps and banknotes of Free France. The motto of the Légion d'Honneur, 'Honneur et Patrie', became that of the Free French when Maurice Schumann used it as the title for his radio programme. French broadcasts on the BBC were designed to shake the occupied French out of their apathy and to persuade them to express themselves through symbolic gestures. One of the most evocative images of the Second World War is that of Churchill raising his hand in a V sign for victory. The originator of this sign was the director of Belgian radio in London who, with the agreement of the BBC, persuaded all the allies to use it. Transcribed into morse, three short notes and a long one, this 'popopopom', reminiscent of the first notes of Beethoven's Fifth Symphony, became the opening theme of the transmission of *The French speak to the French*. The V campaign spread like wildfire. Collective demonstrations of patriotism by the French under occupation were orchestrated from London with the help of the BBC: wearing national colours on 14 July, not going outside at a certain time on 1 January, or keeping silence, always at a particular time, on 11 May, feast day of St Joan of Arc.

To reward the most deserving among the Free French, de Gaulle created the order of the Liberation in 1941, which would be conferred on 1,038 people, five communes and eighteen combat units. The insignia of the order was the cross of Lorraine and the motto *Patriam servando victoriam tulit*, 'By serving his country he has been victorious.' The medal of the Resistance, created in 1943, bears the motto *Patria non immemor*, 'The homeland does not forget.' The medals and insignia were made by the Cartier shop in London.

In 1943 André Gillois, charged by the BBC to direct a new programme specifically aimed at the Resistance, was looking for a new theme tune. For their part, Resistance leaders needed a song to unite the different networks all over France. The two writers Joseph Kessel and Maurice Druon found a song composed by a Slav singer which, with new words, became the *Chant des Partisans*. The harsh words were sung over and over again by the maquisards, prisoners and fighters:

> *'Friend, do you hear the dark flight of crows over our lands*
> *Friend, do you hear the cries of a country in chains*
> *[…] Sing comrades, in the night, freedom will hear us'*[81]

André Gillois used its first notes as the signature tune of his broadcast: it become the anthem of the Resistance.

The war in the airwaves and the press

After the signature of the Munich agreement in 1938, the BBC, to counteract the influence of German radio which was widely listened to in France, began to broadcast news bulletins in French, prepared by a team of French-speaking francophiles. In France at the beginning of the Occupation, the Germans set up a bureau of propaganda. Radio-Paris and Radio-Vichy, under their tight control, attacked all the obvious targets: the Jews, the Freemasons, the French in London, the English – all with the aim of suppressing any will to resist. On 14 July 1940, the BBC decided to include

in its 9.15 p.m. bulletin a broadcast prepared by a French team. The
first five minutes were reserved for General de Gaulle and directed
by his spokesman, Maurice Schumann, who named the broadcast
'Honneur et Patrie'. The next half-hour was provided by Jacques
Duchesne, who came from a theatrical background, backed by
seven colleagues with hardly any radio experience. According to
the recollections of one of them, they included the Protestant
Pierre Bourdan who 'feared nothing'; Jean Marin, a Catholic
Breton; Jacques Borel, or 'Brunius', the 'melancholy poet'; the 'dis-
organised' van Moppès, or 'Momo', a Jew of Dutch origin, who
'resembled Charlie Chaplin without the moustache'; the 'charming' Pierre Lefèvre, who was the youngest, Duchesne's pupil; and
finally Jean Oberlé, the draughtsman whose Parisian accent at the
microphone was the despair of his producer. Later they were
joined by Pierre Dac, a caustically eloquent singer; Frank Bauer, a
jazz-lover; the ex-diplomat Louis Roché, whose wife's cordon-
bleu talents delighted the team; the deadpan and energetic André
Gillois, as well as several 'speakers', one of whom was a woman,
Geneviève Brissot. Almost all worked under pseudonyms to protect their families in France.

They were all Resistants, but not all were Gaullists and *The
French speak to the French* was fiercely independent from 'Honneur
et Patrie'. Improvised at the beginning, it was such a success that
Radio-Paris responded with a similar programme. There followed
a war of the airwaves in which the London team countered
German propaganda with humour and satire, with sketches ridi-
culing the collaborators and inciting resistance. Their texts were
examined before being broadcast by a largely tolerant and obliging
BBC team. Duchesne received many letters from France thanking
and encouraging him, and decided to set aside a part of the programme each week to read out these letters. Between 1939 and
the end of 1944, the French broadcasts increased from half an hour
to six hours, and the English and French staff from four to 111. The
last broadcast took place on 22 November 1944.

Personal messages, often in code, were read out for families in
France, and from May 1941 the English and French secret services

began inserting odd phrases as messages to the French Resistance. The first one was the optimistic 'Lisette is well.' Others were humorous or eccentric: 'The hippopotamus is not a carnivore,' 'Melpomène is scented with hawthorn,' 'The devil is decorating his cave.'[82] These odd phrases were a source of anxiety to the Germans, who tried in vain to decrypt them. The signal to the Resistance that the greatest landing in history was about to take place was Verlaine's famous line, 'Les sanglots longs des violons de l'automne.'

Several French newspapers were started in London during the war but, like any foreign paper, they had to pass through the British censors. The French daily *France* came out as early as 20 August 1940, under the auspices of the Association of French in Great Britain, and with the blessing of the British government. Its offices were at 85 Fleet Street, and it benefited from the services of Reuters and the *Daily Telegraph*, which printed it. Its editor was Pierre Comert, the ex-press attaché. This four-page paper, with Socialist leanings, was very popular with the French community and with French-speaking English people. It continued to appear until the FFL were transferred to North Africa in 1943. The monthly *La France libre*, operating from premises at the French Institute, was appreciated for its high stylistic standards and perceptive analysis. Its title was misleading, as it was completely independent of de Gaulle. It was, above all, loyal to republican ideals. Its editor, André Labarthe, was helped by the contributions of eminent sociologist Raymond Aron. On the whole, the editors of these papers dreaded the influence of de Gaulle, who decided to start his own paper, to be edited by François Quilici. Founded in June 1942, the weekly *La Marseillaise* was eventually closed down by the British government because of its intransigeant positions and its over-critical attitude towards the American allies.

The secret services and the Resistance

General de Gaulle placed the organisation of the French secret service in the hands of Colonel Dewavrin. Limited to information only at the beginning, this 'second bureau' became a military and counter-espionage service, taking the name Bureau central de ren-seignements et d'actions (BCRA). For their safety, the agents chose pseudonyms from Paris metro stations: Saint-Jacques, Barbès, Corvisart, Bienvenue. Dewavrin became Colonel Passy, and his operation was installed first at Carlton Gardens, and then at the beginning of 1942 in an old building at 10 Duke Street, near Oxford Street, before expanding throughout London. Colonel Passy's second-in-command was naval officer Honoré d'Estienne d'Orves who, with agents such as Colonel Rémy and the Socialist Pierre Brossolette, played a crucial role in the organisation of the Resistance in France. The BCRA recruited over a thousand French agents: the first, Jacques Mansion, was dropped on the Cotentin coast on 20 July 1940. Amateurs at first, these agents later received proper training in several stages – sabotage, parachuting, survival and communication. On his return from a mission to France in 1941, Georges Bergé created a specialist survival training school at Inchmery House in Hampshire, with the help of the British Special Operations Executive (SOE).

Great Britain was desperately in need of information about the installations, plans and movements of the German army in France. Its Intelligence Service asked de Gaulle for help; he put them in touch with Colonel Passy, and thus began a long and sometimes rivalrous collaboration. The Intelligence Service found potential agents during their interrogations at the Patriotic School, and wanted to recruit them for themselves. In July 1940, Churchill created a new service, in parallel with the Intelligence Service, specialising in sabotage behind enemy lines – the SOE, funded by the Ministry of War. The French-speaking francophile Maurice Buckmaster was appointed to run its French section (F), based at 1 Dorset Square in Marylebone. It consisted of around 300 French agents, mostly recruited during interrogations at the Patriotic School or through BCRA. One of the most famous was Violette Szabo, whose mother was French.

This competition for recruits created tension between Colonel Passy's BCRA and F Section. A number of French candidates, through suspicion of or outright hostility to de Gaulle, preferred to join the British army or secret service, although the great majority remained within the French organisation. The radio messages, too, were a source of friction, since the French services needed the English transmitters, but the latter could then intercept their information.

Tension between de Gaulle and the Intelligence Service reached crisis point with the Muselier Affair. In January 1941, the admiral commanding the FNFL was arrested by the British, treated as a criminal and incarcerated in HMP Pentonville. He had been falsely accused of having betrayed the Free French and of working for Vichy, but was released once the conspiracy was exposed. Some English people, tired of de Gaulle's arrogant demands, tried to use the affair to discredit him. Soon after this, Admiral Muselier made a vain attempt to supplant the General as leader of the Free French, and was subsequently sidelined.

Despite the rivalries, BCRA, F Section and the Intelligence Service were obliged to cooperate, particularly with regard to the training of agents who, once on the ground, set aside their various allegiances for the sake of their common cause. At the beginning an agent's training consisted only of learning to use codes and to manage a parachute drop. However, after 1941 more training took place, after a rigorous selection process, in a series of courses in large houses outside London. They were kept secret at the time, but are now known about: Ringway, near Manchester; Beaulieu Castle in Hampshire, and Elford near Birmingham. These sessions were designed to test the recruits' physical and psychological endurance; they learned how to handle firearms, sabotage and survival techniques, and parachuting. A good number of them were eliminated, and the 'chosen' became specialised according to the type of mission they were to be given: sabotage of road and railway communications, radio operating, and so on. Ian Fleming, creator of James Bond, was one of the many instructors. Joël Le Tac, who underwent training, was surprised by the experience: 'There was a series of "Professor Nimbuses", all dressed as officers, who had come from the universities where they taught, and who would try out their inventions, with us or on us. I discovered a totally unexpected world of traps and practical jokes.'[83] When an agents was ready, he or she would be given a whole new identity and papers with fictitious family photographs. Some had to go to the dentist to have any English fillings removed, or even visit plastic surgeons. Their last appointment would be in the basement of the Natural History Museum, where they would be supplied with clothes suited to their new identity selected from a vast depot of clothing and accessories.

Before they left, agents would spend their last night isolated from their friends. Buckmaster made it a point of honour to visit them and give them a small gift. Then, after the short training period, the adventure would begin: a rendezvous under a full moon at a military airport, and receipt of the final piece of equipment – a cyanide capsule, to prevent betrayal in the face of torture.

In January 1942, Jean Moulin was entrusted by de Gaulle with the mission of coordinating all the different resistance movements in France. In May 1943 he created the Conseil National de la Résistance (CNR) which regrouped all the movements, parties and union organisations, thus ensuring de Gaulle's legitimacy for the allies, particularly the Americans. At the time of the Normandy landings, Eisenhower said that the Resistance had done as much for victory as six allied divisions, recognising the exceptional intelligence provided on the ground by Colonel Passy and his teams. The CNR became the cornerstone of the new French government after the Liberation.

Churchill and de Gaulle – from love at first sight to old married couple

As Maurice Druon wrote: 'The Churchill–de Gaulle couple, the strangest and yet most symbolic of the whole Second World War, began with a meeting, then love at first sight, then intoxicating courtship, a hasty marriage and stormy conjugal life, ending up as an old ménage inseparable in the face of History.'[84] The British statesman immediately recognised in the French officer his own courage and strength of character, and put his trust in him. He described what they had in common in his usual acerbic style: 'De

Gaulle, a great man? Pah! He is dominating, vain, egotistical, intransigeant, has a bad character . . . exactly like me!'[85] In June 1940 they agreed on the extraordinary idea of a Franco-British union, which was eventually abandoned. However, the General was fiercely determined to safeguard the independence of Free France. By nature touchy and unyielding, he became all the more so thanks to the weakness of his position. It made him wary in his attitude to his allies, for fear of being ruled by them. 'Of all the crosses that I bear, the cross of Lorraine is the heaviest,' Churchill said one day, dealing wittily with his exasperation. In September 1940, when a British–Free French naval expedition tried and failed to take the Vichy-controlled port of Dakar in Senegal, the Prime Minister sought to replace de Gaulle with General Catroux as the head of the Free French; the latter was more accommodating, but refused to oust his leader. De Gaulle particularly dreaded English interference in the French colonies and protectorates. When the United States entered the war, tensions increased as Churchill prioritised his relationship with the great power without whom he could not win the war, while Roosevelt regarded de Gaulle merely as a power-hungry general and an impostor. Under American influence, Churchill's attitude to de Gaulle became positively insulting at times: thus he did not inform him about the Normandy landings until a few hours before the event. De Gaulle, having expressed his admiration for the preparations, was indignant at not being treated as befitted the head of the French provisional government.

Despite memorable quarrels, the two great men maintained a profound respect for one another. They corresponded right up until Churchill's death in January 1965, and de Gaulle came to London for the funeral. But although the British allies' generosity was never in question, the British government's attitude towards de Gaulle, Free France and the French in London was sometimes equivocal. Churchill and his cabinet were careful at first in their handling of the Pétain government, and remained in contact with it through back channels, such as a Canadian minister or the British embassy in Madrid. In October 1940 a French philosopher,

Louis Rougier, came to London to meet Churchill in the hope of
establishing the basis for a secret agreement to continue the fight
against Hitler. This 'gentlemen's agreement', approved by both
Churchill and Pétain, was never formalised, but the British
remained careful not to criticise the Marshal directly, especially in
the BBC's French broadcasts.

Life in London during the blitz

Of all the French people living in London during the war, history
tells us only of those who rallied to the cross of Lorraine; as far as
the rest are concerned, the lack of sources makes any study difficult. Before the great upheaval created by the Free French, the
French community in London was estimated at 7,000: diplomats,
businessmen, shopkeepers, journalists and so on. They were a
mostly conservative group and most regarded with suspicion the
impetuous general who claimed to represent the true France. Very
few of them joined him, although some joined the Resistance
outside his sphere. The French embassy lay at the heart of this
problem: the ambassador, Corbin, resigned on 26 June 1940,
shortly followed by his chargé d'affaires, Roger Cambon – after
Mers-el-Kébir, Cambon withdrew to a property outside London
where he spent the war receiving anti-Gaullist members of the
Resistance. Marshal Pétain had reacted to the Algerian disaster by
recalling the embassy staff on 8 July. The consulate in Bedford
Square, which worked under the Vichy regime, was reduced to a
minimum, as were its branches in the rest of the country. The soldiers and refugees who arrived after June 1940 were often demoralised by the situation in France and by their own precarious
situation. Many found it hard to decide which path to follow:
Pétain or de Gaulle? Vichy or Free France? Or simply put oneself
at the service of the English? Elisabeth de Miribel, an early Free
French recruit and secretary to General de Gaulle, described their
difficult situation: 'Almost all our compatriots returned to France.
Some thought that they could continue the fight in North Africa.
Others were convinced that England would quickly be invaded
and defeated. Others struggled with their consciences: should they

return to protect their families, or remain and fight a rearguard action?'[86] Reflecting the country itself, these rival clans would tear one another apart, riven by intrigue and slander.

The French landed in England in a piteous state: morale among the wounded escaping refugees was at rock-bottom. Those who had escaped death were immensely relieved to find themselves on English soil, but the relief was short-lived when they were quickly sent to camps, or placed under surveillance before being interrogated at the Patriotic School. Those who joined the Free French were incorporated into a structure that provided them with food, shelter and work. The rest were helped and supported by Franco-British benevolent groups. Problems were exacerbated by the Blitz atmosphere in Britain: London was heavily bombed from 7 September 1940 onwards. Bombs fell relentlessly until dawn for 78 consecutive nights until mid-November, and the attacks continued until 10 May 1941. Everybody carried a gas mask and had to obey black-out regulations, and people spent their nights in shelters or underground stations. Several French buildings suffered, some with loss of life: the church of Notre Dame de France, the French women's volunteers' barracks, and the Maison de l'Institut de France.

The refugees were anxious about their families back in France, about whom they had no news. The BBC's personal messages were a great source of comfort. The city was crowded with foreign soldiers and civilians and there was an active social life: 'Despite the worst bombardments, despite the deaths, the arrests, the betrayals, we lived and we lived well. It never occurred to anyone to be shocked by this.'[87] Between bomb alerts, people would go to the pub, the cinema, the theatre, or to dance at the Dorchester. Soho was the centre for night-life, and the French nostalgic for their cuisine would gather at restaurants such as Gaudin's Escargot, Herbodeau's Ecu de France and Berthaud's Coq d'Or. They also went to Chez Rose in Greek Street, which was very popular with sailors, to enjoy horse-steak and chips, or the legendary Victor Berlemont's French House. For those feeling melancholy, the music at the French Club in St James's Square, with its cosy basement restaurant, offered a warm embrace. One inevitable consequence of this intense social life was the many love affairs, serious or illicit, which filled the emotional void and resulted in many marriages and births. Madame de Gaulle was godmother to many babies at that time.

The French community already had several mutual aid groups, such as the French hospital, the Société Française de Bienfaisance, the French Red Cross and the Committee for the aid of the families of French soldiers. By May 1940 more groups were formed, the two most important being the FGB, Français de Grande-Bretagne, a Gaullist group which imposed its authority on smaller organisations, and the CEAF, the French Mutual Assistance Committee. Although originally French, the latter was taken over by an energetic Englishwoman, Lady Warwick, who maintained good relations with both the British government and the Vichyite French consulate.

One Anglo-French association, the Friends of French Volunteers, had the backing of General de Gaulle to coordinate all offers of help for volunteers coming from Great Britain and elsewhere. All these organisations were in competition with one another and there were plenty of quarrels. They were finally placed under the authority of French Welfare, which was put in place by the British government in August 1940. It was installed at the Savoy Hotel and remained in place until 1944. French Welfare looked after all French soldiers and civilians, whether they needed to be repatriated, or to join allied forces, or simply to survive in Britain. It provided lodgings, food, medical care and met any other needs. French refugees were housed with English families at the expense of the British government. Resistance worker Lucie Aubrac was among many who benefited from the services of French Welfare. Brought to England after having organised her husband's escape from a German prison, exhausted and eight months pregnant, she was 'taken to a luxury hotel, the Savoy, where a good room and bathroom with hot water awaited me'.[88]

Christmas was a time of homesickness for the refugees: Masses were held in the barracks, with choirs singing traditional carols.

There were large gatherings at the Albert Hall, for anniversaries such as 18 June or 11 November, where 4,000–5,000 French people would be moved by the speeches of the General. For the national day and St Joan of Arc's feast day, there were processions; on 14 July 1940 the French flag flew from the tower of Westminster Abbey.

The French observed the 'extraordinary calm'[89] of the British and their sang-froid under all circumstances with surprise. Imperturbable shop-keepers would put up signs on their bombed-out shops saying, 'Business as usual'! Apart from the sometimes unkind attitude of the British government, what most of the French living in wartime London remember is the warm welcome they received from the British during their darkest hour. When de Gaulle went out into the streets passers-by expressed their respect and admiration. The English were also extremely compassionate towards the many destitute refugees and the soldiers and sailors who arrived after the fall of France. The survivors of Dunkirk were greeted with flowers and presents as they came off the boats, and during their train journey these exhausted and starving men were fed by the local population and greeted with cheers when they reached Victoria or Waterloo. Conductors on trams and buses would say, 'Frenchies don't pay!' In restaurants throughout the war they were often not presented with a bill, or would find that it had been anonymously paid by a fellow diner.

Despite rationing, the English supplied their unfortunate allies with clothes, meals and money, and invited them into their houses. 'During every leave, English families would invite French soldiers and volunteers to their homes, because they knew that on the whole they had no families in England. It was so kind of the English, who had to feed us even though there was rationing for all civilians.'[90] The rich offered their properties to be used for housing or hospitals: Lord Bessborough opened Stansted House in Hampshire for soldiers returning from Dunkirk. Charity sales were held for French causes. A 1792 bottle of Madeira bought by Napoleon and found at Longwood was auctioned for the record sum of £1,300.

Some stories of the London French

De Gaulle's own family was not immune from the trials and tribu-
lations of refugee life – during his stay in Britain they endured
many moves and separations. The General lived at first in a small
two-room flat lent to him by Jean Laurent, his private secretary in
Paris. Madame de Gaulle set sail from Brest with her three children and her handicapped daughter Anne's nanny and arrived in
Britain on 20 June. Their eldest son, Philippe, who was nineteen,
joined the Free French navy on arrival and fought throughout the
war. As the flat was too small, the family stayed briefly at the
Rubens Hotel near Victoria Station and then accepted the hospitality of the director of Cartier, who rescued them until the
General was able to rent a Tudor-style three-bedroomed house at
41 Birchwood Road, Petts Wood in Orpington. Madame de
Gaulle sent her daughter Elisabeth to board with the Sisters of
Sion at Shrewsbury in Shropshire. The family lived modestly and
the General commuted by train to Victoria. The house in Birchwood Road was close to a railway hub and Anne was terrified of
the bombing. In August 1940, while the General was trying in vain
to persuade Dakar to join the Free French, his wife, daughter and
nanny left London for Ellesmere in Shropshire, not far from Elisabeth in Shrewsbury but four hours by train from London. The
house, Gladlas Mall, was not comfortable but had an agreeable
garden. De Gaulle could not live so far from London, and on his
return from Dakar he rented a small furnished flat at 15 Grosvenor
Square, near Carlton Gardens. He visited his family about once
every six weeks, sometimes by train, sometimes by car. In September 1941 he moved into a suite on the top floor of the Connaught
Hotel in Mayfair. Madame de Gaulle then moved nearer to
London, to the charming historic town of Berkhamsted, where
William the Conqueror had accepted the surrender of London in
1066. Finally, after one last move in September 1942, the family
was reunited and spent their final months in London at 65 Frognal
Road in Hampstead, until de Gaulle's departure for Algiers at the
end of May 1943.

Throughout their English stay, the de Gaulles protected their privacy and never entertained. Madame de Gaulle led a retired life, although she did have her own occupations, and was president of a crèche for the French volunteers. She and the General were often asked to be godparents to the children born of marriages between French volunteers. Faithful to its long tradition, the royal family expressed its goodwill towards the leader of the Free French: the Queen received Madame de Gaulle at a private audience in June 1943 and she was also warmly received by Mrs Churchill.

Exceptional people emerge from exceptional circumstances, and this was certainly the case for some of the London French during the war.

Michel Saint-Denis (1897–1971), a.k.a. Jacques Duchesne of the BBC, revolutionised the theatre in the twentieth century. His influence was felt not just in France and Great Britain, but in the rest of Europe and in Canada. Born into a theatrical family in Beauvais, he was trained by his uncle Jacques Copeau, founder of the Vieux-Colombier theatre in Paris. In 1930 he formed his own troupe, the Compagnie des Quinze, with whom he experimented and tried out his new ideas. His fame grew in Paris and he came on tour to London every year. Backdrops and accessories were abandoned in favour of mime and symbols; in one scene, in which women were weaving and sewing, there were neither threads nor needles and the actions were suggested through mime.

In London he founded the London Theatre Studio in 1935, which was both a theatre and a school, training English actors, directors and designers. He took over an old Methodist chapel in Islington which was modernised by Marcel Breuer, one of the Bauhaus architects, creating a 200-seat theatre. Among his pupils and collaborators were Peter Ustinov, Laurence Olivier, Alec Guinness and other great actors of the time. He put on plays by Shakespeare, Giono, Garcia Lorca and Chekhov, all with great success.

Saint-Denis's theatrical career was interrupted by the outbreak of war. He was mobilised and served as liaison officer with a British regiment. After being evacuated from Dunkirk in June 1940 he joined the BBC French service, and after the 18 June appeal was put in charge of the programme eventually entitled *The French speak to the French*. He adopted a pseudonym to protect his family, and used his theatrical experience to form his team. At the end of the war he went back to his real name and returned to France where, using his BBC experience, he created an English service for French radio.

In 1945 he was invited back to London by Laurence Olivier to direct *Oedipus Rex* at the Old Vic. He then inaugurated a theatrical complex that included the Old Vic Theatre School, the Young Vic theatre for children and an experimental theatre. The original Old Vic theatre having been badly damaged during the war, the company used the New Theatre (now the Noël Coward Theatre). The restored Old Vic reopened in 1950 and Michel Saint-Denis left in 1951. He returned to London in 1962, this time invited by Peter Hall and Peter Brook to co-direct the prestigious Royal Shakespeare Company for three years. He was charged with creating a training studio with theatrical research facilities. Michel Saint-Denis died of a heart attack in London in July 1971.

Another remarkable story is that of the career officer André Dewavrin (1911–98), who was teaching the art of fortification at Saint-Cyr when the war broke out. He took part in the Norwegian campaign and the evacuation of Narvik in May 1940, and on his return to Brest decided to re-embark in order to continue the fight. At Southampton he was transferred to the camp at Trentham Park; having decided to join de Gaulle, he was received by the latter with his usual frosty manner. However, the General did appreciate the talents of this highly educated officer who spoke fluent English, and he put him in charge of the secret service, the Deuxième Bureau which became the BCRA in 1942. Dewavrin, with very few means at the beginning, managed to establish an intelligence service, recruiting agents from military camps and hospitals in the south of England. The first were sent to France as early as July 1940.

Dewavrin also adopted a pseudonym in order to protect his wife and children who had remained in France: he chose the name Passy after a metro station near his home. He was taught the principles of secret warfare by Sir Claude Dansey of the Intelligence Service, and this young man of twenty-nine, with piercing blue eyes, soon became a true professional with a reputation for ruthlessness. Instead of sending foreign agents to find out about the situation in France, he developed his own system, using the French who were already on the spot and who, without moving, could put their talents and any information they could gather to the service of the Free French cause. This method was more efficient and less risky, and resulted in the creation of a French network of agents.

The BCRA was an essential link between the Free French and the French Resistance, but also worked with the English SOE, which created various tensions. Colonel Passy insisted on a special code to prevent French messages from being intercepted by the English. They responded by sending them in the middle of the night, whereupon Passy would summon them to his office at odd hours for unimportant messages. Luckily, this game did not carry on for long. Passy himself travelled on missions to France: with Pierre Brossolette on the Arquebuse-Brumaire operation he was able, from February to April 1943, to make contact with all the Resistance leaders in the north of France and so create the Conseil national de la Résistance (CNR). As General Koenig's chief of staff, he was parachuted into Brittany in August 1944 to join the local Resistance and participate in the liberation of Paimpol, during which 2,000 Germans were taken prisoner.

After the war, in 1945, General de Gaulle made him head of the Direction générale des études et recherches (DGER), which became the Service de documentation extérieure et de contre-espionnage (SDECE), but he resigned when the General left in 1946. The following year he published his three-volume memoirs. After the honour and glory of the war years there came a dark period in his life: he was accused of having failed to inform his successor at the SDECE of the existence of secret funds, and was imprisoned for several months in the fortress of Metz. He was also wrongly suspected by the Communists of involvement in an extreme right-wing plot. Freed without condemnation, he later worked in the private sector. In 1969 André Dewavrin played himself in Jean-Pierre Melville's film *L'Armée des Ombres*. Colonel Passy was highly decorated by the British: he received the DSO and the MC. In France he was a Compagnon de la Libération, and also received the medal of the Resistance, the Croix de Guerre and the Grand Croix de la Légion d'Honneur.

Some women volunteers left moving accounts of their lives in London during the Blitz. Tereska Torrès (1920–2012) grew up in Paris. The war caught her just as she was doing her baccalaureate in June 1940. Her father joined the Polish army and she and her mother escaped. After a dangerous journey to Portugal and then Gibraltar, she heard General de Gaulle's appeal and decided to join the women's forces. She arrived in London during a bombing raid in October 1940 and immediately signed up with the first contingent of female Free French volunteers. She was twenty. Her enthusiasm helped her get through the tough training that the first volunteers got in Bournemouth with the Women's Land Army. Back in London the volunteers moved into 42 Hill Street, a house in Mayfair lent by the Rothschild family. Tereska Torrès recorded all the smallest details of this life in her diary, vividly describing a brutal coming of age for a hitherto sheltered adolescent.

In April the barracks were hit by a bomb which killed one of the volunteers. The unit moved to Moncorvo House in Kensington, the residence of the Duc d'Aumale at the end of the nineteenth century. Tereska became secretary at the propaganda and foreign affairs desk at Carlton Gardens, as well as participating from time to time in BBC broadcasts on women's subjects. Despite the war there was a kind of routine to life, and social life was just as intense as work, with outings, films, dances and so on. Despite moments of deep gloom, she never regretted her commitment to the Free French and she became as fond of London as she had been of Paris: 'I love London where I loved and suffered so much. I feel as though the city is a kind of companion at arms. Paris is my childhood, London is war and life itself.'[91]

In 1943 Tereska was transferred to the BCRA and after special training was made sub-lieutenant. In December she met Georges Torrès, a Free French cadet, whom she married in May 1944 at Our Lady of Victories in Kensington High Street. Their marriage could not take place without the consent of Georges's father, a lawyer who had taken refuge in New York. Undaunted, they knocked on the Prime Minister's door and appealed to Mrs Churchill, who solved the problem. Georges died five months later in Alsace during the Liberation, and Tereska gave birth to a daughter, Dominique, in February 1945. Married again in 1948 to an American writer, she fulfilled her dream of becoming a writer herself and published fifteen books. One of them, a novel inspired by her experiences in the barracks which had lesbian characters, caused a scandal in America; she would not allow it to be published in France for fear of tarnishing the image of the Free French women volunteers. *Une Française libre*, her 1939–45 diaries, published in 2000, describes the everyday life of the French refugees in London, their hopes and their fears.

Another life, another story. Jeanne Bohec (1919–2010) passed her baccalaureate in Angers at the beginning of the war. Interested in chemistry, she joined a gunpowder factory in Brest, where she analysed the chemical components of gunpowder for the war effort. Her life changed on 18 June 1940 when the factory closed and the Germans arrived at the gates of the city. She returned home to fetch a suitcase and found a boat going to England that was willing to take her on board. It was only when she arrived in England that she heard about General de Gaulle. She joined the women's volunteer corps in January 1941. In the first year she was assigned as secretary to the technical and armament office at Carlton Gardens. In her free time she formed a Breton dance group with fellow Bretons, which made successful tours of Cornwall and Scotland.

Using her experience in chemistry she joined a team developing sabotage techniques, which were then shared with the French Resistance. She worked in the laboratories of the French Lycée, whose pupils had been evacuated. Jeanne asked to be transferred to the BCRA as she wanted to be sent to France, but they had never used women. After several attempts, she was finally accepted and underwent rigorous training at various English establishments. In order to protect her identity, she was given the name Râteau ('rake'), a gardening code name used by sabotage instructors, and the Christian name Micheline.

She was one of the first French women to be parachuted into France. The radio announced her arrival with the words, 'When the boa uncurls it will bring you its baby.' The resistance fighters awaiting her arrival were surprised to find that the 'baby' was a young woman just 1.49 metres tall! Her mission was to train members of the Resistance in Brittany, which she toured for several months by bicycle, so as not to be noticed. After the war she married a Free French airman with whom she had a son. She became a maths teacher and deputy mayor of the 18th arrondissement in Paris, remaining an active member of ex-service associations. Her memoir *La Plastiqueuse à bicyclette* is an evocative account of the everyday life of a volunteer, the training of agents in England, and of her Resistance work in France.

Places to visit

THE SECOND WORLD WAR

Imperial War Museum. Many pieces of memorabilia and objects relating to the Free French forces and to life in London under the bombs. One room, the Blitz Experience, has special effects of the ground shaking, sirens and explosions, and the bitter smell of smoke.

Cabinet War Rooms

Clive Steps, King Charles Street SW1
Shelter built to protect Winston Churchill and his war cabinet from German bombs. Churchill had a room here and it was the operational headquarters from 1939 until 1945. The rooms have been kept exactly as they were. The adjoining Churchill Museum is a mine of information about the war. Several mentions of the difficult relationship between Churchill and de Gaulle.

French Medical Centre

3 Harrington Gardens SW7
Based first at 14 Grosvenor Gardens, the centre was created to help the French wounded escaping from Dunkirk in 1940. It still serves the French community, under the name Medicare.

Windsor Castle. In the room next to the Queen Mary's Doll's House Room are two dolls, France and Marianne, with their trousseau, which were given by the children of France to the two princesses, Elizabeth and Margaret, during King George VI's official visit to Paris in July 1938. The 360-piece trousseau contains dresses and accessories from Parisian haute couture houses such as Lanvin, Lancôme, Guerlain, Hermès, Cartier, Vuitton, Duvelleroy . . . They were exhibited in Paris, London and Canada, as ambassadors for French fashion and for the British royal family, and became symbols of the Entente Cordiale during the difficult pre-war years.

D-Day Museum

Clarence Esplanade, Southsea, Hampshire
Museum of the Normandy Landings, opened in 1984 on their 40th anniversary.

ADDRESSES AND REMINDERS OF FREE FRANCE

St Stephen House (Portcullis House)
Victoria Embankment, Westminster SW1
First offices allocated to General de Gaulle. They were dark and shabby and the Free French soon moved to Carlton Gardens. Nowadays, the new building is occupied by MPs' offices.

4 Carlton Gardens SW1. Graciously lent by the British government, this elegant stucco house opposite St James's Park became the heart of Free France in August 1940. Ceremony held each year on 18 June to commemorate the famous appeal of June 1940.

- **Plaque with Cross of Lorraine**
  On front of the building.

- **Statue of General de Gaulle**
  Opposite the building, unveiled in 1993.

17–19 Hill Street, Mayfair W1
Commissariat à l'Intérieur de la France Libre
Building still exists.

Bank of England Museum. The French National Bank functioned from inside the Bank of England, which had placed its resources at their disposal. Objects and documents pertaining to the Free French.

Moncorvo Close

Ennismore Gardens, Kensington SW7
Address of Female Volunteers after they were bombed out of their first house at 42 Hill Street in Mayfair. A fine house, the residence of the Duke d'Aumale in the nineteenth century, it was demolished in 1964. The name Moncorvo Close is all that remains.

Olympia

Hammersmith Road W14
Free French troops were recruited and put up in the vast exhibition hall.

Institut Français. Plaque in the entrance in memory of Special Forces killed between 1939 and 1945.

Lycée Français Charles de Gaulle. Plaque commemorating the presence of the head-quarters of the French air force in the school playground. School renamed Lycée Français Charles de Gaulle in 1980, at the unveiling of the new building on Harrington Road.

St Clement Danes
Strand WC2
Built by Christopher Wren in 1682 and destroyed by a bomb in 1941, restored and dedicated to the RAF in 1958. Gold cross of Lorraine in case at entrance. On the side walls inside the church, list of all the aviators killed in action. In alphabetical order and according to period, the Free French aviators have next to their names the letters 'Fr'.

BBC
Portland Place W1
Bush House, Aldwych WC2
BBC foreign broadcasts, including those of Free France, had been based in Portland Place since 1938. After a bombing raid in 1941, they were transferred to Bush House.

Imperial War Museum. In a case, uniform of a Free French volunteer.

The French House. Gathering place for the French: crowded, noisy, smelling of Gauloises. They mixed with the regulars and the 'fifis', local French prostitutes, who knew they would be protected when they came into the pub.

SECRET SERVICES

Olympia. Recruitment centre. First selection area for French secret services.

Royal Patriotic Building (or Patriotic School)
Trinity Road SW18
Run by MI5 (counter-espionage), the Patriotic School or London Reception Centre was an imposing Gothic-style building in which refugees of all nationalities were received during the Second World War. All had to go through interrogation before being allowed to live in England. Windowless cells under a courtyard held spies before they were transferred to Wandsworth Prison across the road to be executed. The building is now divided into flats, with a French restaurant, Le Gothique, in one of the courtyards.

Oak Lodge School
101 Nightingale Lane, Balham SW12
During interrogation at the Patriotic School, the women were housed in this building. It was destroyed by two bombs and rebuilt in 1968.

Mount Royal Hotel
Bryanston Street W1
Near Duke Street, where the headquarters of the French Secret Service was based, agents and resistance workers who arrived in London lived in this hotel, now part of the Thistle chain.

Alliance Française
1 Dorset Square NW1
Section F of the SOE (French section of the Special Operations Executive, agents working for the English secret services). Agents spent their last night in this building before being parachuted into France. Now the Alliance Française, which joined de Gaulle early on.

SOE Memorial
Lambeth Palace Road SE1
Monument commemorating SOE agents, unveiled in 2009. Chosen to represent them is the Franco-British agent Violette Szabo, whose portrait is carved on the pedestal.

Stockwell War Memorial
Stockwell Road SW9
A large mural, painted in 2001, dedicated to Violette Szabo, representing people of the area who died in the Second World War.

Blue plaque
18 Burnley Road, Stockwell SW9
Home of Violette Szabo. Inscribed on the plaque: 'Secret Agent, lived here. She gave her life for the French Resistance.'

Westminster Abbey. In the cloister, monument commemorating the SOE, unveiled by the Queen Mother in 1996.

Prisons

HMP Pentonville, Caledonian Road N7
HMP Wandsworth, Heathfield Road SW18
HMP Holloway, Parkhurst Road N7
Several unlucky French people ended up in these prisons.

Book and film

Joseph Kessel's book *L'Armée des Ombres* was inspired by the author's own experience as a resistance worker in France, as well as anecdotes gleaned from French intelligence agents he met in London. The book, depicting the heroism of the resistants, was an immediate success. Director Jean-Pierre Melville, himself an ex-Resistance fighter, made a sombre and heroic film of it in 1969, in which Colonel Passy played himself and General de Gaulle made a brief appearance.

FRENCH BUILDINGS DESTROYED IN THE BLITZ

Notre-Dame de France. Bombed in November 1940. French volunteer Tereska Torrès describes the destruction in her diary: 'This morning, Sunday, we wanted to go to Notre Dame de France church [. . .] Two two hundred and fifty kilo bombs have hit the church, reducing it to rubble. It is horrible to see something that one has seen whole the day before suddenly destroyed.'

Maison de L'Institut de France. See pages 191–92.

The French House. Facade of Victor Berlemont's café was destroyed by a bomb in 1944. He sold the establishment but carried on managing it after the building was repaired.

GENERAL DE GAULLE

When he was away from his family, de Gaulle chose lodgings close to Carlton Gardens so that he could walk there.

7 Curzon Place

(previously 7–8 Seymour Grove), Mayfair W1
General de Gaulle's first address in London, a flat lent to him by his private secretary from Paris.

41 Birchwood Road

Petts Wood, near Orpington, Bromley, Kent
First home of de Gaulle family, in south-east suburb of London.

15 Grosvenor Square, Mayfair W1
After the 1940 Dakar expedition, when his family was living near Shrewsbury, de Gaulle rented a small flat in this smart area.

Connaught Hotel. General de Gaulle occupied a suite on the top floor from September 1941. He sometimes entertained guests in the hotel restaurant and continued to do so after he had given up the suite.

Rubens Hotel

39 Buckingham Palace Road SW1
De Gaulle chose this practical and agreeable address for his family when they arrived in London on 19 June 1940.

Cartier. The director, Monsieur Bellenger, placed the Cartier offices and his car at the General's disposal during his first days in London.

St Mary's, Hampstead. Catholic chapel built by refugees from the French Revolution; General de Gaulle and his family's parish during their stay in Hampstead.

Blue plaque

Frognal House, 99 Frognal,
Hampstead NW3
Final residence of de Gaulle family in London. Now a hostel for foreign students.

MICHEL SAINT-DENIS

British Library. Michel Saint-Denis's archives in the British Library contain a quantity of documents and letters relating to his activities in London, both at the BBC during the war, with transcripts of his broadcasts, as well as in the theatre, with his Theatre School.

Old Vic Theatre, Waterloo Road SE1
Young Vic Theatre, The Cut SE1
Michel Saint-Denis worked in both these theatres, which remain active and much admired.

EPILOGUE

'Paris is the capital of one aspect of humanity,
London is capital of the opposite one.
Magnificent and sombre city.
Tumultuous activity, an ant-heap of people.
There you are both free and interlocked.
London is orderly chaos.'

VICTOR HUGO, *William Shakespeare*, 1864

Artists and intellectuals in search of inspiration, émigrés in search of a safe refuge, those curious for new impressions, or simply a new way of life – all these people found this in London. The French newcomers brought in exchange their own *savoir-faire* and their culture as well as a certain lightheartedness and *joie de vivre*. Over the centuries their contribution and their influence were integrated into the fabric of London.

Since the Second World War the French have continued to visit London and settle there: some simply for some particular cultural or professional project, others to make money and thereby contribute, as before, to the economic prosperity of Britain. There are nowadays as many French businesses and artistic or cultural enterprises as there ever were in the past. Anglo–French relationships have been strengthened by the European Community and many French industries now operate in England. But the finest Franco–British achievement must surely be the construction of the Channel Tunnel, opened in 1994. This common project was not a new idea: it had existed since the beginning of the nineteenth century, despite all the mutual distrust. Eurostar, which links Paris to London, has become the symbol of the union between France and England, which has succeeded in spite of all differences and political and economic difficulties. As Victor Hugo said: 'England will always be a sister to France.'[92] Exchanges and visits have multiplied and made integration as easy for the French in London as for the English in Paris.

Today, London is the sixth largest French city: at least 400,000 French people have chosen to live there. They work in every conceivable field, as the Huguenots did before them. Young French graduates from the *grandes écoles* are sought after by London banks; following the legendary Eric Cantona and Thierry Henry, French footballers play for English teams, notably Arsenal with its famous manager Arsène Wenger; the ballerina Sylvie Guillem has been a star of Covent Garden; the big names of French fashion still thrive in London, and French gastronomy continues its great traditions with the Roux brothers, Raymond Blanc and many others. It is a long list. French schools, a good barometer of the French presence in London, have multiplied since the war, and can now be found in Hammersmith, Clapham, Fulham and Kentish Town. The last one was inaugurated in 2015 in Wembley and, as a counterpart to the Lycée Charles de Gaulle in South Kensington, it is called the Lycée Winston Churchill, a reminder of the strong bond between the two countries when faced with difficult times.

Of all the French people in London now, how many of them will merit a commemorative plaque or statue of their own? Only time will tell! The hero of this book is without doubt the city of London itself: it does not judge, but assimilates all these French people tolerantly and without flinching, once again belying the image of 'perfidious Albion'.

ALLIANCES BETWEEN THE ROYAL FAMILIES OF ENGLAND AND FRANCE

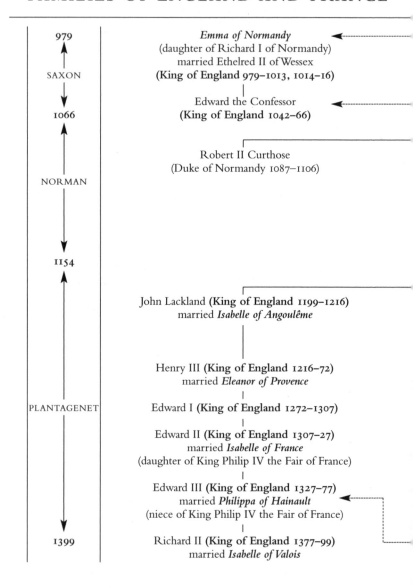

979 | *Emma of Normandy* ⟵
(daughter of Richard I of Normandy)
married Ethelred II of Wessex
(King of England 979–1013, 1014–16)

SAXON

Edward the Confessor
(King of England 1042–66) ⟵

1066

Robert II Curthose
(Duke of Normandy 1087–1106)

NORMAN

1154

John Lackland **(King of England 1199–1216)**
married *Isabelle of Angoulême*

Henry III **(King of England 1216–72)**
married *Eleanor of Provence*

PLANTAGENET

Edward I **(King of England 1272–1307)**

Edward II **(King of England 1307–27)**
married *Isabelle of France*
(daughter of King Philip IV the Fair of France)

Edward III **(King of England 1327–77)**
married *Philippa of Hainault* ⟵
(niece of King Philip IV the Fair of France)

1399 | Richard II **(King of England 1377–99)**
married *Isabelle of Valois*

Bold = Kings and Queens of England
Bold italic = introduction of French blood to the throne of England
Bold italic sans serif = the Bourbons (French)

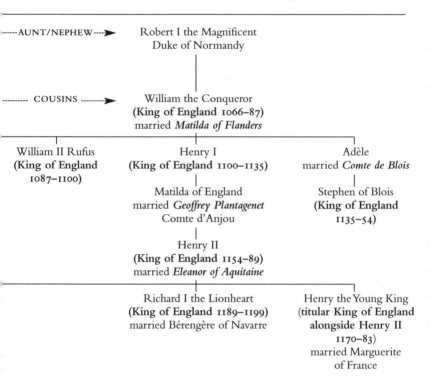

------AUNT/NEPHEW----▶ Robert I the Magnificent
Duke of Normandy

---------- COUSINS ---------▶ William the Conqueror
(King of England 1066–87)
married *Matilda of Flanders*

William II Rufus
**(King of England
1087–1100)**

Henry I
(King of England 1100–1135)

Matilda of England
married *Geoffrey Plantagenet*
Comte d'Anjou

Henry II
(King of England 1154–89)
married *Eleanor of Aquitaine*

Adèle
married *Comte de Blois*

Stephen of Blois
**(King of England
1135–54)**

Richard I the Lionheart
(King of England 1189–1199)
married Bérengère of Navarre

Henry the Young King
**(titular King of England
alongside Henry II
1170–83)**
married Marguerite
of France

---- GRANDPARENTS -------------------▶ Henry IV
GRANDSON **(King of England 1399–1413)**
House of Lancaster
married *Jeanne de Navarre*

continued overleaf

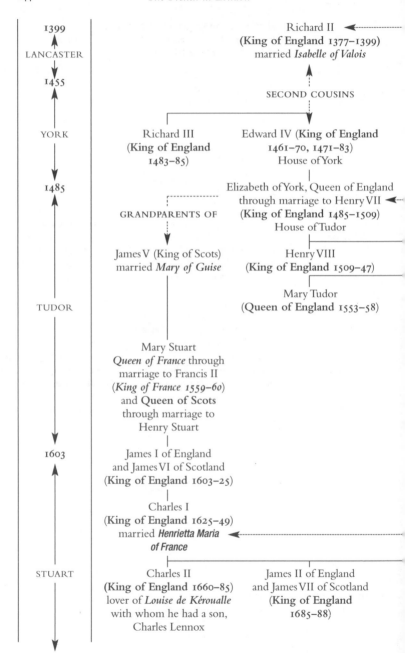

1399

LANCASTER

1455

YORK

1485

TUDOR

1603

STUART

Richard II
(King of England 1377–1399)
married *Isabelle of Valois*

SECOND COUSINS

Richard III
(King of England
1483–85)

Edward IV (King of England
1461–70, 1471–83)
House of York

Elizabeth of York, Queen of England
through marriage to Henry VII
(King of England 1485–1509)
House of Tudor

GRANDPARENTS OF

James V (King of Scots)
married *Mary of Guise*

Henry VIII
(King of England 1509–47)

Mary Tudor
(Queen of England 1553–58)

Mary Stuart
Queen of France through
marriage to Francis II
(*King of France 1559–60*)
and Queen of Scots
through marriage to
Henry Stuart

James I of England
and James VI of Scotland
(King of England 1603–25)

Charles I
(King of England 1625–49)
married *Henrietta Maria
of France*

Charles II
(King of England 1660–85)
lover of *Louise de Kéroualle*
with whom he had a son,
Charles Lennox

James II of England
and James VII of Scotland
(King of England
1685–88)

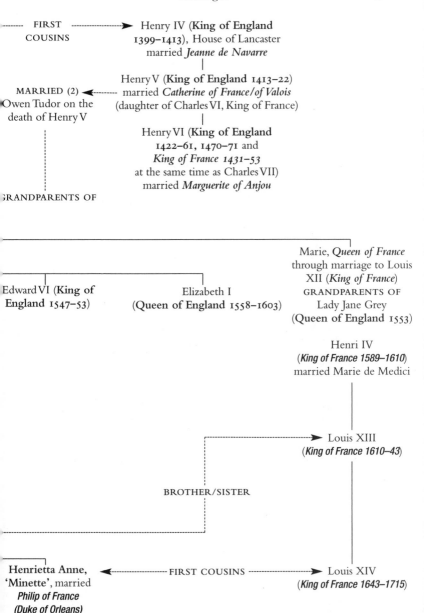

------ FIRST ------➤ Henry IV (**King of England**
COUSINS **1399–1413**), House of Lancaster
married *Jeanne de Navarre*

Henry V (**King of England 1413–22**)
MARRIED (2) ◄------ married *Catherine of France/of Valois*
Owen Tudor on the (daughter of Charles VI, King of France)
death of Henry V

Henry VI (**King of England
1422–61, 1470–71** and
King of France 1431–53
at the same time as Charles VII)
married *Marguerite of Anjou*

GRANDPARENTS OF

Marie, *Queen of France*
through marriage to Louis
XII (*King of France*)
GRANDPARENTS OF
Edward VI (**King of** Elizabeth I Lady Jane Grey
England 1547–53) (**Queen of England 1558–1603**) (**Queen of England 1553**)

Henri IV
(*King of France 1589–1610*)
married Marie de Medici

------➤ Louis XIII
(*King of France 1610–43*)

BROTHER/SISTER

Henrietta Anne, ◄------ FIRST COUSINS ------➤ Louis XIV
'**Minette**', married (*King of France 1643–1715*)
*Philip of France
(Duke of Orleans)*

NOTES

1. Quoted in André Maurois, *Histoire d'Angleterre,* Fayard, Paris, 1937, p. 77.

2. William of Malmesbury, quoted in André Maurois, *La Conquête de l'Angleterre par les Normands,* coll. 'Le Memorial des Siècles', Albin Michel, Paris, 1968, p. 160.

3. Anglo-Saxon Chronicles of 1087, quoted in *La Conquête de l'Angleterre par les Normands,* op. cit., p. 138.

4. William of Malmesbury, quoted in ibid., p. 157.

5. William of Malmesbury, quoted in ibid., p. 160.

6. Quoted by William of Newburgh in Alison Weir, *Eleanor of Aquitaine: By the Wrath of God, Queen of England,* Vintage Books, London, 2007, p. 76.

7. Samuel Pepys, *Diaries,* 17 February 1669.

8. Charles d'Orléans, *L'Écolier de mélancolie,* Rondeau LI (51).

9. Quoted in Josephine Ross, *The Men who would be King: Suitors to Queen Elizabeth I,* Phoenix, London, 2005, p. 177.

10. Quoted in Bryan Bevan, *Charles the Second's French Mistress: a biography of Louise de Keroualle, Duchess of Portsmouth (*1649–1734*),* Robert Hale, London, 1972, p. 125.

11. Quoted in Yves Jaulmes, *The French Protestant Church of London and the Huguenots,* French Protestant Church of London, 1993, p. 7.

12. Saint-Simon, *Mémoires,* vol. 1, ed. Yves Coirault, Folio Classique, Gallimard, Paris, 1990, p. 380.

13. 11 November 1783, quoted in *Voltaire's England,* ed. Desmond Flower, The Folio Society, London, 1950, p. ix.

14. Tobias Smollett, *Travels through France and Italy,* letter VII, OUP, 1935, p. 63.

15. Marquise de la Tour du Pin, *Mémoires d'une femme de cinquante ans,* vol. I, Librairie Chapelot, Paris, 1914, p. 165.

16. Voltaire, *Zaire: tragédie,* coll. 'Classiques' Larousse, Paris, 1985, p. 19.

17. Montesquieu, *De l'esprit des Lois,* XX, 7 1748.

18. James Boswell, in his diary, gives a lively description of his meeting with Paoli in Corsica. F. Brady and F. Pottle, *Boswell on the Grand Tour: Italy, Corsica and France, 1765–1766,* William Heinemann, London, 1955, pp, 152–332. In his book *The Life of Samuel Johnson* he often mentions Paoli, with whom he lodged for a time in London and who often saw Johnson. James Boswell, *The Life of Samuel Johnson,* Penguin Classics, London, 1986, pp, 255–324.

19. Duchesse de Gontaut, *Mémoires,* Librairie Plon, Paris, 1890, p. 30.

20. In 1791 the Revolutionary government in France introduced the Civil Constitution of the Clergy, according to which priests were forced to sign a deed of loyalty to the new regime.

21. Abbé Baruel, *Histoire du Clergé,* quoted in Émile Gabory, *L'Angleterre et la Vendée,* vol. 1, Perrin, Paris, 1930, p. 22.

22. Comtesse de Boigne, *Mémoires de la comtesse de Boigne, née d'Osmond*, vol. 1, coll. 'Le Temps Retrouvé', Mercure de France, Paris, 1986, p. 1035.

23. Chateaubriand, *Mémoires d'outre-tombe*, coll 'Classiques Garnier', Bordas, Paris, 1989, vol. I, book X, Chapter 6.

24. Quoted in Claude Gamblin, *L'immigration française en Grande-Bretagne, 1789–1815*, coll. 'l'aire anglophone', L'Harmattan, Paris, 2000, p. 105.

25. Chateaubriand, *Mémoires d'outre-tombe*, op. cit., chapter 6, p. 647.

26. Marquis de Valoux, *Sur les routes de l'Émigration, Mémoires de la duchesse de Saulx-Tavannes (1791–1806)*, Paris, 1834, p. 46, quoted in Kirsty Carpenter, *Refugees of the French Revolution. Emigrés in London, 1789–1802*, Macmillan, London, 1999, p. 80.

27. Quoted in T. H. R. Cashmore, 'The Orleans family in Twickenham, 1800–1932', *Journal* 49, Twickenham Local History Society, Twickenham, 1997, p. 6.

28. Vicomte Walsh, *Souvenirs de cinquante ans*, Paris, 1862, p. 155, quoted in Kirsty Carpenter, *Refugees of the French Revolution,* op. cit., p. 87.

29. Chateaubriand, *Mémoires d'Outre-Tombe*, Édition du Centenaire, Flammarion, Paris, 1982, vol. II, book I, chapter 3, p. 15.

30. Charles Dickens, *The Old Curiosity Shop*, 1841.

31. Mme Vigée-Lebrun, *Souvenirs*, vol. 2, coll. 'Écrits d'hier', Éditions des femmes, Paris, 1986, p. 141.

32. Quoted in Andrew Roberts, *Napoleon and Wellington*, Phoenix Press, London, 2002, p. 163.

33. Quoted in Marc Vion, *Perfide Albion! Douce Angleterre? L'Angleterre et les Anglais vus par les Français du XIVeme siècle à l'an 2000*, Alan Sutton, Saint-Cyr-sur-Loire, 2002, p. 112.

34. 'Nic' was one of the English nicknames for Napoleon.

35. Quoted in Marc Vion, *Perfide Albion!*, op. cit., p. 126.

36. Quoted in Margery Weiner, *The French Exiles, 1789–1815*, John Murray, London, 1960, p. 195.

37. Quoted in Pierre de la Gorce, *Louis XVIII*, Librairie Plon, Paris, 1926, p. 5.

38. From Captain Gronow, *The Reminiscences and Recollections of Captain Gronow, being anecdotes of the camp, court, clubs and society, 1810–1860*, Bodley Head, London, 1964, p. 82.

39. Comtesse de Boigne, *Mémoires de la comtesse de Boigne née d'Osmond*, op. cit., p. 255.

40. Quoted in J. Lucas-Dubreton, *Le comte d'Artois Charles X*, Librairie Hachette, 1927, p. 171.

41. Letter from Queen Victoria to her uncle, the King of the Belgians, 1 March 1848, in *The Letters of Queen Victoria (1837–1861)*, vol. II, John Murray, London, 1908, p. 155.

42. Letter to Baron Stockmar, 1 September 1855, in *The Letters of Queen Victoria*, op. cit., vol. III, p. 139.

43. *Queen Victoria's Journals*, 27 March 1871.

44. Quoted in A. Augustin-Thierry, *Le Prince Impérial*, Grasset, Paris, 1935, p. 174.

45. This attack was the inspiration for Joseph Conrad's *The Secret Agent*, published in 1906.

46. William Thackeray, *The Adventures of Philip on his Way through the World*, 1862, chapter XXI.

47. Quoted in Dominique Lobstein, *Monet et Londres*, Editions À Propos, Garches, 2004.

48. Quoted in ibid., p. 17.

49. Ibid., p. 28.

50. Ibid., p. 33.

51. *Queen Victoria's Journals*, 25 June 1853.

52. Peter Hughes, *The Founders of the Wallace Collection*, The Trustees of the Wallace Collection, London, 2006, p. 53.

53. Paul Verlaine, from the poem 'Londres'.

54. Jules Verne, *Round the World in Eighty Days*.

55. Letter to Henri Cazalis, 30 November 1862, quoted in Marc Vion, *Perfide Angleterre!*, op. cit., p. 180.

56. Paul Verlaine, 'Londres', op. cit.:
    'On a summer Sunday, when the sun is out,
    London is a feast for sensitive souls:
    the sturdy round trees on the delicate soft greenery
    appear so far from the mists and the fumes,
    they seem to grow in peasant earth.
    Light sunshine against the delicate, hardly blue sky.
    One is as if bathed in the soft scent of slowly infusing tea.'

57. Captain Gronow, *Reminiscences*, op. cit., p. 256.

58. Ibid., p. 60.

59. Quoted in the biography of Carême to be found at http://chefsimon.lemonde.fr/articles/litterature-marie-antoine-dit-antonin-careme.

60. Lady Morgan, *Lady Morgan in France*, Oriel Press, London, 1971, p. 235.

61. A remark by the banker Otto Kahn, quoted under Ritter, Carl, 60, in the *Encyclopedia Britannica*, 2002.

62. Pierre Hamp, *La Peine des Hommes: Mes Métiers*, coll. 'N.R.F.', Gallimard, Paris, 1930, pp. 156, 157.

63. Jules Verne, *Les aventures du capitaine Hatteras*, first part: 'Les Anglais au Pôle Nord', chap. XXI, coll. 'Folio Classique', Gallimard, Paris, 2005, p. 229.

64. Quoted in Gordon Brook-Shepherd, *Uncle of Europe: The social and diplomatic life of Edward VII*, Collins, London, 1975, p. 193.

65. Letter from Napoleon III to Mr F. Campbell, translator of M. Thiers, *L'Atlas de l'Histoire du Consulat et de l'Empire*, 1859, quoted by Queen Victoria in *The Letters of Queen Victoria*, op. cit., chap. XXIV.

66. Quoted in G. P. Salvy-Guide, *Fachoda. La mission Marchand*, Nathan, Paris, 1977, p. 176.

67. Quoted in Gordon Brook-Shepherd, *Uncle of Europe*, op. cit., p. 193.

68. World War I document archive, 1914.

69. Quoted in Marc Vion, *Perfide Albion!*, op. cit., p. 198.

70. Paul Cambon, letter to his mother dated 28 January 1901, in *Correspondance 1870–1924*, vol. II, Grasset, Paris, 1940–46, p. 52.

71. Paul Cambon, letter to his son dated 11 May 1910, in *Correspondance*, op. cit., p. 302.

72. Quoted in the catalogue of the exhibition *Face to Face: One hundred years of photographs from the Institut Français Archives*, on the occasion of the Centenary of the Entente Cordiale, Institut Français du Royaume-Uni, London, 2004, p. 8.

73. Paul Cambon, letter to his brother Jules Cambon dated 19 May 1909, in *Correspondance*, op. cit., p. 286.

74. *The Times*, 17 January 1905.

75. Paul Cambon, letter to his brother Jules Cambon dated 19 May 1909, in *Correspondance*, op. cit., p. 286.

76. André Maurois's *Ariel* was the first Penguin paperback to be published.

77. Quoted in Marc Vion, *Perfide Albion!*, op. cit., p. 242.

78. Extract from the appeal of 18 June 1940.

79. Quoted in André Gillois, *Histoire secrète des Français à Londres de 1940 à 1944*, Hachette, Paris, 1973, p. 50.

80. Quoted in Tereska Torrès, *Une Française Libre: Journal 1939–1945*, coll. 'Le vif du sujet', Phébus, Paris, 2000, p. 156.

81. The complete lyrics may be easily found on the internet.

82. Quoted in Dominique Decène, *Ici Londres . . . La lune est pleine d'éléphants verts: histoire des messages de Radio-Londres à la Résistance française, 1942–1944*, J. Lanzmann & Seghers Éditeurs, Paris, 1979, p. 77.

83. Quoted in André Gillois, *Histoire secrète*, op. cit., p. 123.

84. Chapter by Maurice Druon in *Conseil franco-britannique, L'Entente cordiale dans le siècle*, Odile Jacob, Paris, 2004, p. 131.

85. Quoted in Jules-François Blondel, *Entente cordiale*, Caduceus Press, London, 1971, p. 43 (and mentioned in the Churchill Museum at the War Cabinet Rooms).

86. Élisabeth de Miribel, *La Liberté souffre violence*, Librairie Plon, Paris, 1981, p. 38.

87. Jean Pierre-Bloch, *Londres, capitale de la France libre*, Éditions Carrere et Michel Laffont, Paris, 1986, p. 57.

88. Lucie Aubrac, *Ils partiront dans l'ivresse*, Éditions du Seuil, Paris, 1984, p. 246.

89. Jean Oberlé, *Jean Oberlé vous parle . . .*, La Jeune Parque, Paris, 1945, p. 68.

90. Tereska Torrès, *Une Française libre*, op. cit., p. 203.

91. Ibid., p. 134.

92. Victor Hugo, *Cromwell*, act II, scene 2, 1827.

BIBLIOGRAPHY

General

Arkell, David, *Ententes Cordiales, The French in London and other adventures*, Carcanet Press, Manchester, 1989

Baker, Margaret, *Discovering London Statues and Monuments*, Shire Publications, 2002

Cendre, Anne, *Les Peintres de Londres*, Edita S.A. Lausanne, 1990

Cruikshank, Dan, *Invasion, defending Britain from attack*, Pan Macmillan, 2001

Drabble, Margaret, ed., *The Oxford Companion to English Literature*, Oxford University Press, 1998

Gibson, Robert, *Best of Enemies: Anglo-French relations since the Norman Conquest,* Impress Books, Exeter University, 2004

Maurois, André, *Histoire d'Angleterre*, A. Fayard, 1937

Miquel, Pierre, *Histoire de la France*, Fayard, 1976

Rennison, Nick, *The London Blue Plaque Guide*, Sutton Publishing, 2003

Richardson John, *The Annals of London*, Cassell, 2001

Sumeray, Derek and John Sheppard, *London Plaques*, Shire Publications, 2010

Tagholm, Roger, *Walking Literary London*, New Holland Publishers (UK), 2004

Tombs, Robert and Isabelle, *That Sweet Enemy*, William Heinemann, London, 2006

Van Tieghem, Philippe, *Les Influences Etrangères sur la Littérature Française 1550–1880,* Presses Universitaires de France, Paris, 1961

Vion, Marc, *Perfide Albion! Douce Angleterre? L'Angleterre et les Anglais vus par les Français du 14ᵉ siècle à l'An 2000*, Editions Alan Sutton, 2002

Weinreb, Ben and Christopher Hibbert, *The London Encyclopedia,* Macmillan, Papermac, 1993

Woodrow, Alain, *Tout ce que vous avez toujours voulu savoir sur les Anglais . . . sans jamais oser le leur demander*, Editions du Félin, Paris, 1997

Historical publications on districts of London (Soho, Covent Garden, Wandsworth, Marylebone, Greenwich, etc.), Historical Publications, Whitstable, Kent, www.historicalpublications.co.uk

1 Norman England

Barber, Charles, *The English Language. A historical introduction*, Cambridge University Press, 2000

Bragg, Melvyn, *The Adventure of English. The Biography of a Language,* Hodder and Stoughton, London, 2003

Dean and Chapter of Westminster, *Westminster Abbey*, official guide, 1997

Hallam, Elizabeth, ed., *Chronicles of the Age of Chivalry*, Greenwich Editions, London, 2002

Lamy, Michel, *Les Templiers*, Editions Aubéron, Bordeaux, 1997

Leguai, André, *La guerre de Cent ans*, Editions Fernand Nathan, Coll. Université, 1974

Maurois, André, *La conquête de l'Angleterre par les Normands*, Albin Michel, 1968

Ross, Cathy and John Clark, *London, the illustrated history*, Museum of London, Penguin, 2008

Seward, Desmond, *The Hundred Years War. The English in France, 1337–1453,* Robinson, London 1988

Soyez, Jean-Marc, *Quand les Anglais vendangeaient l'Aquitaine*, Fayard, 1978

Walter, Henriette, *Honi soit qui mal y pense*, Robert Laffont, Livre de poche, 2001

2 Exceptional people

Deviosse, Jean, *Jean Le Bon*, Fayard, 1985

Dupuy, Micheline, *Françaises Reines d'Angleterre*, Librairie Académique Perrin, 1968

Fraser, Antonia, ed., *The lives of the Kings and Queens of England*, Weidenfeld & Nicholson, London, 1998

McLeod, Enid, *Charles d'Orléans: Prince and Poet*, Chatto & Windus, London, 1969

Villehardouin, Geoffroy de, Jean Froissart, Jean de Joinville and Philippe de Commynes, *Les chroniqueurs français*, La Renaissance du Livre, Paris, Jean Gillequin éditeurs, 1910

Weir, Alison, *Eleanor of Aquitaine*, Vintage Books, London, 2007

Williamson, David, *Kings and Queens of Britain*, The Promotional Reprint Company for Bookmart, Leicester

3 Bourbons and Stuarts

Airy, Osmund, *Charles II*, Longmans, Green, and Co., London, 1904

Bevan, Bryan, *Charles the Second's French Mistress. A biography of Louise de Keroualle, Duchess of Portsmouth*, Robert Hale, 1972

Cassavetti, Eileen, *The Lion and the Lillies. The Stuarts and France*, Book Club Associates, 1977

Chapman, Hester W, *Privileged Persons: four seventeenth century studies*, London, Jonathan Cape, 1966

Charlanne, L., *L'Influence Française en Angleterre au XVIIème siècle. Le Théâtre et la Critique,* Société Française d'Imprimerie et de Librairie, Paris, 1906

Harris, John, Stephen Orgel and Roy Strong, *The King's Arcadia: Inigo Jones and the Stuart Court,* Catalogue of Inigo Jones, exhibition, Arts Council of Great Britain, London, 1973

Pepys, Samuel, *Journal*, French translation by René Villoteau, coll. 'Le Temps Retrouvé', Mercure de France, 1985, 1987

Plowden Alison, *Henrietta-Maria: Charles I's Indomitable Queen*, Sutton Publishing, 2001

Ross, Josephine, *The Men Who Would be King: Suitors to Queen Elizabeth I*, Phoenix, London, 2005

4 A Country for the Huguenots

Avery, Charles, *Hubert Le Sueur*, The Walpole Society, vol. 48, Pitman Press, 1982

Cottret, Bernard, *Terre d'exil – L'Angleterre et ses réfugiés 16ᵉ–17ᵉ siècles*, Aubier, 1985

Gwynn, Robin, *Huguenot Heritage. The history and contribution of the Huguenots in Britain,* Sussex Academic Press, Brighton Portland, 2001

Gwynn, Robin, *The Huguenots of London*, The Alpha Press, 1998

Ingamells, John and Robert Raines, *Philip Mercier*, The Walpole Society, vol. 46, Pitman Press, 1978

Jaulmes, Yves, *The French Protestant Church of London and the Huguenots,* London, 1993

Le Roy de Sainte-Croix, *Vie et ouvrages de L. F. Roubillac, sculpteur lyonnais*, Paris, 1882

Murdoch, Tessa, *The Quiet Conquest: The Huguenots 1685 to 1985,* Museum of London exhibition in association with the Huguenot Society, Museum of London, 1985

Shaw, Richard, Robin Gwynn and Peter Thomas, *Huguenots in Wandsworth*, Wandsworth Borough Council, 1985

Starkie Gardner, John, *A new book of drawings, invented and designed by Jean Tijou*, London, 1896

Van der Cruysse, Dirk, *Chardin le Persan*, Fayard, 1998

5 Enlightenment vs 'Siècle des Lumières'

Croft-Murray, Edward, *Decorative Paintings in England 1537–1837 (Louis Laguerre)*, Country Life, London 1962

Flower, Desmond, *Voltaire's England*, The Folio Society, London, 1950

Kinne, Willard Austin, *Revivals and importations of French comedies in England, 1749–1800*, AMS Press, New York, 1967

Mossiker, Frances, *Le collier de la reine*, René Julliard, Paris, 1963

Mourousy, Paul, *Le Chevalier d'Eon, Un travesti malgré lui*, Ed. du Rocher, 1998

Prévost, l'Abbé, *Mémoires d'un homme de qualité*, vol. V: *Séjour en Angleterre*, Librairie ancienne Honore Champion, Paris, 1927

Voltaire, *Le Siècle de Louis XIV*, Les classiques de Poche, 2005

6 Refugees from the Revolution

Bellenger, Dominic Aidan, *The French exiled clergy in the British Isles after 1789*, Downside Abbey, Bath, 1986

Bernard, Jack. F., *Talleyrand: A Biography*, Collins, London, 1973

Boigne, Comtesse de, *Mémoires*, coll. 'Le Temps Retrouvé', Mercure de France, Paris, 1986

Carpenter, Kirsty, *Refugees of the French Revolution. Emigrés in London, 1789–1802*, Macmillan Press, 1999

Chartrand, René and Patrice Courcelle, *Émigré and foreign troops in British service (1), 1793–1802*, Osprey Military Men-at-Arms, No. 328, Osprey Publishing, 1999

Chateaubriand, François-René de, *Mémoires d'Outre-Tombe*, Classiques de Poche, Bordas, Paris, 1989

Eagles, Robin, *Francophilia in English Society, 1748–1815*, Macmillan Press, 2000

Gabory, Emile, *L'Angleterre et la Vendée: Granville – Quiberon – l'Ile d'Yeu – d'après des documents inédits*, Librairie Académique, Perrin & Cie, Paris, 1931

Gamblin, Claude, *L'immigration française en Grande-Bretagne, 1789–1815*, L'Harmattan, 2000

Kelly, Linda, *Juniper Hall: an English refuge from the French Revolution*, Weidenfeld and Nicholson, London, 1991

La Tour du Pin, Marquise de, *Journal d'une femme de cinquante ans, 1778–1815*, 2 vols., Librairie Chapelot, Paris, 1914

Monlosier, Comte de, *Souvenirs d'un Emigré, 1791–1798*, Hachette, 1951

Portalis, Baron Roger de, *Henry Pierre Danloux, peintre de portraits et son journal durant l'émigration*, Paris, pour la société des bibliophiles français, E. Rahir, 1910

Powell, Christabel, *Augustus Welby Pugin, Designer of the British Houses of Parliament. The Victorian quest for a liturgical architecture*, The Edwin Mellen Press, 2006

Ransom, Teresa, *Madame Tussaud: A life and a time*, Sutton Publishing, 2003

Tames, Richard, *Isambard Kingdom Brunel*, Shire Publications, 1992

Troughton, Jane, *French Connections. French émigrés in Richmond upon Thames*, exhibition at Orleans House, London Borough of Richmond upon Thames, 1989

Vigée-Lebrun, Elisabeth, *Souvenirs*, Edition des Femmes, Paris, 1986

Weiner, Margery, *The French Exiles (1789–1815)*, John Murray, London, 1960

Williams, Guy, *Augustus Pugin versus Decimus Burton: a Victorian architectural duel,* Cassell, 1990

7 Napoleon, the mortal enemy

Bowle, John, *Napoléon,* Great Lives series, Book Club Associates, Weidenfeld and Nicolson, 1973

Bryant, Julius, *Apsley House: The Wellington Collection,* English Heritage, 2005

Chamberlain, Paul, *Hell Upon Water: Prisoners of War in Britain, 1793–1815,* The History Press, 2008

Gronow, Captain Rees Howell, *The Reminiscences & Recollections of Captain Gronow, being anecdotes of the camp, court and society, 1810–1860,* Bodley Head, 1964

Howarth, David, *Trafalgar. The Nelson Touch,* Collins, 1969

Maine, René, *Trafalgar: Napoléon's Naval Waterloo,* Thames and Hudson, London, 1957

Pocock, Tom, *The Terror before Trafalgar. Nelson, Napoleon and the Secret War,* John Murray, London, 2002

Roberts, Andrew, *Napoleon and Wellington,* Phoenix Press, 2002

Seymour, William, Jacques Champagne and Eberhard Kaulbach, *Waterloo, Battle of Three Armies,* ed. Lord Chalfont, Sidgwick and Jackson, 1979

Thackeray, William Makepeace, *The English Humorists,* Smith, Elder & Co., London, 1853

Tulard, Jean, *Napoléon, ou le Mythe du Sauveur,* Fayard, 1977

8 London, a sanctuary for the politically persecuted

Aprile, Sylvie, 'Exil et exilés français sous le Second Empire', in *Hommes et Migrations, Trajectoires d'exils,* no. 1253, January–February 2005

Aprile, Sylvie, 'Les proscrits français et l'Angleterre', in *Figures de l'Exil,* no. 38, 2000/1

Arjuzon, Antoine d', *Victoria et Napoléon III. Histoire d'une amitié,* Atlantica, Biarritz 2007

Cashmore, T. H. R., *The Orleans Family in Twickenham,* Twickenham Local History Society, 1997

Guest, Ivor, *Napoléon III in England,* British Technical and General Press, London, 1952

Lucas-Dubreton, Jean, *Le comte d'Artois Charles X, le Prince, l'Emigré, le Roi,* Librairie Hachette, Paris, 1927

Mansell, Philip, *Louis XVIII,* Blond & Briggs, London, 1981

Mostyn, Dorothy A., *The Story of a House: Farnborough Hill,* St Michael's Abbey Press, Farnborough, 1980

Queen Victoria, *The Letters of Queen Victoria (1837–1861),* John Murray, London, 1908

9 Romantic visitors

Adler, Kathleen, *Pissarro in London,* National Gallery, London, 2003

Ash, Russell, *James Tissot,* Pavilion Books, London, 1995

Bann, Stephen and Linda Whiteley, *Painting History: Delaroche and Lady Jane Grey,* exhibition catalogue, National Gallery, 2010

Cairns David, *Berlioz: Servitude and Greatness 1832–1869,* Allen Lane / Penguin, London, 1999

Carse, Adam, *The Life of Jullien,* W. Heffer & Sons, Cambridge, 1951

Duvelleroy, King of Fans, Fan Maker to Kings, exhibition catalogue, Fan Museum, 1995

Fletcher, Pamela, 'Creating the French Gallery: Ernest Gambart and the rise of the commercial art gallery in mid-Victorian London', *Nineteenth-Century Art Worldwide,* vol. 6, no. 1, Association of Historians of Ninetenth-Century Art (AHNCA), spring 2007

Hayes Tucker, Paul, *Monet in the '90s: The series paintings*, Yale University Press, New Haven, for the Museum of Fine Arts, Boston, 1989

Hughes, Peter, *The Founders of the Wallace Collection,* The Trustees of the Wallace Collection, London, 2006

Jeancolas, Claude, *Passion – L'album d'une vie: Rimbaud,* Editions Textuel, 1998

Lobstein, Dominique, *Monet et Londres,* Editions À Propos, Paris, 2004

Lodge, Suzanne, 'Géricault in England', *Burlington Magazine,* vol. 107, no, 753, December 1965

Mackworth, Cecil, *English interludes: Mallarmé, Verlaine, Paul Valéry, Valéry Larbaud, 1860–1912,* Routledge & Kegan Paul, 1974

McWatters, K. G. and C. W. Thompson, *Stendhal et l'Angleterre*, Liverpool University Press, 1987

Matyjaszkiewicz, Krystyna, *James Tissot*, Phaidon Press and Barbican Art Gallery, 1984

Moreau, Marcel, *Le romanticisme français en Angleterre de 1814 à 1848*, Librairie Ancienne Honoré Champion, 1933

Morris, Edward, *French Art in Nineteenth Century Britain*, Yale University Press, 2005

Pages, A. and O. Morgan, *Guide Emile Zola*, Ellipses, 2002

Reed, Nicholas, *Camille Pissarro at Crystal Palace*, Liburne Press, London, 1995

Shanes, Eric, *Londres Impressionniste*, Editions Abbeville, Paris, 1994

Shawe-Taylor, Desmond, *Dulwich Picture Gallery – A Visitor's Guide*, 2000

10 The great invasion of the nineteenth century

Bajac, Quentin, *The Invention of Photography: the first fifty years*, Thames and Hudson, 2002

Brandon, Ruth, *The People's Chef: Alexis Soyer. A Life in Seven Courses*, John Wiley and Sons, Chichester, West Sussex, 2004

Camm, Dom Bede, *A Sacrifice of Praise: Marie-Adèle Garnier and the founding of Tyburn Convent,* St Michael's Abbey Press, Farnborough, 2006

Cathcart Borer, Mary, *Mayfair: the Years of Grandeur,* W. H. Allen, London, 1975

Escoffier, Auguste, *Ma cuisine,* introduction by André L. Simon, Paul Hamlyn, London, 1965

Foulks, Nick, *Last of the Dandies: The Scandalous Life and Escapades of Count d'Orsay*, Little, Brown, London, 2003

Haworth-Booth Mark, *Camille Silvy: Photographer of Modern Life*, exhibition catalogue, National Portrait Gallery, London, 2010

Whitting, Philip D., *A History of Hammersmith based upon that of Thomas Faulkner in 1839*, Hammersmith Local History Group, 1965

11 Allies and brothers-in-arms

Audoin-Rouzeau and Becker, *Encyclopédie de la Grande Guerre 1914–1918,* Bayard, 2004

Bell, P. M., *France and Britain, 1900–1940. Entente and estrangement*, Longman, 1996

Cambon, Paul, *Correspondance, 1870–1924*, volumes II and III, Grasset, 1940 and 1946

Conseil Franco-Britannique, *L'Entente Cordiale dans le siècle*, Odile Jacob, 2004

Cooper-Richet, Diana and Michel Rapoport, *L'Entente Cordiale – Cent ans de relations culturelles Franco-britannique (1904–2004)*, Edition Creaphis, 2006

Lemonnier, Léon, *Edouard VII: le Roi de l'Entente Cordiale*, Hachette, 1949

Olivier, David, *Hendon Aerodrome: A history*, Airlife Publishers, 1994

Pearce, Robert, *Britain and the European powers, 1865–1914*, Hodder & Stoughton, 1996

Salvy-Guide, G. P., *Fachoda. La mission Marchand*, Fernand Nathand, 1977

Vaïsse, Maurice, *L'Entente Cordiale de Fachoda à la Grande Guerre*, Edition Complexe – Ministère des Affaires Etrangères, 2004

12 A shared modernity

Aston, Elaine, *Sarah Bernhardt: A French actress on the English stage*, Berg Publishers, 1989

Beattie, Susan, *The Burghers of Calais in London: the history of the purchase*, Arts Council of Great Britain, 1986

Boulestin, Marcel, *A Londres Naguère*, Librairie Arthème Fayard, Paris, 1946

Cacan, Felician, Bruno Foucart, Claude Petry and Jane Roberts, *Jacques-Emile Blanche, peintre, 1861–1942*, Musée des Beaux-Arts, Rouen, 1997

Ceri Richards, Peter Olivier, Jacques-Emile Blanche, V. J. Champion, exhibition catalogue, Redfern Gallery, London, 1957

Delvaille, Bernard, *Essai sur Valery Larbaud*, Poètes d'aujourd'hui, Pierre Seghers, 1963

Fawkes, Sandy, *The French, a Personal History*, Lewis/Botham French House, London, 1993

Gaunt, William, *Paintings from 1882 to 1938 by Jacques-Emile Blanche*, exhibition catalogue, Leicester Galleries, London, 1969

Gruetzner Robins, Anna and Richard Thomson, *Degas, Sickert and Toulouse-Lautrec, London and Paris, 1870–1910*, Tate Publishing, 2005

Guyard, Marius-François, *La Grande-Bretagne dans le Roman Français, 1914–1940*, Librairie Marcel Didier, Paris, 1954

House, John and Mary Anne Stevens, *Post-Impressionism: Cross-Currents in European Painting*, exhibition catalogue, Royal Academy of Arts / Weidenfeld and Nicolson, 1979

Kellerman, Michel, *André Derain: Catalogue raisonné de l'œuvre peinte*, Editions Galerie Schmit, 1992

Kilburn, Mike, *London's Theatres*, New Holland, London, 2011

Macworth, Cecily, *English Interludes: Mallarmé, Verlaine, Paul Valéry – Valery Larbaud in England, 1860–1912*, Routledge & Kegan Paul, London, 1974

Upstone, Robert, *Modern Painters: The Camden Town Group*, exhibition catalogue, Tate Publishing, London, 2008

13 London, capital of Free France

Accoce, Pierre, *Les Français à Londres, 1940–1941*, Editions Balland, 1989

Atkin, Nicholas, *The Forgotten French: Exiles in the British Isles, 1940–44*, Manchester University Press, 2003

Bergot, Erwan, *Les Cadets de la France Libre*, Presses de la Cité, 1978

Bohec, Jeanne, *La plastiqueuse à bicyclette*, Editions du Félin, 1999

Bourdan, Pierre, *Carnet des jours d'attente, Juin 40–Juin 44*, Editions Pierre Trémois, Paris, 1945

La Caisse Centrale de la France Libre. De Gaulle's Bank in London, Bank of England Museum and Education Resources, 2011

Cointet, Michel and Jean-Paul, *La France à Londres, 1940–1943*, Editions Complexes, 1990

Corbett, A. and D. Johnson, *A Day in June: Britain and de Gaulle, 1940*, Franco-British Council, British Section, 2000

Crawley, Aidan, *De Gaulle*, The Literary Guild, London, 1969

Decèze, Dominique, *Ici Londres . . . La Lune est pleine d'éléphants verts*, J. Lanzmann & Seghers, Paris, 1979

Gaulle, Charles de, *Mémoires de guerre: l'Appel, 1940–42*, Plon, 1954

Gillois, André, *Histoire secrète des Français à Londres, de 1940 à 1944*, Librairie Hachette, 1973

Kersaudy, François, *De Gaulle et Churchill. La mésentente cordiale*, Perrin, 2001

Luneau, Aurélie, *Radio-Londres 1940–1944. Les voix de la liberté*, Editions Perrin, Paris, 2005

Oberlé, Jean, *Jean Oberlé vous parle . . .*, Editions La Jeune Parque, Paris, 1945

Passy, Colonel, *Souvenirs,* vol. 1: *2ᵉ Bureau de Londres,* vol. 2: *10, Duke Street*, Editions Raoul Solar, Monte-Carlo, 1947

Torres, Tereska, *Une Française Libre: Journal 1939–1945*, Edition Phébus, London, 2000

PICTURE CREDITS

Plates after page 144

1, 13 Wikimedia Commons
3 Wikimedia Commons / British Library
4, 7, 11© National Portrait Gallery, London
5 Wikimedia Commons / Auckland Art Gallery
6 Courtesy of the Garrick Club
8 © Bibliomane / Courtesy of Field Studies Council of Juniper Hall
10, 14, 18 Photo Robert Morrison
12 Bibliomane – Chateau d'Eu / Photo by kind permission of Bruno Senard

15 Bottom right courtesy of Restaurant Kettner
Line drawing on page 155 Wikimedia Commons / BnF

All other pictures are courtesy of the authors or out of copyright. Every effort has been made to contact copyright holders; any errors or omissions are inadvertent and will be rectified in future editions upon notification to the publishers.